BIG MUDDY

Other Books by B. C. Hall

BIG MUDDY

DOWN THE MISSISSIPPI THROUGH AMERICA'S HEARTLAND

B. C. Hall and C. T. Wood

A DUTTON BOOK

DUTTON
Published by the Penguin Group
Penguin Books USA Inc., 375 Hudson Street,
New York, New York 10014, U.S.A.
Penguin Books Ltd, 27 Wrights Lane,
London W8 5TZ, England
Penguin Books Australia Ltd, Ringwood,
Victoria, Australia
Penguin Books Canada Ltd, 10 Alcorn Avenue,
Toronto, Ontario, Canada M4V 3B2
Penguin Books (N.Z.) Ltd, 182-190 Wairau Road,
Auckland 10, New Zealand

Penguin Books Ltd, Registered Offices:
Harmondsworth, Middlesex, England

First published by Dutton, an imprint of New American Library,
a division of Penguin Books USA Inc.
Distributed in Canada by McClelland & Stewart Inc.

First Printing, August, 1992
10 9 8 7 6 5 4 3 2 1

LIBRARY OF CONGRESS CATALOGING-IN-PUBLICATION DATA
Hall, B. Clarence, 1936-
  Big Muddy : a journey to America's heartland / B.C. Hall and C.T. Wood.
    p.   cm.
  Includes bibliographical references and index.
  ISBN 0-525-93476-6
  1. Mississippi River.   2. Mississippi River Valley.   I. Wood, C.T. (Clyde Thornton)   II. Title.
F351.H16   1992
977—dc20   92-3489
                                                                       CIP

Printed in the United States of America
Set in ITC New Baskerville
Designed by Julian Hamer

For Ed Stewart
and
for Lucy-Anne and Martha Rose

ACKNOWLEDGMENTS

The authors thank the following people for their help and kindness: Carl Brucker, Wanda Choate, June and Freddie Rood, John and Odessa Wood, Marcia Studler, Ruby Bisher, Ella Chitwood, Juanita Kelly, Jeffie Crawford, Beatrice Hall, Tom Royals, Bruun Whitehead, Nathan Austin, Mary Catherine Cole, Carolyn Foshce, Garry Garner, Mindy Hudson, Connie Koenes, Yoshi Matsura, Linda McDougal, Lisa Millard, Patti Millard, Margie Moore, Michael Morris, Judith Stolz, Faye Crumpler, Deanna Smith and Teresa Willoughby.

Contents

The basin of the Mississippi is the body of the nation.

—From Mark Twain's
Life on the Mississippi

Introduction:
Getting in the River

"The Mississippi is well worth reading about. It is not a commonplace river, but on the contrary is in all ways remarkable."

—*First lines of* Life on the Mississippi

Once upon a time, in an epoch as different from today as chalk is from cheese, the Mississippi was a pure, unspoiled river. Its catch basin stretched west to the Rockies, east to the Alleghenies and south to the Gulf of Mexico. Ultimately it would cover all or parts of thirty-one states and would feed and clothe America for generations while providing the means by which the country could be explored and settled. Without it, our nation wouldn't be what it is today. Then as now, the river began and flowed through America's heartland, the most productive farmland on the face of the earth, with soil like granulated licorice.

Mark Twain sailed on America's river. His greatest achievement in writing was the river itself, for the Mississippi endures as his worthiest character. His works evoke the promise of the New World, though they also reflect the country's persistent weaknesses, which have exhibited themselves since man first touched the river.

Our earliest exposure to the Mississippi River was, like that of most schoolkids, through the reading of *Adventures of Huckleberry Finn;* in those pages we first learned something of the river's symbolic and mythic qualities. Twain told us that the Mississippi basin is "the body of the nation," and T. S. Eliot once called the river itself "a great brown god." Yet when we came to the river we found that both of these visions sounded too much like eulogies. We decided to let the river be our teacher, our pilot, and to trust it to guide us through the snags and deadfalls we might face—even though a more sinister eulogy is beginning to be preached with the current warnings about massive toxic pollution of the grand old river.

The sweep of any river is engaging, but the Mississippi's is rhapsodic. It begins in the cold north country and flows past towering bluffs that reach the height of skyscrapers. It moves over banks where shattered relics and eroded mounds whisper of past cultures. It channels through the plains and pours over a dangerous faultline that threatens to cut America in half. It bends and curves and surges, eating away billions of tons of earth. It dances and swells and changes the pitch of its rhapsody to the throaty blues and casual violence of the south. Finally it begins to unravel itself for a last push to the sea.

In young Samuel Clemens's time the dream of boys living along the river was to grow up to be steamboat pilots. Maybe the deeper dream was just to be on the river in any capacity. Something about the river, something magnetic and inscrutable, got inside young Sam Clemens's heart and never left him completely. Though he was to surrender to wanderlust during his long years, some unnameable call of the river brought him back again and again. Only on the river could he reclaim the true boy's heart inside him and be the only thing he always needed to be, Mark Twain. He gave us wonderful gifts. Tom Sawyer and Huck Finn, the Duke and the Dolphin, Captain Bixby, and the premier father figure in all of American literature, Jim. Most importantly, he gave us the river.

Traveling along the river, we hit upon a common trait. The people who live on and near the levees have a need to be interpreters of the river. They savor this necessity even though they take it for granted. It is a river fever and the river traveler can't come to the banks of the Big Muddy without feeling its flush. At each city, haven and port we learned new lessons about the dynamic impact the river has upon daily lives. The more we searched, the more we began to sense a deep-rooted commonality among the river's people—from the stony-poor folk living in gloomy shanties along the Southern levees to the business executives in penthouse offices overlooking the river's spectacular sweep. The people of the river taught us that the Mississippi is truly democratic, self-creating, uniquely American.

The spirit of Huck Finn pulls even after a hundred years, and if we were going to travel down the length of Mark Twain's river we knew the ideal way to do it would be the way Huck and Jim did it, like free spirits running the river on a homemade raft. But this is hardly possible today. The upper river is throttled by locks and dams; the lower river, always perilous, is choked by an endless flux of barges, commercial craft, bridges and the long-existing threat of river rats still as low and mean as John A. Murrell's pirates of the 1820s.

We had rafted the river once as teenagers. We thought we had to do it because it was our river and we had lived all of our youth near it. We had learned to swim in the river's clear coves, we had flown down the snow-packed levees in winter on washtub toboggans, we had learned about hunting and fishing in the bayous and bottoms. And we read Mark Twain beside the river and dreamed of sweeping off yonder to the ports and places of our imagination. So, one summer we struck out into an easy current as though we were La Salle or Mark Twain. But the river beat us. We broke our backs paddling out of swells made by long barges; the parching sun baked our flesh and at night we suffocated in muddy beds of vermin and in clouds of insects. We found ourselves stuck in the snaky bog of a river-made lake somewhere in the state of Mississippi. We hadn't experienced anything of the river except mile after mile of muddy, unfriendly water.

Now, years later, we came back to the river because we could never quite shed the notion that it belonged to us. We still weren't ready to give up the wish to sail the Mississippi, and we tried some modern-day river travel. We booked passage from one port to another, went for excursions on pleasure cruisers and even the new casino boats. All manner of river trips are available nowadays out of ports from St. Paul to New Orleans; the tours range from one-hour spins to full-river journeys. The amenities are upscale and include dining, dancing and brushing up against celebrities. It is all pleasant, relaxing, unsatisfying. You don't see the true river.

So we looked around for an alternative and found one, a great riparian road still very much in use. The road is known as U.S. Highway 61, though sometimes it's called the Great River Road. The states it serves down through the Mississippi Valley have spruced it up with parks and signs and tour guides, but Old 61 is still the same old bumpy, eclectic, dangerous road that Bob Dylan raised to a measure of immortality in his musical folklore. Many American highways have carried with them an aura of historical importance or adventure or both: El Camino Real, the Natchez Trace, the Texas Road and Route 66. El Camino Real was a dirt track supposedly linking the few outposts of Spanish authority in eighteenth-century California; the Natchez Trace was becoming obsolete even before it was carved from the wilderness between Natchez and Nashville early in the nineteenth century; the Texas Road wound from the lower Missouri River bend through Indian Territory into east Texas in the 1830s; Route 66 will always be recalled as the escape artery for thousands of Okies and Arkies as they undertook the white man's version of the Trail of Tears during the Great Depression.

Old 61 remains a solid entity with a presence that has persevered through generations of American culture. This old river road was once a migratory trail beaten by tribes native to the river, and dozens of Indian mounds still exist along Old 61's route—from the upper reaches in Wisconsin to the Cahokia Mounds near East St. Louis and descending through the Mississippi Valley to the Emerald Mound at the end of the Natchez Trace. Old 61 at once connects the vestiges of America's oldest culture and affords a glimpse of our true ancestors. And despite a conspicuous pattern of abuse and neglect, the fellow travelers—the greatest of river roads and the greatest of rivers—somehow still breathe and cling to life.

If we had a design in mind for our journey, it was to see what life on the Mississippi is like today and how people are treating the river; we also meant to keep in mind some important aspects of history and see how they have affected the river, and maybe how the river has affected them. For our voyage we chose a fifteen-year-old Lincoln touring car. We cleaned it up and tuned it up and painted it until it vaguely resembled a land-yacht befitting the floating river palaces of old. We christened it the *Grant II* because it was good company and drank a lot.

In 1882 Mark Twain spent some time on the river gathering material for *Life on the Mississippi,* and what he found was not the river of his boyhood days but a river sustaining drastic changes in man's continuing struggle to tame it. More than a hundred years

later, many of the landmarks Twain saw are still there. Sadly, much
of what he saw has either vanished or changed beyond recognition.
But the conflict between man and the river rages on. Were Twain
here today he would be heartsick over some of the things he'd see.
But he'd be eager to get down on the river where a funny and
earthy and sad new world of writer's material would be waiting for
him.

The people of the river are not just those who live on or near
its shores. Almost everywhere we journeyed on the Mississippi we
encountered crowds. Hundreds of thousands visit the headwaters
at the remote little lake of Itasca in Minnesota. Up and down the
river, events attract people in almost unbelievable numbers—
seventy-five thousand to a blues festival in tiny Helena, Arkansas;
upwards of a million to the Fourth of July celebration in St. Louis;
ten thousand to a jazz festival in Davenport, Iowa; a quarter of a
million in Memphis strutting the Chickasaw Bluff, eating barbecue;
and the granddaddy of them all, months of partying along the
levee in New Orleans starting with Mardi Gras where millions turn
out. Talk about your river fever.

This fever was never more in evidence than on a seemingly commonplace night in December 1990. On that night an event took
place down the full length of the Mississippi and up most of its
tributaries that was bedazzling in its merit and spontaneity. The
event happened only a few days after the great bogus earthquake
on the New Madrid Fault. Troops of newspeople had assembled
on the river for an event that never took place. They dispersed,
but they should have hung around, for they missed an impressive
show. In the little hamlets, towns and cities along the river thousands were gathering to take part in an impromptu celebration
that was in essence a tribute to the river's place in American civilization.

By chance on that night we happened to be traveling along the
Ohio headed toward Cairo and the Confluence of America—the
Ohio and Mississippi—the historic route of the first steamboat
journey. Our first inkling of what was going on came from listening to long-haul truckers talk back and forth on their CB radios;
they were planning something, a noisy demonstration. One husky
voice was encouraging other truckers to make a racket that could
be heard "way over on that old Persian Gulf." A little later every

trucker on the road began blasting his air horn to the heavens. Pretty soon every other vehicle along the way joined in. From the CB talk it was apparent that truckers all the way from Pittsburgh on the Ohio to New Orleans on the Mississippi were doing the same thing, at precisely the same time. We were coming to Paducah, Kentucky, and we hurried to the riverfront in time to see a candlelight procession winding down to the river landing. The people were taking part in an event called "Lights on the River." Most towns along the Ohio and Mississippi were joining in; people stood with glowing candles and sang "The Battle Hymn of the Republic." Church bells all over Paducah were ringing and we could see searchlights from the river barges sweeping over the river.

These river gatherings were put together as patriotic observances to honor the troops going to the Persian Gulf. The instinctive response of so many towns and so many people up and down the rivers said something about these far-flung, mostly unmentioned places. What started out as a simple candlelight event spread like a flood, from the green country of Henderson, Owensboro and Cairo on the Ohio to St. Louis, New Madrid, Memphis and past Vicksburg on the Mississippi. The rivers joined them and gave them sudden spirit. The length of the Mississippi, like some protracted torch procession, became for a few minutes one brilliant shower of light. No single individual could see it all, though all of those folks felt it. River fever.

River folks, those whose everyday lives are affected by the Mississippi, have more than just a special relationship with the river. It's akin to the feeling you might have for a sweet old aunt and an outlaw uncle, all at the same time. You love them and depend on them and respect them and fear them. The best way of expressing it is what an old codger told us about the river: "By God, it's family." And like all family life, gossip about its members turns into oral history, legends if you will. There's the apocryphal story of the Old Man and the River. An elderly gentleman was fishing from an old flat-bottom boat in the backwaters of the river and he hooked into the granddaddy catfish of them all, five or six hundred pounds or more. The great fish (a modern-day leviathan heralded from prehistory by the first tribes) pulled the old man up and down the river for days. Some time during this combat the man collapsed from heart failure. When he was found, he had a smile on his face.

Yet another "river family" story came to us at Baton Rouge, where we met a modern-day riverboatman, a hobnail-hard fellow of fifty who works on the Ohio barge line as a boilerman. He talked about the most frightening experience he'd had on the river. He spoke of riding out hurricanes down close to the Gulf, of fires on the boats when everybody panics, of heavy fogs that make a boat helpless. "The worst time for me was back during the flood of seventy-two or seventy-three. A bunch of barges broke loose and tore up the docks and the boats and damned near took the bridge down. Some people got killed, but you expect that on the river. The scariest thing is the river all by itself. It's a mean mother, but, hell, it's *our* mean mother."

The Father of Waters *is* a mean mother. It can and surely does flood with the best of them, despite all of man's efforts to contain it. The Mississippi was in flood when De Soto crossed it in 1541. It was in flood when the first steamboat, the *New Orleans,* came downriver in 1811. It flooded at least every five years throughout the nineteenth century. But in 1927 the Mississippi went berserk and tried to erase the puny works of man overnight; the levees crashed and melted in the water, houses disappeared, crops were inundated and people died by the thousands. The river tried again in 1937 with almost the same force and nearly the same results, and again in 1948. The river is indeed mean.

Floods on the river have given rise to still another kind of fever, man's rage to impose his control on the river in all its seasons. The U.S. Army Corps of Engineers has been and is still America's tool for this work. The Corps claims full expertise in river hydrology. It has even claimed to be able to control the river by changing its course at will. Mark Twain heard these arguments in the 1880s and reflected on them as he came downriver. In *Life on the Mississippi* Twain uses the curmudgeonly voice of Uncle Mumford, a thirty-year veteran on the riverboats, to express his disdain: "Well, you've got to admire men that deal in ideas of that size and can tote them around without crutches; but you haven't got to believe they can *do* such miracles, have you?"

In the years since the great flood of 1927 the Corps has assumed

total responsibility for the Mississippi. Most recently it has suppressed its ideas for changing the course of the river. The Corps
still believes it can do it, but all the river's history is against it.
Nowadays the Corps is into damage control and risk management:
it seeks to protect the Mississippi by controlling the somewhat more
amenable tributaries. The Corps is keeping itself busy damming
up the rivers feeding into the Big Muddy. Making lakes and creating an environment for leisure-time activities and lakefront estates, the Corps, unwittingly or not, is proving to be the best friend
land developers have ever had.

America's environmental community believes the Corps is building a time bomb. Creating dams and lakes on the river and its
tributaries amounts to waging a war against nature, according to
such organizations as Greenpeace, the Sierra Club, the Izaak Walton League, the American Rivers Association. Wetlands, the very
center of regeneration, are being destroyed by clear-cutting and
soil erosion. The dams become repositories for all the richness of
the eroded lands; the silt is so thick that fish cannot survive in it.
And, of course, the dams trap the chemicals and poisons dumped
in by industrial wastewater and cropfield runoff. The great irony
is that the Corps' risk management program has not factored in
the environment; the Corps suffers from such lock-and-dam vision
that the future of nature hangs in the balance.

One of the consistent stories of the river is a joke you can hear
at most any town or courthouse on the Mississippi. People will tell
you that before the Corps came around with its fancy flood con-
trols, the basements in town stood six feet deep in floodwaters;
after the Corps had finished its work, the basements only had four
feet of water.

Even in Mark Twain's time the Mississippi never lent itself to
easy definition, and such a caveat is even more valid today. The
river undulates sometimes sleepily, sometimes stormily, a protean
tendency reflected by its human tenants since they first tried to
harness it and bridge the gulf between savagery and civilization.
The river's culture draws upon immigrants whose disparate histories coincided in only one aspect, the elimination of the native
tribes.

About three hundred years ago French explorers from the Canadian north began searching for a legendary river that would lead

them to the enigmatic Vermilion Sea and the fabled riches of the Orient. This continuing fantasy was nurtured by an almost total ignorance of the topography of North America. Distance, whether by land or water in winter or summer, was measured in days, with the calculation of leagues left to an arbitrary assignment, by either the explorer or an Indian guide. And neither the neolithic tribesmen nor their European cousins were ever noted for their accuracy. But distance, hostile tribes and impenetrable forests could keep back only those without vision, no matter how clouded and illusory that vision may have been. By the end of the seventeenth century the fantasy had taken on an existence of its own; the seekers acquired an almost total, sleepwalker's sense of security in pursuit of their vermilion grail.

The names of the seventeenth-century searchers fill the histories of the epoch: Joliet, Marquette, Dulhut, Hennepin, Tonti, De La Forest, and of course René-Robert Cavelier Sieur de la Salle, the first white man to travel the Mississippi to the Gulf. The old dream of extracting reality from the myth by discovering a Northwest Passage didn't die until two more centuries had dawned.

Just after Thomas Jefferson's Louisiana Purchase in 1803, American explorers continued to backtrack the early French adventurers in their search for a route to the Orient. Indulgent Indians had assured the seventeenth-century French that there was indeed a great river to be found running an east-west course, emptying into an even greater water source. The French were aware of the Ohio River and its direction; they knew it joined with a greater river in flowing south. Marquette and Joliet had mentioned the Missouri and the Arkansas in their journals a few years before La Salle's journey to the Gulf of Mexico in 1682. But the western rivers were flowing in the wrong direction and would not fit the fantasy. The French did not make the connection between the westward-flowing Ohio and the eastward-flowing Missouri. Nor did the Americans a century later.

Concrete evidence about the western rivers, particularly the Missouri, was not authoritatively accumulated until Lewis and Clark completed their 1804–06 expedition. Had Lewis and Clark completed their journey before Lieutenant Zebulon Pike erroneously claimed to have found the headwaters of the Mississippi, Mark Twain's fondest dream would have been realized: the source of the

Mississippi would have been in Montana, not Minnesota, and the Mississippi would truly have been the longest river in the world, as Twain claims in *Life on the Mississippi*. This dream was long known as *Mechesebe,* an Algonquin word meaning "great water."

Commerce today on the Mississippi is very much alive, to an extent unheard of even during the prime days of pre–Civil War steamboat trade. Despite his acerbity, Twain was ever an optimist about his river and relied upon it for rejuvenation. He'd be appalled at its condition today, though maybe he would hope, as do the growing ranks of river devotees, that not all is lost, that there is still some worth in the venerable adage, "You can't pluck a flower without troubling a star."

As we started our journey down the Mississippi, we moved in the shadows of all that has happened in the river's past. We knew the shadows would sometimes come a little too close and have a chilling effect. Sometimes we would be able to see Thomas Jefferson's bright dream, and sometimes that dream would be obscured. The dark side was presaged in 1776 by John Adams when he said: "There is so much venality and corruption, so much avarice and ambition, such a rage for profit and commerce that I doubt there is public virtue enough to support a Republic." Yet to take solely the dark view would be to overlook the good in Mark Twain and the other people of the river.

So here by a sweet little stream in the far north country, we began *Life on the Mississippi* revisited, a journey down the river through America's heartland.

CHAPTER 1

The Heritage
of the Mechesebe

"The very ink with which all history is written is merely
fluid prejudice."

—*From Twain's* Following the Equator

The history of the Mississippi River is a dreamworld with prizes of
riches and empire being the rewards of fantasy. In *Life on the Mississippi,* Twain introduced his beloved, personally sustaining river
with just a few passing sketches of its history from the pre-
steamboat epoch. Twain's casual, flippant references to the often
cloudy time between the middle of the sixteenth century and the
beginning of the nineteenth were deliberate snubs to things not
American. In a word, these people and their histories were *foreign,*
their every action predicated upon European points of reference.

The nineteenth-century Americans for whom Twain wrote knew
that they were making history, true American history, on a daily,
almost hourly basis. Twain understood his countrymen's intoler-
ance for any memorials that couldn't be orally recounted by their
grandparents. Because of this jealousy, *Life on the Mississippi* dis-
poses of three centuries of history in less than nine pages of highly
selective, rather dismissive commentary. Well, the demanding pace
of the nineteenth century and the building of the United States
have shifted emphasis, and late-twentieth-century Americans can
afford to reflect more on the history of their nation. Perceptions,
too, have changed, in the more than a hundred years since Twain
wrote his rhapsody to the Mississippi. At the time of publication
the genocide of the American Indians was still in progress; both
the Civil War and its most palpable cause, the slavery of black

Africans, had ended only eighteen years earlier, and the memories and guilt still hurt too much; and the contemptible web of peonage in which poor whites and blacks were being trapped was just beginning to be spun. These were all contentious issues that Twain chose not to address. Perhaps they were too contemporary to the times to allow reflection and judgment.

Mark Twain didn't believe the appearance of De Soto on the Mississippi in 1541 was important (except to establish a respectable lineage for North America). Twain didn't choose to delve very deeply into the whys and wherefores of the Spanish expedition. If he had, he would have found that De Soto was an archetypal conquistador fresh from the campaigns that had conquered and enslaved the Incan civilization. De Soto came to North America for the sole purpose of taking by force of arms any and all movable wealth from Indians he knew could not defend themselves.

The Mississippi River basin in the sixteenth century was a relatively peaceful part of the world. To be sure, its inhabitants were engaged in constant fighting, but the populations of the tribes were too small to bring warfare up to the scope of the known civilized world. As you can learn from the journals of the early explorers, the social and political fabric of the tribes was very loose-knit. Each tribe had many, too many, leaders. They had no fixed abode and tended to go their own way, with no regard for land or ownership. The tribes were all adept at torturing their enemies, just as their European counterparts were, but the Indians viewed cannibalism as a natural consequence of being captured (the greater your prowess as a warrior, the more likelihood of gracing your opponent's cooking pot). A great mysticism lived along the river—enchanting rites and bitter potions were said to give the Indians' spiritual leaders magical powers; they could plunge their arms into boiling water without injury, pick up and hold hot coals, conjure balls of fire from the air, make stones wheel and dance, and render warriors impervious to the enemy's weapons. Legends, surely, but evidence of a way of life in harmony with the natural order of things. But the idyll was over. Civilization was about to show its bestial face in the figure of Hernando de Soto.

De Soto landed at Tampa Bay in August 1539. His entourage required 17 vessels and he brought upwards of 1,000 soldiers, 223 horses, 13 priests, a notary, dozens of war dogs, plus assorted knights and noble adventurers, carpenters, blacksmiths, scores of attendant slaves and herds of swine. Pig meat was the food of choice of the Spanish. For centuries Spain had fought the Muslim civilization in Iberia. Only recently had the Moors been expelled from Spain, and pork was a forbidden food to the Muslims. The Spanish took delight in ridiculing the pagan beliefs of their historic foe. The wild hog population of America owes its existence to De Soto and the Spanish bigotry.

De Soto also brought along several cannons. He wasn't going to engage Indians without the full force of European civilization's art to back him up. The expedition encountered nothing but difficulty from the outset. Hostile Indians were everywhere. The entourage had to slog through swamps, boggy creeks, rivers of poisonous snakes, still more swamps inhabited by huge alligators and still more hostile natives. The Spanish soldiers found it easy enough to overwhelm the Indian villages and to take many slaves, but the new slaves were unruly; they broke loose and ran away and had to be chained together for the forced march. In the end the slaves were as burdensome to transport as the useless cannons.

De Soto brought slaves with him to America and took many more on his doomed march, a natural acting out of the Spanish mind-set in the New World. It was standard practice for any Spanish expedition to, in a sense, read the Indians their rights before they were enslaved or slaughtered out of hand. The rights were precious few: the Indians could either accept Christianity on the spot and be enslaved or reject Christianity and be murdered. In a book published in 1552, a Dominican priest named Bartolomé de las Casas exposed the brutality, the atrocities and the nascent genocide being practiced by the Spanish on the Indians. The whole history of Spain versus the tribes in the New World came to be known as the Black Legend.

The Spanish government ignored de las Casas's book but the work was translated and used by England and France to blackguard the name of Spain; more importantly, it justified the buccaneer operations of the English and French against the Spanish treasure fleets. The righteous indignation of the English and French did not stop these empire builders from following the Spanish example. Various degrees of genocide were practiced by all Europeans in the New World. The emergent American nations

simply picked up where their sponsors left off after the struggles
for independence, the United States no less than Argentina or
Mexico. Civilization and exclusive property ownership were in;
Stone Age savages of no fixed abode were out. Spain bequeathed
to the New World a choice among genocide, slavery and peonage
not only for the Indians but for the soon-to-come black slaves and
the poor whites as well, in a pernicious system of bondage that
would last into the twentieth century.

Roughly 140 years after De Soto came to the Mississippi, the
French rediscovered the Father of Waters. They were searching for
a water route to the fabled Vermilion Sea. Common belief in Europe and in the New World colonies held that just over the horizon
were to be found Japan, China and the Spice Islands. What was
needed was a river to take the questing Europeans there. The obvious answer was to ask the Indians; the Indians answered, "Yes,
there are waters flowing to the sun and away from the sun." This
ambiguity kept the dream alive all the way into the nineteenth
century.

Francis Parkman, the finest historian of the American West, au-
thenticated the dream in his book *La Salle and the Discovery of the
Great West*. Working in retrospect in the late 1860s, Parkman had
the uncanny ability to meld a keen insight into past events with
his own intuition as to the importance of seemingly trivial legends
and lore. He seemed to sense that there was something historically
important in all the mythmaking, no matter how fantastic. Parkman related the story of Jean Nicolet, a French trapper living with
the Nippissings in the 1630s.

Nicolet had heard of a new kind of people, without hair or
beards, who came from the West to trade with an Indian tribe
somewhere on the Great Lakes. In common with all French *voya-
geurs* in New France, Nicolet was an enterprising soul, and he set
out for Green Bay immediately. His canoe glided to the shore and
the surprised Indians saw their first white man, dressed in a sump-
tuous damask gown and with a pistol in each hand. Nicolet could
find no Chinese trader, no prince of Cathay, only a squalid little
Winnebago Indian village. His failure did nothing to dampen the
dream, and the search for the water route continued. The name of
Nicolet carries the same historical importance in present-day Wisconsin and Minnesota as does the name of De Soto in the south.

Though equally naive, Frenchmen of higher stature were soon to come to the river. Joliet and Marquette, both priests and merchants, carved their names into history by discovering not only the Mississippi but also the Missouri and Arkansas rivers, in 1673. French imperial ambitions in the New World under Louis XIV were heating up. All expeditions in Canada were designed to find or at least gather word of the storied river.

No matter how historically inaccurate the notion, to most people it is La Salle who discovered the Mississippi River. What La Salle really did was to prove that the Mississippi emptied into the Gulf of Mexico, not into the Vermilion Sea. Strangely enough, this confirmation suited the purposes of the French king. Louis XIV was not interested in long-term developments; he was dead broke and needed money as fast as it could be poured into the royal coffers.

When La Salle discovered the estuary of the river in 1682, he made his way back to the court at Versailles to plead his case for new settlement in what was called Louisiana. But Louis had his eyes on the Spanish gold and silver mines (in what is now Mexico). Cleverly, La Salle must have decided to use Louis's desire for instant wealth as an excuse to establish a full-blown colony at the mouth of the Mississippi. He promised the king that he would raise an army of fifty thousand Indians and use it to march on the Spanish gold mines, if Louis would finance the Mississippi colony. Louis agreed. La Salle returned to the Gulf in triumph; he was outfitted with four ships, a hundred soldiers, dozens of gentlemen volunteers and artisans, families of settlers, and even thirty teenaged girls swept from the streets of Paris with the promise of becoming "the little mothers of New France."

The grandiose scheme, grounded in Louis's lust for gold and La Salle's compulsive drive for fame, ended in failure for the simplest of reasons—as he sailed in from the sea, La Salle couldn't find the Mississippi. He knew the longitude but not the latitude and his expedition overshot the river by four hundred miles, landing on the cold, uninviting Texas coast at present-day Matagorda Bay. Within two years the colony would be destroyed by disease, starvation and raids by fierce, cannibalistic Indians. La Salle himself would be murdered by a conspiracy of the last survivors of the colony. His murder is one of the great unsolved mysteries of the New World. Parkman, in his biography of La Salle, comes closest of all the historians to pointing the finger; in his masterful but overly gentle analysis of La Salle's enemies, Parkman points out that the Jesuits hated him, the court intrigued against him, and the vice-regal government in New France schemed for his downfall. A close reading of Parkman establishes a strong case that the leaders of the conspiracy were La Salle's older brother (a Jesuit priest) and a close family friend.

It had taken more than 170 years but by 1720 the European fortune hunters had at least provisionally decided that the wealth of the Mississippi Valley could be extracted only by long-term development. Settlers had to exploit the potential with hard work. Furs could be profitable but only if they were brought downriver to New Orleans and its deep-water port. The French had been making sporadic attempts at colonization with De Bienville and D'Iberville, the gentleman backwoodsman brothers from Canada who are credited with founding the first settlements in and around New Orleans. Still, get-rich-quick schemes held the stage in Louisiana.

The most notorious scheme in the crowded annals of avarice and arrogance on the Mississippi River is known to history as the Mississippi Bubble. It was put together by a con artist without peer, John Law. This Scotsman had fled England early in the eighteenth century with a price on his head for having killed a man in a duel over a prostitute. Law sought refuge in the famed Paris bordello of Madame Duclos. In the gambling salon of this bawdy house, Law met the Duke of Orléans, the future regent of France. The duke and Law became fast friends because Law saw to it that his royal acquaintance won heavily at his faro table.

When Louis XIV finally died, the new regent inherited an exhausted treasury; he turned to his new companion, Law, to save the fortunes of France. Incredibly, Law did just that. He took over the bank of France, stabilized the currency and began to bring France out of debt. He was so successful that he became the de facto minister of finance, and it was from this position that he put together the notorious Mississippi Investment Company.

Law found the perfect foil to promote his scheme, an old soldier who claimed to have been with La Salle. This adventurer, named Sagean, came to Paris from New France with tales of gold and silver mines, gemstones lying on the shores of the Mississippi and beaver begging to be trapped. Law created an eighteenth-century propaganda blitz extolling the virtues of Louisiana and the fortunes to be had for the taking. He flooded Europe with brochures that claimed, "The land is filled with gold, silver, copper, and lead mines ... we will hunt for herbs and plants for the apothecaries and soon we shall find healing remedies for the most dangerous wounds, yes, also, so they say, infallible ones for the fruits of love."

Almost everyone in Europe fell for the scheme, with the exception of one man who knew the truth. He was an old soldier by the name of De Cadillac who had served as an officer in New France. De Cadillac had been all the way down the river to Louisiana and knew Sagean's claims to be false, and when he tried to tell the truth, Law had him arrested and thrown into the Bastille.

Law carried on a whirlwind trade in the shares of his new company. Anyone who was anybody, or wanted to be, came to Law at his apartments on the Rue Quincampoix, which soon became known across Europe as "Mississippi Street." Law could not walk down the street or even enter a toilet without people begging for the opportunity to invest in his Mississippi Company. The mother of the Duke of Orléans was scandalized when a duchess kissed Law's hand in public; the duchess was thanking him for allowing her to invest half a million francs. The Duke's mother wrote in her diary: "If a duchess will kiss his hand, what will not other women kiss?"

Law's company was all a paper chase. There was never any investment in Louisiana and the assets of the company were a small fraction of the money sold in shares. The chimerical bubble popped in 1720; the economy of France collapsed, setting off a bitter depression all across Europe. The story was still common currency more than a hundred years later, and even American writer Washington Irving was moved to include Law's bubble in one of his monographs.

John Law unwittingly gave the first real impetus to serious colonization on the Mississippi with his fabulously crooked promotions. As many as ten thousand Alsatian Germans, Dutch and Belgians believed his brochures and actually paid for the privilege of sailing to the Gulf Coast to settle the river above New Orleans. Their dreams of riches, freedom and comfort met the stark reality of an austere life of privation, disease and starvation.

Despite the influx of new colonists in the Lower Mississippi Val-

ley, the almost total absence of an economic base upriver meant
that New Orleans was not yet a truly viable settlement. By 1763
France paid for her failure to settle New France in any substantive
numbers; the English colonists were in the hundreds of thousands,
while the French could count just a few tens of thousands. Sheer
numbers forced the French to abandon Canada. In the aftermath
England caused the removal of around five thousand French families from Acadia in Nova Scotia to Louisiana. Though only a brief
footnote in history, this act had far-reaching and interesting cultural effects, for these Acadian French people became the Cajuns,
and their rich culture has been the keystone around which the
state of Louisiana has developed.

When France lost Canada it managed to save Louisiana from the
English by giving it to Spain, if only for a short while. France
reacquired Louisiana just at the turn of the nineteenth century.
Napoleon coerced the weak and corrupt Spanish throne into giving back the land, and for a time he flirted with the idea of putting
an army in New Orleans in order to invade Mexico and steal the
gold and silver of New Spain. It was Louis XIV's scheme all over
again. Coming events would make this second attempt impossible.
Napoleon had no real interests in the New World anyway, other
than what loose change he could pick up from the sugar trade; so
he looked around for a buyer for his vast American holdings. No
sooner did he entertain the thought than Thomas Jefferson was
knocking on the door.

Americans from the fledgling United States had begun to settle
the lands west of the Alleghenies, using the Ohio River as their
natural conduit. The easiest path by which these new settlers could
get their goods to market was down the Ohio and Mississippi rivers
to New Orleans. The time had come for a practical and profitable
use of the deep-water port. Jefferson was a visionary and a very
shrewd businessman. He knew that without the control of New
Orleans, America would not grow. He offered to buy the port and
wound up owning the entire Louisiana Territory, doubling the size
of the nation. Jefferson in essence started the real American Dream.

Amazingly, Jefferson still believed in the magical existence of a
Northwest Passage. After buying the land, his next act was to commission the famous Lewis and Clark expedition, whose dual purposes were to find the river connection to the Pacific Ocean and

to figure a way to take away the lucrative Canadian fur trade from the English. Jefferson's second act was to forbid French, English and Spanish fur traders from operating anywhere in American territory. For all practical purposes, this restriction conferred the entire fur trade upon the German-born fur trader, capitalist, and robber-baron John Jacob Astor and was the making of the Mississippi's great upriver port, St. Louis.

One last serious empire builder was to come to the Mississippi. He was Aaron Burr, the man without a country. He had a country in mind, though, and it was to stretch from the Arkansas River south and west through what is now Louisiana, Texas and northern Mexico. It was the third and last version of Louis XIV's dream of Spanish gold.

Burr was just as good a politician as Jefferson and just as keen a visionary. He had easily figured out that with the growth of America, the Mississippi River and its great port, New Orleans, would be the most valuable piece of real estate in the new republic. He was equally determined that he would carve an empire from the newly purchased territory and establish himself as the once and future King Rex of New Orleans. With his co-conspirator, General James Wilkinson, Burr set about drumming up support for a popular rebellion in New Orleans.

Before he set out on his voyage of empire, Burr settled an old score with his long-standing rival, the great Federalist, Alexander Hamilton, a man who had his own dream of empire, with himself as a New World Napoleon. The two men had been at crossed swords since the Revolution, but Hamilton finally went too far and ruined Burr's bid to become governor of New York in a dirty-tricks campaign as bad as any in the history of American politics. Burr called Hamilton out and in a duel along the banks of the Hudson River gunned him down.

Burr journeyed to the headwaters of the Ohio and boarded his specially built luxury river-yacht, an outsized keelboat the likes of which had never been seen on the river. Along the way, he found considerable support for his conspiracy among the landed gentry. His new reputation as a duelist did him no harm—Hamilton was despised in the new American West, and Burr had become a hero to the independent-minded frontiersmen. In a short while Burr had recruited more than enough men to build a personal army. In

Tennessee Andrew Jackson greeted Burr warmly as a brother in the *code duello* and actually agreed to take part in Burr's plan for empire. An obscure note gives a hint of the two men's characters— an ironic sidelight on their meeting was that Jackson understood perfectly when Burr told him the only regret he had about the Hamilton affair was that he "hadn't shot the son of a bitch right between the eyes."

Burr floated on into New Orleans, arriving to a hero's welcome. The French population was thoroughly disenchanted with its new American masters and enthusiastically joined in the conspiracy. The bishop of New Orleans and the prioress of the abbey were firmly in the Burr camp and used their influence to get Burr wide support. With his base secured, Burr returned to the East to raise capital for the enterprise; Wilkinson as territorial commander set the plan in motion by sending Zebulon Pike to scout for gold mines in Mexico.

James Wilkinson had long been in the pay of Spain (to help stop American settlement west of the Alleghenies) and unknown to Burr was prepared to betray everybody. When Burr returned to the Mississippi to start the uprising, Wilkinson had sold him out to Jefferson. Burr was arrested and taken east to face charges, but escaped Jefferson's revenge through congressional acquittal. Wilkinson got yet another reward and was made commander in chief of the U.S. Army. Pike became a noted explorer but was killed by Indians in the War of 1812. And Andrew Jackson became the first populist president of the United States.

If Burr had waited about five years, he could have arrived in New Orleans in real style. In the early spring of 1812 the first steamboat on the Mississippi arrived in New Orleans. It was called the *New Orleans* and had been built and captained by Nicholas J. Roosevelt, the great-grand-uncle of Teddy Roosevelt. Robert Fulton receives credit for inventing this steamboat and New York chancellor Robert Livingston (Burr's old friend and the man Jefferson chose to negotiate the Louisiana Purchase) was the financial backer and political muscle. The combination of Livingston, Fulton and Roosevelt was yet another conspiracy on the Mississippi, this one to secure control of the river's commerce.

The combine rightly estimated the massive potential of the Ohio and Mississippi rivers for the shipping trade, but there were no roads to take the produce from the Ohio Valley back to the markets on the East Coast. Flatboat and keelboat traffic was enormous but slow and inefficient. The new steamboat was truly a visionary answer. Most of the flatboats and keelboats ended up in New Orleans and its sister port Algiers as building material, for it wasn't practical to try to get them back upriver. The colorful keelboat era, as symbolized by frontiersman Mike Fink, was over by the end of the 1820s.

The illegal attempt at a steamboat monopoly fell apart within two years. Even though the *New Orleans* had made it all the way downstream from Pittsburgh, and through the disastrous earthquake of 1811–12, it was only because of the high flood levels that the deep-draft vessel was successful. The real competition arrived in the spring of 1814. Henry Shreve, a former keelboat master, pulled into New Orleans in a Da Vinciesque creation called the *Enterprise,* the first true river steamboat. Shreve's boat would revolutionize transportation on America's rivers, while the Fulton design was restricted to oceans. Though competitors, the *Enterprise* and the *New Orleans* would fight side by side at the Battle of New Orleans in the War of 1812. According to legend, the first steamboat race on the river took place between these bitter rivals, though there's no record of the outcome.

The settlement and economic exploitation of the Mississippi Valley went hand in hand with the steamboat. By the 1830s hundreds of *Enterprise*-like boats were plying the Mississippi and Ohio rivers, and the great cotton plantations were coming on stream. Subsistence farming was transformed into corporate-scale production. The boom was on and cotton was king.

The dark side of Jefferson's dream was a product of the almost unrestrained commercial growth: the economic boom created many victims. To get the land for the plantations, Americans had to eliminate the Indian tribes. Andrew Jackson relentlessly expanded James Madison's modest removal schemes and instituted an out-and-out policy of eradication. Indians were simply in the way. To till the soil, black slaves were imported in waves. Slavery already held sway on the Tidewater but the genteel, "peculiar institution" on the Atlantic coast was a sideshow compared to the body count for the Mississippi delta. The port of entry for such

slave ships as the *Black Joke* was New Orleans, and a wharf called
Vieux Carré (where jazz was born) was the largest slave market in
the civilized world.

Yet another side of the dark dream to feed off the emerging
commerce on the Mississippi was the man-made plague of piracy,
and the river seemed almost designed to foster the trade. Its loops,
bayous, backwaters and islands perfectly concealed the nests of the
robbers and cutthroats who infested it. The two most notorious
pirate princes on the Mississippi did business in about the same
time span. Jean Lafitte, the buccaneer, preyed on oceangoing ships,
while John Murrell chose the riverboats.

Murrell was a criminal with the stamp of genius. In *Life on the
Mississippi,* Twain makes a comparison between Murrell and Jesse
James. Twain claims Murrell was the equal to James "in pluck,
rapacity, brutality, heartlessness" and "in general and comprehen-
sive vileness ... and very much his superior in some larger aspects ... James was a retail rascal; Murrell, wholesale." Murrell
roamed the river in the early days of the steamboats and gained
notoriety by assembling a large band of followers known as "the
Mystic Clan." The estimated size of the clan rivaled that of the U.S.
Army at the time, with upwards of five thousand members and all
sworn to secrecy. Murrell waylaid, robbed and murdered victims
on flatboats, keelboats and steamboats, but his best game was stealing slaves and putting them up for resale. He gulled the poor blacks
with the promise of freedom into first running away from their
owners; after reselling them two or three times, he murdered them
and sank their bodies in hidden bayous.

Murrell hatched a scheme of empire-like proportions. He
planned to raise the slaves in the Lower Mississippi Valley in a
rebellion; they were to rob and kill their masters and march on
New Orleans, where Murrell would rule over them in his new kingdom of Louisiana. Seemingly preposterous, this plan might have
succeeded, for the blacks far outnumbered the whites. But a traitor
turned state's evidence and got Murrell convicted and sentenced
to prison for fourteen years. Twain does not tell us the ultimate
outcome of Murrell's scheme or his fate. The plan never got off
the ground. After serving his term in a Southern prison dungeon,
Murrell lived out the rest of his life as a village smith in a back-
woods town near the Natchez Trace.

Lafitte wasn't really a pirate, at least not a free-lance one; he was a licensed privateer, commissioned by the French to rob the Spanish and by the Spanish to rob the French, and by both countries to rob the English. Lafitte was likely the true hero at the Battle of New Orleans in 1815. According to his biographer, Lyle Saxon, he was a consummate entrepreneur and organizational genius. Lafitte's enterprise provided the powder, muskets and cannon that repelled the British. Not only that, Lafitte's business associates manned the ramparts along with Andrew Jackson's ragtag militia. Though he was the toast of New Orleans, Lafitte was an embarrassment to Washington. His unsavory reputation meant that the lion's share of the credit for the victory went to Jackson. All Lafitte got out of it was a presidential pardon from James Madison.

The lesser cousins of the pirates were the Mississippi river rats. These people committed dreadful crimes, but in small bands or individually and with no grand plan. Perfect models of these villains of the river were the infamous Harpe Brothers, Big and Little. Oral tradition has it that these brothers perpetrated perhaps hundreds of sickening atrocities from the Ohio to the Gulf. The usual victims lived on isolated farmsteads far from help. The notoriety of Big and Little Harpe was such that a town was named for one of them. Their usual ploy was to pose as itinerant preachers, and they kept their doxies in tow to assist in psalm singing and to allay the suspicions of their intended prey. They came to a household on the Green River and gained entry with a promise to conduct divine services. Their singing was so sweet that the husband of the family felt safe enough to leave the Harpes in his home as he went to the nearby market town. No sooner was the man away than the Harpes raped and murdered the wife and children. They stole everything that might be sold for gain and moved out in the opposite direction from the town. When the husband returned to the brutal scene, he swore revenge and pursued the violators. He caught up with them, but the brothers separated, and the man could only ride down Little Harpe. Harpe begged for his life, but the man put the muzzle of his musket to his chest and pulled the trigger. Although Little Harpe died instantly, it wasn't enough for the weeping husband. He took out his Bowie knife and sawed Little Harpe's head off; he stuck it on a nearby sapling, and thereafter the Kentucky town on the Green River was called Harpe's Head.

The four decades between 1830 and 1870 attracted another breed of people to the Mississippi River who worked hard at making an easy buck. This free and easy era saw a concentration of gambling never matched anywhere else in the world. Up and down the developing Mississippi basin, just about everyone gambled and on virtually anything—cock, pit bull and pimp fights, horse, mule and boat races. Of all the forms of wagering, riverboat gambling came to be gambling in style.

Some gamblers, knights of the river, became so famous that their names still live: Jimmy Fitzgerald, Dick Hargreaves, Canada Bill, John Powell, Elijah Skaggs, Charlie Starr, George White, and one impostor going by the name of Mark Twain—this man actually brought a lawsuit against Sam Clemens, claiming that Clemens had stolen his rights to the pen name Mark Twain. The suit was dismissed as a nuisance, as Twain reports in *Life on the Mississippi.* Most of the gamblers, even the famous ones listed here, faded from the scene with the coming of the railroads. The railroads were all business and had no time for the lesser, if more interesting, pursuits of man.

The last hurrah of the steamboats came much more quickly than anyone expected. The pre–Civil War traffic on the rivers built up and became even greater during the decade after the war. Yet the passing of an era was at hand and the steamboat would have its valedictory in the form of the most famous race in history, the contest between the *Robert E. Lee* and the *Natchez,* which took place in 1870. The race excited the attention of the whole world, it seemed, and you might have expected the famous boats to be enshrined in a hall of fame forever. The *Robert E. Lee* ended up as a derelict paint locker at the wharf of Little Rock on the Arkansas River, and the *Natchez* was condemned to become a maintenance warehouse on the docks at Vicksburg. There was simply no use for these celebrated steamboats; the railroads had driven them out of business.

Although Lincoln freed the black slaves in 1863, implementation of this long-overdue humanitarian act was deferred until the end of the Civil War in 1865. Even then the slave was free in name only. Echoes of the Spanish attitude toward the Indians in the New World resounded once more, over three hundred years later.

After 1865, more than three million freed slaves lived in the Mississippi Valley. Almost all of them were out of work, no longer serving masters who had an obligation to feed, clothe or house them. The empty gift of emancipation was no recompense for their inability to earn a living. The federal government which had freed them did nothing to preserve their liberty. They had no future.

Throughout the Lower Mississippi Valley bands of blacks wandered hopelessly. Some managed to make it to the larger Southern cities, where they began a dismal existence in shantytowns and ghettoes. Only a few were able or were even allowed to migrate into the North; the white cities of the North didn't want them and wouldn't take them. Memories of race riots in New York City and elsewhere were too fresh. The Union Army forcibly restrained coffles of former field hands from traveling the roads; blacks had to have passes from their "owners" to get by the patrols.

The overwhelming need was for food, but little was to be had, only greens from the forest and gleanings from the field. The dream of "Forty Acres and a Mule," promised by the Freedman's Bureau, never reached the Mississippi delta. A man could feed himself and his family with the produce of forty acres, but no land reform came to the South. The desperate situation facing the blacks was just as bleak for the poor white Southerner, and his only solace was his own presumed racial superiority.

The South had been fed by the produce of the North before the Civil War and had paid with the earnings from its cotton plantations. The reorganization of production in the deep South, as well as the re-creation of a productive and malleable work force, took from three to five years in the Mississippi Valley. The key to this miraculous turnaround was the imposition of a system of peonage; the Spanish encomienda, a brutal system of forced, unpaid labor, had returned to haunt America's southlands. The system was simple. The peons worked from dawn to dusk, though the people called it "from can to can't." They received the barest subsistence. No wages, no frills, no fancy hats. No hat at all. By the turn of the twentieth century 90 percent of the land in the South was tenanted by sharecroppers, black and white.

Around this time, Washington decided to renege on the Proclamation. Jim Crow laws and separate-but-equal court rulings became the accepted practice. These egregious acts tightened the melancholy grip on the inmates of peonage. Black families' sole consolation was in gathering in clapboard sheds they called their churches, where they made no heavy demands on their God. As despicable as it was, peonage would continue as an institution in the South until well into the 1960s. Its vestiges are still recognizable.

There are some famous Americans who haven't been mentioned in this brief survey of the Mississippi's heritage, famous but damned. The names of De Soto, La Salle, Fulton, Jackson, Burr, Jefferson, Joliet, Marquette, Law can all be found in the histories of the United States. But where can you find the names of Little Turtle, Tecumseh, Black Hawk, the Prophet, Pontiac. In several anthologies these Indian chiefs and leaders are hardly viewed as Americans.

These real Americans are often treated by history as aliens—wronged ones, to be sure, but still aliens. The excuse of the white man has always been that *they were in the way.* The practical impact was that nearly any method could be used to get them out of the way. One such seminal event took place in 1763 way up the Ohio River. It was a small thing, hardly a footnote to history, just a correspondence between an English general and a Swiss mercenary colonel, both of whom were serving in the American colonies. The episode speaks to the mind-set of the people who settled and built America.

A supreme war chief, Pontiac, challenged the expansion of the English colonies beyond the Alleghenies. His friends the French had lost to the English and had been expelled from the lands east of the Mississippi. Pontiac had pledged his heart to his French father over the sea. He believed that if he could only defeat the English, the French would return. Like so many of the chiefs, Pontiac was a man of his word. He raised a hellish rebellion on the frontier; he captured British forts, wiped out white settlements and eliminated as many farmsteads as his braves could reach. His rebellion was the most significant attempt by the Indian nations to throw off the encroaching white civilization.

Pontiac's warriors besieged the fort at Pittsburgh so effectively that the English General Amherst was reduced to writing to Colonel Bouquet: "Could it not be contrived to send the Small Pox among those disaffected tribes of Indians? We must on this occasion use every stratagem in our power to reduce them." Colonel Bouquet followed Amherst's orders by infecting stacks of trade blankets with smallpox virus and distributing the blankets to Pontiac's people during a peace parlay. A smallpox epidemic swept through the tribes in 1763 and 1764. Again historian Francis Parkman provides us with the documentation; the first recorded act of germ warfare had been committed in America. As horrendous as it was, this act would be repeated time and again, in one form or another, during the bitter history of the Indians against the white man on the river. The conflict would culminate with the Trail of Tears. With the death marches of the Five Civilized Tribes on "The Trail Where They Cried," the heritage of the Mechesebe ends. The Father of Waters was no longer the home of the redmen; it would flow on as the Mississippi and become for the next generations the best promise of the white man's dream.

CHAPTER 2

The Star
of the North

"Tom Sawyer wouldn't back out now, and so I won't either;
I'm agoing to see what's going on."

—*From* The Adventures of Huckleberry Finn

Stepping-stones stretch across the little stream coming out of Minnesota's Lake Itasca. In less than a minute a visitor here can maneuver across the stream and witness the continuous birth of the Father of Waters. You'll probably get your feet wet; the stepping-stones are smooth and slippery and the water is icy until summer. Right away the stream begins to make a rushing sound as if it knows it's going to become a big river. No other sense of grandeur pervades the air. No brooding cloud of menace foreshadows the impending power, no hint of vitality and richness disturbs the scene—just a sense of beginning.

A sign fashioned from a tall modeled log, standing by an asphalt walkway, says it all: HERE 1475 FEET ABOVE THE OCEAN THE MIGHTY MISSISSIPPI BEGINS TO FLOW ON ITS WINDING WAY TO THE GULF OF MEXICO.

Lake Itasca is not a grand water paradise in comparison to others in this land of ten thousand lakes, but then Walden was just one pond among many and the Merrimack and Concord hardly deserved the appellation of river. As we came north we conducted our own poll as to the number of people in ten who could name Lake Itasca as the headwaters of the Mississippi. The answer is one. A café waitress down in Albert Lea didn't know where Lake Itasca was but said she vacations at Hibbing because "it's real pretty."

It's real pretty at Lake Itasca too. It's a mile-long, spring-fed lake

Headwaters at Lake Itasca, Minnesota.

in appropriately named Clearwater County surrounded by timber-land of red and white pines. The Cousteau Society visited the lake in 1986, tested the water and declared Lake Itasca the purest part of the Mississippi River. The lake was not always thought to be the river's source. In 1805 an ambitious young army officer named Zebulon Pike claimed he had found the headwaters at Leech Lake. Pike received undeserved credit for his "discovery" and a big boost to his career, but he was a little premature. Some twenty-seven years later Henry Schoolcraft, an amateur explorer and collector of Indian lore, announced that the true source was here at Lake Itasca, roughly seventy-five miles to the west.

The state park attendant was an untalkative woman named Mickey. She did tell us that Lake Itasca gets more than half a million visitors each year and that they were preparing for six-hundred thousand this season. We asked if most visitors walked across the river on the rocks.

"Not all. Most use the footbridge. Some people don't mind getting their feet wet. It's the Mississippi." Mickey smiled, warming up. She said the park fills up in summer; it's a popular place for canoeists to put in. "People come here from every state. It doesn't matter if they're from Minnesota or Massachusetts, they love the idea that they're at the very top of the Mississippi."

Stand by the little stream that gives life to the powerful river and you can look off across Lake Itasca and visualize the plains of Ole Rölvaag's *Giants in the Earth*. This land had certainly presented a delusory picture of itself to all those Scandinavian pioneers who braved the dreads of the wilderness to settle the region. How cruel it proved in reality. "The border of utter darkness," Rölvaag called it. "A grey waste, an empty silence, a boundless cold."

"If you'll excuse me," Mickey said and went about her business. She had a clear, clipped Minnesota accent, and we guessed she had come from Norwegian stock. A park attendant told us the state park was getting ready for its centennial celebration. There'd be pioneer wagon train parades, marathon races, nature tours. "Ought to come back in summer," she said. "We'll have lumber sawing, threshing, straw bailing, grain shelling. All the way the settlers did it. My grandpa was a little boy in those days, a champion thresher. And the kids put on the snow snake games, kind of like hockey and tug-of-war. We used to win it every year."

Mickey gave us a brochure from which we learned that Itasca State Park owes its existence to a pioneer named Jacob Brower, a man who devoted his life to preserving these environs back before the turn of the century. Brower had campaigned to stop clear-cutting during a time when Minnesota was strip-mining itself to death. "You won't see any of that stuff going on in Minnesota," the attendant said. "Too many people against it." Minnesota, as well as its neighbor Wisconsin, enjoys a good national reputation for its handling of environmental issues; its legislature is known for its comparatively innovative laws. The progressive citizens of this north country lead their lawmakers by example.

A couple of new campers had come into the park but we mostly had the river to ourselves. Paying homage to the nascent river became a quiet ritual. We stood and looked and then looked a little more. And wondered if climate isn't everything to the American personality. The country's highest civility now lives in this northern zone. Emerson once wrote that "wherever snow falls there is usually civil freedom but where the banana grows man is usually sensual and cruel." We'd see both extremes before our river trip was finished.

Out of Lake Itasca, the Mississippi takes a meandering tour up to Bemidji and through more lake country to pick up several streams and little rivers; by the time it has sluiced through Grand Rapids it has taken on the aspects of a real river. The towns and villages along the way hold the demeanor of true blue Minnesota: clean, wholesome, solid, with no ostentation and no squalor, no racket and no litter. Always there are the homologous farmsteads on the landscape—plain, useful houses stuck up against huge red barns, tall red silos, all fixed upon glacial rolls and surrounded by rich black earth.

In the little town of Crosby we stopped to fill up the land-yacht and talked to an elderly attendant with a friendly tone and non-committal smile. We wanted to fill up our chest with ice but he said his darned ice machine was on the blink.

"It quits just as soon as the spring thaw. In Crosby here we used to have an icehouse, you know, way back when. We'd go out in

Minnesota farmstead, one of thousands on the prairie.

winter and cut blocks of ice out of Bay Lake. Good clean ice back in those days."

"Couldn't trust it now?"

"Nupe."

The old man gave us a free cup of coffee and we stared out into the mist barely coming down. He remarked, "Sure could use that rain. Whole state's hurting for it. Fellow I know with a backhoe went down twenty feet and still didn't hit the table. Minnesota's dry."

We continued on through the land of ten thousand lakes. From one little Minnesota town to another we noticed some of those old two- and three-story houses still using mock-brick siding. There's a prevalence of local taverns, which Minnesota is known for and where old-timers settle in hardwood booths to swig beer and schnapps while they play a Far North card game called buck euchre. We stopped for lunch in one of the taverns and got a tart potato salad and homemade dill pickles. We didn't find any buck euchre players but the waitress said they still played the game here and she showed us a booth where years of slapping cards down had worn the wood into smooth little craters. The prices on the menus were low indeed; the emphasis is on family dining. It's not until the traveler gets down the Mississippi around St. Louis that inflated prices hit the menu.

The river had been slowly widening and as it came into some industrial sprawl at Sauk Rapids it began to change from deep blue to commerce gray. The river's problems begin at Sauk Rapids. We had traveled about a hundred miles from the headwaters without seeing any concentration of industry, but that began to change. We passed several companies along the river that were letting their wastewater back into the river. The EPA has published reports that show the river at Sauk Rapids containing a substantial amount of polychlorinated biphenyls (PCBs). The companies here make electrical components, and that's where the PCBs come from. When the wastewater containing PCBs is let back into the river, the PCBs settle to the bottom. Catfish and northern carp feed there. Slowly, but not too slowly, these northern fish are dying off. Eating them can bring on liver disorders and possible cancer, according to the EPA.

The State of Minnesota has issued warnings against more than

Boyhood home of Sinclair Lewis, Sauk Centre, Minnesota.

a meal or two of fish a month. A spokesman for the Upper Mississippi River Basin Association said that the association warns against consuming any fish from the river between Minneapolis and Cairo, Illinois. The association has been trying to get this reach of the river declared off-limits to commercial fishing. The EPA has long held off declaring a ban.

Where Interstate 94 shoots west out of St. Cloud, we took our first side trip to the little town of Sauk Centre, an incarnation of small-town America in the same way that Oak Park, Illinois, and Oxford, Mississippi, and Monterey, California, used to be, all hometowns of American Nobel prize winners in literature. Sauk Centre was the boyhood home of Sinclair Lewis, America's first literary Nobel laureate.

Sauk Centre today seems to want to look spiffy, maybe because the interstate highway has sullied it with travel marts and tourist stops. The older part of town doesn't look as if it has changed since Lewis used it as a model for his novel *Main Street* back in 1920. We found the folks of Sauk Centre courteous and busy; you can't stir them to much talk. The people are proud that their little town gave the world a great man of letters. Main Street has been renamed Sinclair Lewis Avenue and a sign proclaims it THE ORIGINAL MAIN STREET.

Famous little literary towns like Hannibal and Oxford and Sauk Centre have built self-serving industries on the reputations of men whom they might otherwise have ignored. In Sauk Centre there is a Sinclair Lewis Museum, a Sinclair Lewis Tourist Center, a Sinclair Lewis Memorial Park. Lewis's boyhood home is open for tours in the summer, and you can view life as he lived it with his father, Dr. Lewis, and his mother, Isabel, and his two brothers, Fred and Claude. But none of it lets you get any closer to Lewis than the chamber of commerce building, where a burial urn of Lewis's ashes is displayed in a locked glass case. Lewis died in Rome, Italy, in 1951 but his ashes came home to rest in Sauk Centre, the prairie town that he used as his ticket out. In his childhood Lewis was called Harry by his family, Hal by his friends, and was known around town as Doodle, Mink, Minnie and Ginger. Later his literary friends all called him Red, a good-old-boy nickname that doesn't fit his image.

Red Lewis probably wouldn't find it ironic or amusing that his boyhood home is being used as a museum for gawking tourists. At the visitation center out on the highway, the young assistant was too busy to talk about Lewis; she stayed on the phone lining up an upcoming chamber of commerce banquet. The museum contains the standard leavings of the famous like a medieval reliquary: Lewis's Nobel speech, his autographed first editions and some personal photographs.

Asking around town, we didn't find anyone who'd admit to having read any of Red's works or even with any plans to do so. Coming out of town along the Sauk River, you pass an old railroad bridge and if you take a minute to stop, you can search for Sinclair Lewis's name where he carved it in one of the bridge's timbers. It's there, his barely discernible initials in the creosoted old wood.

Following the river into the Twin Cities, we looked around for mythical Lake Wobegon but couldn't locate it anywhere. We swung into Anoka, hometown of Garrison Keillor, *the* Minnesota funny man. We discovered quickly that Anoka is not Lake Wobegon; it might have been at one time but today it's swallowed up by urban

Falls of St. Anthony, Minnesota, now a lock-and-dam.

sprawl and highway crisscrosses pouring out of nearby Minneapolis. We kept an eye out for the living flag and the sons of Knute Ice Melt and Ralph's Pretty Good Grocery. We wanted to have a Nesbit soda in Dorothy's Chatterbox Café and listen in on some Keillor-like talk or maybe get invited to one of those old-fashioned dances where Norway's sons and daughters used to polka and drink the night away.

St. Anthony's Falls in downtown Minneapolis is nothing more than a series of ripples cautiously flowing from a lock and dam. The falls were once quite imposing; they were named by Father Louis Hennepin in 1680. According to Parkman, Hennepin was a self-serving impostor interested in glorifying his own name. Hennepin once claimed to have discovered the Mississippi River; in his own published work he belittled La Salle and Joliet and Marquette, but mostly he showed contempt for the famous French explorer Dulhut, who actually rescued Hennepin from the Indians at St. Anthony's Falls.

The falls have undergone drastic changes over the years. Parkman describes this part of the river as "gray crags festooned with wild honeysuckle and trees mantled with wild grapevines . . . a wilderness clothed with velvet grass, with forest-shadowed valleys, lofty heights of domes and pinnacles."

We stood in the shadows of skyscrapers and thought of what it might have been like to be with Dulhut or even Hennepin on this part of the river, gliding along in a canoe. But the changes have been too drastic; even when Twain visited the area in 1882 the river had eaten away the soft sandstone cataract, making the dangerous falls as tame as a toothless tabby. The two locks and dams here in downtown Minneapolis were not built to control the river or to protect the citizens of Hennepin County from floodwaters; they're here to aid barge traffic going on upriver to St. Cloud.

Downtown Minneapolis itself is an incidental blend of old and new. Some of the sights Twain remarked on in 1882 remain—old buildings, a stone ridge, remnants of the famous mills that gave rise to the city. These are about the only interesting things to look at in Minneapolis; it's not a pretty town and it's not ugly. It doesn't seem to have a personality at all. Twain was impressed with the town and in *Life on the Mississippi* he remarked about its progress, money and "slash and go." It's an intelligent town; no city in America spends more per capita on education and the arts.

We walked over the old stone bridge and onto the University of Minnesota campus and overheard students in the morning rush to their classes. It was a chilly day but most of the students had peeled down to sweaters and windbreakers. Their thoughts were on upcoming finals and sports, especially hockey. We quizzed a handful of students about their campus, if there were any big issues. They had to think, they shrugged, they said "gay rights, the environment."

"Congress's clean air bill is a farce," a young man said. "They're letting the business sector write its own ticket."

"At least Minnesota passes stronger pollution laws than the rest of the country will even consider."

"Oh, you think so? Some of the worst polluters are right here in the Twin Cities," another young man said. "And we don't stop them."

Once we got them going, they would talk energetically and on any subject. Their names were Susan, Gary, Les and Mark; they went off to their classes in accounting, psychology, marketing. They were arguing sports as they went.

Minneapolis seems able to let itself go only over sports. The hub is out in suburban Bloomington and if one of the professional teams has a chance for a championship, the pubs and watering holes might make you think you're in New Orleans. When we were there the hockey team, the North Stars, were making a run at the Stanley Cup. We tried to wedge into a couple of the popular sports bars, Champp's and Joe Senser's, but they were packed with a thousand rowdy fans, getting drunk. Even so, they were raucous in a controlled way and we never got the feeling they were going to cross the thug-line and tear up the bar.

While we were in Minneapolis we went out to the opening of Canterbury Downs racetrack at Shakopee, a ten-minute drive along pretty lakes south of Bloomington. In the grandstand we scanned a gathering of Minnesota punters and plungers, and what we saw was something close to the composite face of the prairie: broad, clear, open faces etched with Lutheran and German Catholic faith. A little gremlin of a man sitting next to us gave us a good tip. He said, "Gambling money has no home." He was betting two-dollar show tickets.

Overall, it's hard to find fault with the way Minneapolis does things. *Fortune* magazine rates the Twin Cities at or near the top of every category in quality of living. The people seem naturally to do the right thing (though *Fortune* analyses tend to ignore *individual* quality of life concepts).

St. Paul is just a few miles farther along the river from Minneapolis but in some ways it is as far away as the French fur traders who once controlled this land of the north. Twain found that St. Paul was "put together in solid blocks of honest brick and stone, and has the air of intending to stay." Indeed it has. The progressive little city of 71,000 that Twain found here in 1882 has grown to be a partner in a 2.5-million-person metroplex, yet St. Paul has managed to retain its own identity. It seems more laid-back and worldly, whereas Minneapolis is serious and competitive.

Originally St. Paul was Fort Snelling, and in 1836, according to Kenneth M. Stampp in his book *America in 1857,* the fort housed Dred and Harriet Scott, slaves to an army surgeon named Dr. Emerson. The Scotts had lived in Fort Snelling for two years and it was this fact—their living in territory where slavery was prohibited by the Missouri Compromise—that formed the basis of Dred Scott's legal petition for freedom. Scott filed his petition in 1846 but it was not until 1857 that Roger B. Taney, chief justice of the Supreme Court, handed down his famous decision; Scott was ruled not to be a citizen but, in the words of Taney, "a subordinate and inferior class of being ... with ... no rights or privileges."

In the census of 1850, the entire territory of Minnesota had a white population of six thousand, with an Indian population of slightly more than twice that number. By 1858 the Indian population had not increased, but the whites now numbered more than one hundred fifty thousand and Minnesota was admitted to the Union. The eastern Sioux tribes—Mdewakanton, Wahpekute, Wahpeton, Sisseton—had lost more than 28 million acres of their land by treaty. The Indians were to have received annual annuities in the form of money, trade goods and food. As usual the government's signature on the treaty was not worth much and the annuities were seldom paid in full.

Henry Sibley, an Indian trader, and Alexander Ramsey, an Indian agent, were known to have stolen more than half a million dollars from the tribes, says Robert M. Utley in his book *The Indian Frontier*. Sibley and Ramsey became the first and second governors of the state of Minnesota. In August 1862 the Indians took matters into their own hands and went on the warpath at the town of New Ulm on the Minnesota River. The Indians were starving. Andrew Myrick, the Indian agent, had dismissed their claims for food with the comment, "So far as I am concerned, if they are hungry let them eat grass or their own dung." The Indians under Chief Little Crow slaughtered every white man they could lay their hatchets on. Myrick was killed, his body mutilated and his mouth stuffed with blood-soaked grass. The now Colonel Sibley led thousands of state militiamen in conquering the eastern Sioux; he even rounded up the innocent Winnebagos. More than 2,000 prisoners were taken and 303 were charged and convicted of murder. The Minnesotan's plan to hang all these Indians was overturned by President Abraham Lincoln in all but 38 cases, and these 38 were hanged and publicly displayed in December 1862. Little Crow had escaped to Canada but returned to his home grounds the following summer. He was shot to death while picking berries in a field; his

executioner was voted a $500 reward by a grateful Minnesota leg-
islature.

In St. Paul we had arranged to meet an old friend named Burt
Carlton, a native of Minnesota, an artist and former lawyer and
math professor. We found him waiting for us on the steps of the
city library. In his forties now, he had kept his youthful appearance
and looked the very image of F. Scott Fitzgerald: blond, blue-eyed,
with an undisguised look of devilment. As was his habit, he had a
load of books in his arms. When we came up to him on the library
steps, he was thumbing through a volume of Immanuel Kant and
laughing to himself. In the 1960s Burt had dabbled in politics and
protest, had spent two years in the Peace Corps, picked up ad-
vanced degrees in math and law, and had worked in Eugene
McCarthy's campaign.

"It's easy to misread life up here," Burt told us a little later. "Out
in provincial Minnesota the church is strong. And the unbreakable
bond is family. One gets 'in' by family ties and if one has no family
ties, then count on being an eternal outsider, even in friendships."

Burt toured us around the Twin Cities, the old historical parts,
the famous Guthrie Theater, Fort Snelling, Minnehaha Falls, the
huge Cathedral of St. Paul.

"Religion plays a big part in the lives of Minnesotans, and Cath-
olics and Protestants peacefully coexist like they do down in New
Orleans. As long as the bars stay open on Sunday."

We toured some more and Burt continued his epigrams and
aphorisms. "In the big cities, the Twins and Duluth, one gets in by
hard work and hard play. Minnesotans like to talk about the
weather, and in the summer to mention winter is a cardinal sin.
Retired Minnesotans like to get away during the winters and the
favorite retreats are Arizona and south Texas. See, the Minnesotan
is self-insulating and suspicious by nature and chooses to face his
problems alone."

He took us to a tavern in north St. Paul that he said retained
some of the old-country flavor. Inside, the place was barely lit,
though we could see the long zinc bar and the rows of rough-hewn
booths lacquered to a glossy finish. The place was jammed and the
small dance floor at the back thumped with the clacking heels of
couples doing country dancing. We sat in a corner booth and Burt
talked more about the frozen north. "We take our politics seriously

A church in the Midwest.

up here and mostly turn the scoundrels out, as witness last year's governor's race when a candidate was forced to drop out because he'd gone skinny-dipping with a couple of teenyboppers. I'm sure it was in a heated pool," he said, laughing.

We saw a couple of men in the next booth playing buck euchre and slapping their cards down on the wood. It had been a long time since we'd played the game; it's a bit like Rook or bridge and you only play with part of the deck and bid for trumps. The players were having a great time with it and downing a brew with each hand.

On the wall above our booth were two posters, baseball Twins and football Vikings, and another one below that of Kent Hrbek,

the Twins' first baseman, who looked in the poster like Paul Bun-
yan. A pretty blond waitress moved from the pickup window and
glided along the bar with a casual, flirty ease, tolerating the taunts
and come-ons from regulars with the aplomb of one who'd heard
it all a thousand times. One husky fellow reached out and put his
arm around her and we heard him say, "Lady, I only got one thing
to say to you—get them britches off!"

The waitress laughed at him and slipped out of his grasp. At our
booth a minute later she laughed again and told us, "Don't pay
any attention to those rowdies; they're harmless." She cleared
empty beer mugs from the booths and swayed by us and said, "If
I don't drop all this I'll be grace in action." The husky fellow got
up from the bar and staggered toward the men's room, knocking
into our booth. He was very heavy and very drunk. A few minutes
later he came back by and rammed into our booth again. Evidently
he hadn't liked it when the waitress had spoken to us. He squinched
up his face, leaned down deliberately and sneezed right on Burt's
neck.

"That bother you?" he growled on Burt.

"No, it felt cool," Burt said. The guy laughed then and offered
to buy us a beer. He became contrite and wanted to apologize by
sitting in our booth with us and buying more beer, though he soon
lost interest and staggered back to the bar, where they were telling
Ole and Lena jokes, the north woods variety of simpleton humor.

On our way out we noticed a leather dice cup at the cash register. That tradition is long-standing in Midwestern taverns: double
or nothing on your tab according to the toss of the dice. The tradition there was reserved for regulars and the pretty waitress took
our money and said she was sorry for the way the guy had acted
up. "The guys are decent fellows most of the time or we just ignore
them. They're so broke they can't pay attention." She knew we
were not from the area and she asked where we were heading, and
when Burt told her we were on our way down the Mississippi River,
she said, "Oh, that kinda makes us neighbors."

Later Burt guided us around a chain of lakes until we hit Old
Highway 61 at White Bear Lake above St. Paul. Twain had con-
cluded his steamboat journey at St. Paul in *Life on the Mississippi*
and this area was his last point of interest. He called White Bear
Lake "a lovely sheet of water being utilized as a summer resort by

the wealth and fashion of the state." It's still a lovely sheet of water and is surrounded by the gilt of affluence. We passed along marinas, beaches, hotels, golf courses and luxury homes. There are no bears, of course, around White Bear Lake and any of the native inhabitants who might have resided in the vicinity had long been put to flight even before the steamboat days.

Old 61 widens into a busy freeway as it rushes into St. Paul. It is truly a democratic avenue, for before we were down its length we would pass through some of the worst pockets of poverty in America. The river and the highway almost join hands at the enormous port of St. Paul; the Mississippi for the first time began to look like the Father of Waters.

St. Paul is the distribution center of the upper Midwest and we saw proof of the fact in the busy harbor, where dozens of barges were taking on freight for shipment downriver. The water here looks much different than it does just a few miles away over in Minneapolis; it is thick and milky, with that telltale appearance of vigorously treated wastewater.

Our highway follows the Mississippi in St. Paul to Indian Mounds Park and we stopped to look at the turfed man-made hills that begin here in Minnesota and Wisconsin and crop up all the way down the river basin.

Since St. Paul is the state capital, the city is a center for Minnesota's environmental activities. Over the years these public and private groups have campaigned with an almost religious fervor, and as a result Minnesota is a model state for recycling and for water pollution safeguards. Minnesota has a state lottery and 40 percent of the proceeds go to an environmental and natural resources tax fund.

"What really needs to happen," Burt said, "is for the bad old pollution states of the South to adopt a legislative exchange program. Let Minnesota lawmakers go down there and make laws for them and let the good old boys come up here and teach us how to party." We had come back to the heart of St. Paul and we were strolling around the state capitol. Burt took us for coffee into a small restaurant where Minnesota lawmakers and newspaper people hang out. In this haunt some weighty political ideas have been hatched over the years. Eugene McCarthy and Hubert Humphrey came in here, and back in the fifties Adlai Stevenson launched his campaign here.

"Norman Vincent Peale was from Minnesota," Burt said. "Everybody's probably forgotten what Adlai said about Peale: 'St. Paul is appealing and St. Peale is appalling.' "

We sat talking about this north country, and Burt held forth on his home state and spoke about such figures as James J. Hill, America's first railroad tycoon, and J. Paul Getty, the world's richest man for a good part of a century. And Burt's favorite, Frank Kellogg of Minnesota, the man who once sponsored a treaty that actually outlawed war. "Kellogg won the Nobel," Burt said, "and the world went to war." Burt himself had worked for the antiwar candidate, Eugene McCarthy, years ago and had been fond of marching around saying, "Come clean for Gene." Now more reflective, Burt said that all the antiwar demonstrations back in the sixties seemed almost a fad.

"Protest was just trendy," he said. "Just like environmentalism is trendy today.

"I have some good friends who work with the Izaak Walton League in the Twin Cities," he said. "They've been trying to stop those barge lines from using their old single-hull boats. They still use some, you know."

We didn't know anything about single- or double-hull barges and Burt explained something of how it works and what the Izaak Waltons were so concerned about. "Most of the old single-hull boats have been phased out, but the barge lines are still using some of the older ones, I guess because they've still got them and can make a lot of money using them. But the single-hulls are dangerous and everybody knows it. They've been involved in dozens of spills down the river."

Burt told us that he himself had worked as a volunteer gathering names on petitions asking the Coast Guard to quit giving permits to the single-hull barges. "The Izaak Walton League keeps asking the barge lines to take their single-hulls out of operation and the companies keep refusing. So the League took its petition to the Coast Guard. And it was hung up in the typical governmental bureaucracy. But the Coast Guard finally rendered a decision, just this summer. It denied the League's petition. The Coast Guard said the barge lines had too good a safety record to deny them permits. Yeah, right. There are lots of barge lines operating up and down that river and they average fifty spills a year. Fifty! Poor Izaak Walton, the consummate fisherman!"

We stood by the harbor watching other barges pushing along upriver. We wondered what cargo they were carrying, and Burt said that every day the giant tow-barges bring up millions of gallons of petroleum and chemicals, here and over on the Great Lakes. "You watch," he said. "There's going to be a major spill someday, just like the *Valdez*, and a single-hull barge will be involved, but that will get lost in the shuffle. And what's that going to do to the fishing if it happens in Minnesota?"

Burt had on the crazy old-time protest smile that had got him cuffed around once in a march on Washington. We thought that Burt was always going to have a good time. We left him standing by the river, looking. As we backed out in the land-yacht, he came walking toward us again. He leaned down to the window and said, "I forgot one other Minnesota boy. Thorstein Veblen. Now didn't he raise the specter of conspicuous consumption! Just as soon as you get out of St. Paul, you're going to see conspicuous consumption is alive and well on the Mississippi. Hey, you ought to take Veblen along with you down the river, a little ways at least."

We caught a last glimpse of Burt still standing and musing by the river as we turned out into the busy traffic of disguised Old 61. Farther along, the river came back in sight and ran with us for a minute before it jumped off down into the heartland of the country.

CHAPTER 3

The Route of Eagles

"Studying the river shining below, the green swell of trees on either side of the banks, eagles flashing down golden-beaked, talons trailing the wind ... then soaring off with wings beating high."

—*Sam Hamod, American poet*

The Mississippi is not itself between St. Paul and La Crosse, Wisconsin. It's a silk-stocking strip that Twain in *Life on the Mississippi* saw as a "delightful resort of jaded summer tourists." What we saw was an expanse of beautiful, ruinously expensive lake frontage with dozens of manicured estates. The man-made lakes are chock-full of yachts, sailboats, ski rigs, cabin cruisers, with marinas, clubs, lodges and restaurants to accommodate it all. In this nothing had changed since Twain's journey down the river.

The lakes are clear and royal blue, as though strained through a sieve; the river runs through it all somewhere, though it's hard to see. No fewer than eight lock-and-dam systems smother the infant current in less than a hundred miles. These upper stretches of the Mississippi have never been a serious threat to the works of man, and we could only surmise as we passed along the concrete and steel goliaths that the dams are monuments to vested political interest, the pork barrel rolling out of Washington.

The U.S. Army Corps of Engineers has existed as an institution since 1802. It is, as such, the charter member of the military-industrial complex. Over the years the Corps has built roads and fortresses, bridges and dams, and fought meritoriously in every war in which America has been engaged. Generally speaking, since its supervision of the $2-billion Manhattan Project, the primary function of the Corps has been the control of America's waterways.

The incredible disaster of the 1927 Mississippi flood first caused the Corps to be entrusted with complete responsibility for the river. Subsequent major floods in each decade since the 1920s have firmly entrenched the Corps in the role of head plumber of America's water supplies.

The Corps is aware that it cannot exert absolute control over the Mississippi below the confluence with the Missouri. The Corps operates on a self-defined mandate of "damage control" and "risk management," not flood control. As we moved downriver, we spoke with several resident Corps engineers at locks and dams along the way. Each of them told us, as they explained the official Corps policy, that there's a lot of misunderstanding when floods come and people want to know why the dams built and operated by the Corps didn't contain the floodwaters. One engineer interpreted the Corps policy this way: "The business of the Corps is to prevent disaster. We do this by allowing limited and containable backflooding to ensure that loss does not exceed acceptable levels. But people just see the flood damage to their own property and point fingers rather than realizing what the Corps has saved."

Rich bottomland borders the forested bluffs of the river as it keeps pushing southward. We were traveling the middle of the strip and all of a sudden we were in the middle of a basic junior high school geography lesson—but not what you'd think. We couldn't find any wetlands in these bottoms. Wetlands, an issue almost lost in the complex scheme of commerce and progress, are crucial to the survival of fish and wildlife. Wetlands absorb topsoil that washes off high ground; this soil is rich in nutrients and provides food for fish and wildlife as it rejoins the flow of streams and rivers. It's a basic lesson that Mr. Wizard taught us when we were young, and you don't need exhaustive studies to show you that the land—its fish, fowl and wildlife—is paying a price for all the opulence on parade. Congress has passed some wetlands legislation but the implementation of these laws is decades away even to the most optimistic. The problem seems to center on the crossed responsibilities of the diverse and disparate agencies at the federal, state and especially the local level. No one agrees on what should be done, when it should be done or where it should be done. Vested interests are fighting hard to delay implementation.

We stopped at Lock and Dam No. 3 at Red Wing and spoke with

a Corps of Engineers secretary, asking her, "How's business?" She replied proudly that business was super. "Boats pass through the lock every few minutes." She reported more than twenty thousand boats had gone through the lock during 1990 and more than that were expected in 1991. Most of the boats were pleasure craft. That's a lot of pleasure, but the boats are also causing noticeable erosion and a depletion of the river's vegetation.

Along the strip we found several people worried about the damage caused by the dams. "The Corps of Engineers is waging war on nature," said a high school science teacher in Winona County, Minnesota. "We are beginning to see the results along the river. Of course, the dams have been there for some time. They trap the pollution and the fish can't survive in it. But what can be done— tear the dams out?" A botany professor at a Minnesota state college furnished us with the results of startling tests conducted by the U.S. Department of Natural Resources. The Department has tested the fish in the lakes created by the dams in the district and has found substantial particles of a substance called furan. Furan is short for one molecule of poison; a lethal dose for a guinea pig, our botany professor said, can be ten parts per billion, or a thousand times less than the PCB levels found in the lake's fish.

Just out of curiosity, we kept an eye out as we passed along some of the luxury lakes and sure enough we saw a commercial fishing rig busy with nets out in the middle of the lake. Somehow the fish dishes on restaurant menus weren't too appealing.

Old 61 keeps itself in the Mississippi's hip pocket through Minnesota and Wisconsin, and we headed for an old stamping ground at La Crosse. We had expected La Crosse to be more of a hopping place than it turned out to be. In our college days it was lively and rowdy like old Gaslight Square in St. Louis. Cruising along Fourth Street, we found just as many bars as ever, but the street seemed more sedate and had the look of respectability. We did find a deli-bar selling a local specialty called scrapple that we used to buy and gag down years ago, and in this we weren't disappointed. Scrapple is still a compost of the worst-tasting stuff this side of boiled gristle, but just like someone who grew up in the South eating cracklings, every now and then we have to relive our bad taste.

We hadn't intended the record of our journey to become an environmental tract, yet what we saw and heard gave us pause. We had been led to believe that the states on the upper river were environmentally aware. The more we saw and heard, the more we began to understand why the people were leading the legislators. The next story we ran into was unbelievable but all too real. We had read of it in national magazines and seen it on TV, but we wanted to prove it to ourselves.

Out of La Crosse, Highway 61 angles over through the Wisconsin countryside before rejoining the river in Iowa, but we took state roads to stay on the river because there were a couple of locales we wanted to see, the little towns of Genoa and Prairie du Chien. On the surface there's nothing exceptional about either town. They are both small ports on the river, they're only half an hour apart, and they're pleasant places with friendly townspeople. If you asked the towns they'd tell you there's nothing unique about them, yet they stand as microcosms, emblems if you will, of American culture, past and present.

Genoa lives with a daily, agonizing dilemma that has to do with its aging power plant. When it was first built, the plant was powered by uranium, like so many others across the country. A few years ago the plant's owners converted to coal. The burning of coal, about a billion tons a year, is bad enough at Genoa, covering the area with a sooty black pall. But that's not the real hazard. It's the presence of all the radioactive waste built up over the years, thousands of uranium pellets, enough to destroy the heartland of America for ten thousand years.

The plant sits squarely on the banks of the Mississippi and projects a bleak contrast to the pristine surroundings. Though the plant maintains rigid security, you can get close enough to see the main works and the rows of outbuildings squatting by the river. In those dingy structures are stored thousands of bundles of uranium pellets that will continue to do their business until the year 12,000.

The outbuildings are tightly enclosed by chain-link fence and covered over with a mass of barbed wire. It's a hideous sight but one that the two dozen security guards have to face in round-the-clock shifts. Who in the world would want to break into such a place? Someone wanting to make his own atom bomb. You start with plutonium, physicists tell us, and there's plenty of the stuff in those outbuildings.

We drove up as close as we could and stood off to the side

looking down upon the works. Our first thoughts on seeing this place were that it was like a concentration camp or prison. Or a scene from the theater of the absurd. For a minute you got fanciful and thought of Prometheus and his vultures, Sisyphus and his rock. Remembering our youth, we tried to think of when it all started. It began with high hopes and slogans like "Atoms for Peace."

This plant, like scores of others, will have to wait until the government finds a place to store the nuclear wastes, and even the government says that will be well into the next century. In the meantime Genoa abides and the guards keep their vigil. A fellow in town told us the guards make good money and have excellent fringe benefits. "They don't have to worry about their jobs playing out."

Driving away from Genoa and into the Wisconsin countryside, we didn't get a sense of the strength of the nearby river, only a vague feeling of the land's historical locus. Indian mounds kept cropping up and lakes carved out by the Ice Age dotted the landscape of the river basin, falling all the way down from Green Bay, where grimy fur trappers were able in the span of two generations to completely slaughter the beaver of the north country.

Prairie du Chien was the jumping-off point for most of the Scandinavian and Middle European settlers of Rölvaag's northern prairies in the 1850s. It is also the jumping-off point for the renewal of America's heritage and symbol, the rebirth of the great bald eagle in the heartland of the nation.

A poet, Sam Hamod, joined us near Prairie du Chien and spent time with us on the river. We'd known him at the University of Iowa and had made more than one trip here with him to watch eagles fishing in the Mississippi. Sam's a book poet, not a magazine poet, and he has eight volumes to his credit. He teaches at Howard University in Washington, D.C., and was visiting relatives in Iowa when we contacted him; he jumped at the chance to meet us for eagle watching.

We met him at an overlook downriver; he was already scanning the bluffs. "They're not out in numbers," he said, "but they're coming." We stood craning our necks and sharing binoculars while a sharp wind gusted off the river. There's a great old poem by Tennyson about an eagle and as we watched the sky Sam began talking the poem, not quoting it but bringing it alive along the bluffs of the Mississippi. Then we saw one, a strong fellow looping over the bluff. The bald eagle poised aloft for seconds and then plunged; he was Tennyson's thunderbolt coming over the mountain wall. Shivers went through us and it wasn't the frigid wind.

"The family Falconidae," Sam said. "They look ugly in pictures but they're really beautiful. The hind toe is perfectly level with the three front toes. Nothing else will do him. His claws are sharper than knives."

The eagles have made a big comeback along the river. We had thought they were going to die off. DDT and other cropland poisons almost made them extinct as late as the 1970s, but thanks to a small corps of activists in the country, the eagles are surviving, even flourishing to an extent. Eagles like the Mississippi basin; it's always been their habitat because of its bluffs and waterways, where they can practice their art of fishing.

"If they desired," Sam said, "eagles could go so high as to take to the jet stream. They could go into outer orbit and visit the galaxy."

Because we came so close to losing them, eagle watching is now a popular sport. The U.S. Fish and Wildlife Service has estimated that as many as fifteen thousand eagles nest in the country. In the 1970s there may have been fewer than two thousand. Some cities are thinking of introducing eagles to their parks and reservoir areas.

"It all started with *Silent Spring*," Sam said. "We get to watch these fellows today because of Rachel Carson."

Our count that day wasn't enormous, fewer than ten. We stayed by the bluffs most of the morning and saw a few stunning aerial displays. We had the overlook to ourselves for a couple of hours until other people, travelers, came by and took up the watch. We might have stayed for the exhilaration of it all, and for Sam Hamod, poet and lover of the sky's unrivaled fishermen. The air over the river was clean and unmixed. If a spirit lingered from that older time, it might have found a semblance of peace in the flight of eagles.

A few days after one of our river forays, a letter came from Sam in Washington, D.C.; it was refreshing. With the blather that comes from the capital, here was an account of something that matters, an expression of a good feeling:

Writing and driving along the Mississippi are a lot alike. So much washes in time you can't remember if it was in spring that you saw the bald eagles up by Prairie du Chien, or if it was in the fall, studying the river shining below, the green swell of trees on either side of the banks, eagles flashing down golden-beaked, talons trailing the wind, splashing only slightly the surface of the water, then soaring off with wings beating high into the trees on the other side.

And I could tell you about the time we drove Highway 61 without air conditioning; the humid river forced us to open the windows, and in they came, hundreds of mayflies. We beat them out with towels. But always alongside was this quiet river, this wide ranging brown glory of Iowa, Wisconsin, Illinois, that same river that runs down into the sodden, swamped ponds of Louisiana.

The river was like the early times that I knew it when I was a young boy and going to Iowa to visit relatives with my father and mother, driving our old Chrysler, maroon four-door, and it would take so long, for we'd come from Gary, Indiana, across Illinois. My father always stopped when we got to the river and let us look down on some of the river's magic, the long coal boats and ore boats and the fishing scows and the Sunday sailboats and motorboats for skiing. And when we got to the bridge we knew we were almost to Cedar Rapids, almost to Fort Dodge, almost to that other world we went to for reprieve away from the steel mills, the bars, the drunkenness of Gary, and into the clean air, the rolling farmland, the smell of horse and cow manure from the livestock trucks we'd pass. Sometimes we stopped at a farmhouse and asked and received cordially a drink of cold, savory well water. It was as if once we got into Iowa on the other side of the Mississippi, we came into some other sort of haven, maybe a kind of heaven. On some days.

And then later I'd go visit on my own, either taking the train and crossing the river on that old black bridge at Rock Island, always afraid the train would be too heavy for the bridge, but it never fell in. Or by newer car, with air-conditioning to safeguard against mayflies. Then when I went to Iowa to school, traveling in a Ford V-8 two-door, white and maroon flashing into the evening sun off Highway 61, the Mississippi was like a shaman river foretelling one's fate. I remember when I went back to graduate school, my wife and two children and I came through a fierce rainstorm crossing Illinois, and just as we got to the Mississippi River the sun suddenly broke through, and across the river in Iowa we could see this huge, clear, stunning rainbow. There it was, saying: Yes, you are welcome.

Yes, all will go well. And I always remember that time at the river because from then on it did go well.

Sam Hamod

We had begun this reach of the river innocently and were nearly overwhelmed by the darkness of the shadows. Yet with all, the sense of relief brought to life by Sam Hamod's rainbow, by his love of the river, by the return of the eagles, left us with a feeling of good— returned us to Mark Twain's vision of "the shining river, winding here and there and yonder, its sweep interrupted at intervals by clusters of wooded islands threaded by silver channels ... it is all as tranquil and reposeful as dreamland ... nothing to hang a fret or a worry upon."

CHAPTER 4

Black Hawk

"We always had plenty—our children never cried with hunger, nor our people were never in want. Here our village had stood for more than a hundred years, during all which time we were the undisputed possessors of the valley of the Mississippi."

—*From* Black Hawk: An Autobiography

Coming into Prairie du Chien, a town named for the millions of prairie dogs (ground squirrels) found here by the first French explorers, the river traveler doesn't immediately sense anything different about the town. Like Genoa, Prairie du Chien is unremarkable; it tries to be hospitable and would like to expand its tourist trade, but what little town wouldn't?

The town has one big attraction, a baronial mansion called Villa Louis that the locals are quite proud of; it was the home of Wisconsin's first millionaire fur trader. The first wave of white immigrants made quick work of the prairie dogs; their stew pots bubbled for a while and then the little creatures were gone, obliterated like the beaver.

Actually the town of Prairie du Chien has a haunting angle buried in its past, though we could find no marker declaring it the site of one of the most shameful episodes in American history. It was here on the banks of the Mississippi in 1832 that the last battle of the Black Hawk War was fought. It all started over the planting of corn.

Part of Thomas Jefferson's dream was that the Indians and whites could live, if not together, then in splendid isolation. A dreamline was created called the Permanent Indian Frontier and a chain of forts was established to enforce it. But a leader named Black Hawk had no truck with visions of the white men; he crossed the line and all hell broke loose.

Black Hawk is the only man in U.S. history to have a war named after him. He was the last high chief of the proud Sauk-Fox tribes whose empire extended to the greater part of the Upper Mississippi Valley. His holdings were not anchored in the white man's law; the touch of Black Hawk on the land was as the wind and the dew. For many generations his Sauk-Fox nation hunted the nomadic buffalo here, planted corn here, raised their children here and when necessary gathered to defend the land of their birthright. Black Hawk had lived all the days of his life close by the great river that nourished him and his people.

In the coming war, Black Hawk and his small band of warriors would face the best and brightest America had to offer: Lieutenant Robert Anderson, who would later defend the rights of the Union at Fort Sumter in 1861; Lieutenant Jefferson Davis, who would lead the Confederacy in rebellion; General William Henry Harrison, who had built an illustrious career by treating the Indians out of their lands and would ride that fame into the White House; Colonel Zachary Taylor, another noted Indian fighter who took his turn in the generals' parade to the White House in 1849; General Winfield Scott, the longest-serving general in U.S. history (he also ran for the presidency, though not even his Whig Party could stand his fussy soreheadedness); and Captain Abraham Lincoln, whose war-star status helped propel him into the limelight as the Great Emancipator.

The Black Hawk War began at planting time in the spring of 1831. By that year the flush era of steamboat travel was well under way; the country was alive with westward expansion and masses of Europeans were flooding into the Mississippi River Valley. Black Hawk himself had stood on the banks of the river and watched the first steamboat in Northern waters taking military supplies up to Fort Snelling. As he watched the smoke-belching monster, Black Hawk must have realized that his mode of living was going the way of the beaver and the buffalo.

Black Hawk had been a marked man since the end of the War of 1812. He had taken England's side in that war, causing the intruding white settlers and regional authorities no end of misery. Although the adolescent United States could do nothing about

Black Hawk at the time, his punishment was not forgotten; only put off. Who better to carry out the retribution than the hero of the War of 1812, Andrew Jackson himself? Before his years in the presidency were over, Jackson would do far more than punish one chief.

Old Hickory had got where he was, all the way to the White House, by compiling a prime record in eradicating Indians. He had begun by annihilating the Creek Nation, making his beloved South safe for the white man; afterward Jackson directed the campaign to wipe out the Seminoles in Florida. When Jackson came to office in 1829, the first two steps he took were to reorganize (for his cronies) the country's banking system and to set the stage for his official, barefaced policy toward all the native American Indians—open and inexorable genocide.

America's Trail of Tears actually began in the early 1820s under the relocation policies of President Monroe, though removal of the Indians from their lands had started with the arrival of the first European boats. Under Jackson, the liquidation of the tribes took on the zeal of a holy crusade. Diseases such as cholera and measles (not to mention the sadistic and ruthless whites who rushed in) killed thousands of the Indians being relocated, and money promised to the "civilized tribes" never found its way out of the clutches of the federal agents. Congress gave Jackson its official blessing by passing the Indian Removal Act in 1830.

Still, Jackson was a politician and needed a shining victory to buoy his immense popularity with the thousands of Europeans "relocating" in America. When word came to Jackson that Indian trouble was erupting on the Upper Mississippi, his chance for a rekindling victory was at hand. The Indian chief causing the trouble was Black Hawk, who had always been a thorn in the side. Now a man in his sixties and the paramount chief of a dwindling people, Black Hawk would be a fine trophy, and an inexpensive one at that. Ridding Florida of the Seminoles had cost the astronomical sum of $20 million, but putting down Black Hawk would come cheap and easy. Promptly, Jackson dispatched the country's best generals to the Illinois Territory of the Upper Mississippi.

Black Hawk's troubles with white settlers had been going on for several years. As a young chief back in 1804 he had been to St. Louis, had drunk the white man's whiskey and seen his brother

Sauk-Fox tribes swindled out of fifty million acres of their hunting grounds. In the War of 1812 he had fought alongside the great chief Tecumseh and had been with him when he died (and had helped save Tecumseh's body from being skinned by the soldiers).

In a Sauk village (near present-day Rockford, Illinois), Black Hawk was born in 1767, just as America was being born as a nation. As a teenager he was a strong warrior, and he became an able chief by the time of the Indian Wars and the coming of the white settlers. For years he tried to get along with the settlers and took his grievances to the Indian agents in Rockford. Each year saw more and more squatters on his land. In 1829 the situation had grown so acute that, on returning from the winter hunt for food, Black Hawk found white settlers occupying his own village, a family living in his own lodge. The settlers had plowed up the Sauk burial grounds and burned down several lodges. In reply to Black Hawk's protests, the Land Office of Illinois put his land, and even his village, up for public auction—first come, first served. This decision, in total disregard of the existing treaty, was made by Illinois governor John Reynolds, a political opportunist and usurper of the first order.

Remarkably, Black Hawk chose not to fight but remained two more years on his ancestral land, watching the settlers streaming in to squeeze him into a tight little corner at the mouth of the Rock River. But his people were starving and he sent word to Governor Reynolds asking for permission to cross the Mississippi for one last winter hunt. Territorial Indian Commissioner William Clark had refused to provide enough promised government rations to keep Black Hawk's people alive, and the hunt was his last hope. Yet there was no game to be had—white poachers had taken care of that.

So in April 1831, at the beginning of the planting season, Black Hawk crossed over the Mississippi—not to stage a rebellion against the white intruders, but to plant a crop of corn. He was on a desperate search for any vacant stretch of prairie away from the settlers. Small parties of Sauk-Fox squaws and children began tilling the soil and planting seed corn. In actuality the planting of crops by Indians was not prohibited by the treaty dating back to 1804, but the sight of about a thousand of Black Hawk's people on the move from across the river scared settlers to death. Word of this unpardonable sin reached Governor Reynolds and he jumped at the opportunity to call out the militia "to repel the invasion." A Galena, Illinois, newspaper rushed into print with a vehement call for a "war of extermination until there shall be no Indian left in Illinois."

Though Black Hawk didn't know it, the war was on, and the call to arms brought sixteen hundred volunteers and the regular army under General Edmund P. Gaines, a veteran of the wars against the Creeks and Seminoles and Andy Jackson's hand-picked man. But Gaines made the initial mistake of sending Major Isaiah Stillman after Black Hawk first with only volunteers. They caught Black Hawk off guard, with only a handful of warriors, and surrounded him. Far outnumbered, Black Hawk offered a flag of surrender, but Stillman's rough and drunken militia opened fire on Black Hawk's camp, killing a few braves. Here he would die, Black Hawk decided, and instead of running he turned and attacked the volunteers. He led forty warriors into the teeth of three hundred soldiers, and to his surprise, the Illinois militia turned tail and ran. For a long time afterward, the action of the volunteers, who had so bravely marched off to fight the red-man scourge, was known as Stillman's Run. Still, except for the actions of a few whiskeyed-up hotheads, the coming massacre might have been avoided.

Seeing all the soldiers, Black Hawk believed it was kill or be killed. He massed some five hundred warriors and led them across the land, burning settlers' shacks and taking scalps. Hysteria spread along the Illinois frontier and volunteer companies began to form everywhere in Illinois and Indiana. Black Hawk and his last tribes, in all less than two thousand strong, retreated up the Rock River, with thousands of militia men and regular army troops pouring after them. The chase would go deep into the Wisconsin wilderness through June and July. The soldiers came at them from all sides but somehow Black Hawk's people survived through the spring and summer in the swampy wilds on berries, fish and roots.

Clearly Black Hawk had no chance. Close to two hundred thousand settlers lived in the Illinois and Wisconsin territories, and Black Hawk had fewer warriors than he had commanded as a fifteen-year-old brave. Still, he might have held out indefinitely had he not been betrayed by one of his own. A major portion of the Sauk-Fox warriors had followed Chief Keokuk and they were all safely secluded on a preserve in Iowa; Keokuk had made a separate pact with Commissioner Clark. In exchange for promises of food and peace, Keokuk had agreed not to go to Black Hawk's aid.

Keokuk would not fight, but Black Hawk would. In the War of 1812 Black Hawk had been the master of guerrilla tactics, constantly stinging the Americans with lightning raids. But in 1812 he did not have the responsibility of protecting women and children. Then he could hit and run; now he could only run. He led his tribe deeper into the Wisconsin north, swinging closer day by day to the Mississippi River, which had always sustained him. What followed was not war; it was a slaughter of men, women and children, so sickening that it repulsed many of the regular army officers. Black Hawk could not surrender—when segments of his tribe attempted to give up, they were cut down in their tracks. The ultimate enemy, starvation, finally defeated Black Hawk and forced him out into the open. He made one last desperate run toward Prairie du Chien; if he could get his people across the Mississippi again, they might lose themselves in the dense woods until the pursuing soldiers lost their thirst for blood.

Black Hawk made it to the Mississippi but was immediately pinned down by a gunboat, the *Warrior,* and its six-pounder cannon. Not wanting any more of his people to die, Black Hawk raised a white flag, but troops on the gunboat opened fire, picking off the Indians on the riverbank. Black Hawk put up a stout defense and made the *Warrior* retreat downriver. But at that point more than a thousand of the militiamen came charging up the riverbank. Again Black Hawk tried to surrender but the troops fell upon the Sauk-Fox with axes, clubs and guns. Here the real slaughter of the Black Hawk War began. Called later the Massacre at Ax River, the carnage lasted eight full hours, and in the end the soldiers took only thirty-nine prisoners out of two thousand who had fled into the wilderness.

Despite his ferocious rear-guard stand, Black Hawk could only watch as his people were cut down. Some two hundred, mostly women and children, did manage to swim or thrash their way across the river, only to be met by a force of mercenary Sioux who had been paid by Commissioner Clark to finish off the dirty business. The Sioux, an old and bitter enemy of Black Hawk's, earned their pay with relish. They killed and mutilated the last of Black Hawk's tribe.

Black Hawk and four or five others escaped the slaughter and sought haven with Winnebago Indians in northern Wisconsin. These Winnebagos sold Black Hawk to the authorities for a reward of twenty horses and a hundred dollars. Black Hawk and three of his sub-chiefs were transported down the Mississippi by steamboat to St. Louis, where Commissioner Clark kept them in chains for a year. The last chief of the once-strong Sauk-Fox tribes was taunted and spat upon; he might have been tortured except for the kindness of a young officer named Jefferson Davis. In any case, the dirty little war was finished. It had been staged for the benefit of ambitious politicians and greedy white settlers.

When news of the great victory reached Washington, the press applauded America's new conquering heroes. Highest honors were heaped upon these rugged, death-defying liberators of the West. The military leaders would soon be rewarded beyond even itchy Andy Jackson's expectations. Obscure political figures found their careers soaring. These eager men of easy opportunity taught a lesson to future rank-and-file office seekers—they need only buy themselves a military commission and get some battlefield experience, and if a useful little war was not available, one could be created. The Black Hawk War set a pattern that would last well beyond the nineteenth century.

During the year when Black Hawk and his three chiefs were imprisoned in St. Louis's Jefferson Barracks, Clark made them the center of attention. Everyone who was anyone—from city fathers to schoolchildren—paraded through the stockade to view the dreaded Black Hawk. Washington Irving and Count de Pourtalès, beginning their tour of the prairies, were permitted a gawking interview (Irving, ill at ease, did not mention the meeting in his writings, and in a way he was sending a message that polite society cared nothing for the harsher realities of the American frontier).

As the year wore on, Clark began to fret over rumors of a possible rescue of Black Hawk, and the commissioner was much relieved when President Jackson sent orders to have Black Hawk and his chiefs transferred to Fort Monroe, the great Eastern seaboard fortress. Actually Jackson had other plans. He had the chiefs brought instead to Washington, where the Black Hawk tragedy took on the aspect of a Roman triumph, with Andy as Caesar to Black Hawk's Vercingetorix.

As it turned out, Old Hickory had overplayed his hand. The defeat of Black Hawk was supposed to have been Jackson's crowning glory in the nation's eyes, and it started out that way. Andy trooped out the Indian chiefs, pinned medals on them, and preened about as the acknowledged Indian fighter of all time. But the political orchestration began to take on negative aspects. The public had had its fill of gory heroes; some of the Eastern newspapers were openly critical, saying that Jackson's laurels were bathed in too much Indian blood. Jackson went on with it; he had Black Hawk and his chiefs paraded, in chains on some occasions, through the major cities of the East. In the offbeat way in which American society often reacts to such staged events, Black Hawk became something of a beau ideal. He was applauded wherever he went. His regal demeanor appealed to the mannered folks of Philadelphia and New York and Boston. He sat for portraits, smiled and bowed with grace, and spoke eloquently about the American way of life. Clearly he was turning the tables and beating Jackson at his own game.

With pressure mounting on him to unchain and free the chiefs, Jackson finally relented. After spending most of the year as a sideshow freak, Black Hawk was sent back to live in Iowa. He would never again be free to live on his land, hunt or provide for his people. For the rest of his days he was closely watched and had to obey every command of his betrayer, Keokuk, who now served as the paramount chief of the Sauk-Fox tribes, what little was left of them.

Black Hawk died destitute in the winter of 1838. His last recorded words were, "I was once a great warrior. I am poor now. Keokuk has been the cause of my present situation." Black Hawk was buried according to the custom of his ancestors, sitting erect inside a small mausoleum of undressed logs. His grave was soon despoiled and his skeleton displayed proudly by Iowa's governor at his mansion in Des Moines. The skeleton remained on display in the "Hawkeye Capital" for some years until more decent Iowans, recoiling at the bad taste of it all, protested and had Black Hawk finally laid to rest.

Black Hawk's death in 1838 marked the close of a three-hundred-year epoch and the end of the Mechesebe as the native tribes knew it. Yet one tragic drama remained to be played out along the banks of the aboriginal river. In the year of Black Hawk's death, the white leader in Washington went forward with his obsession to remove all the tribes east of the Mississippi.

The fertile valley of the Tennessee River was simply too rich to be wasted on the Cherokee tribes, though they had lived in harmony with their white neighbors for decades. Their civilization up and down the pristine river valley was a model of good citizenship much like that of the Incas, which Pizarro and De Soto had destroyed right before the Spanish incursion into America. The Cherokees had carved out for themselves a piece of what would be the American dream. Their communities were prosperous, clean and orderly—they had good schools, sawmills, blacksmith shops, textile mills, city halls, a court system, miles of public roads. They supported the U.S. government, paid their taxes and had their own tribal constitution. Many of their young people were capable students with ambitions to become doctors, nurses and lawyers.

Their peaceful existence came to an abrupt end in 1832, just after the end of the Black Hawk War, when Andrew Jackson defied the U.S. Supreme Court ruling that the Cherokees had every right to their land. Greedy Georgia crackers kept up raids into the Cherokee Nation and brought so much pressure upon the state and national governments that Jackson got his way. He set the final removal date for May 23, 1838, and the army was ordered to begin building log cages for the Cherokee roundup. General Winfield Scott was again in charge and at his command were seven thousand soldiers. Although Scott had ordered his troops to show "every possible kindness" to the Cherokees, when the roundup began some of the soldiers robbed and raped and murdered members of the tribes. The roundups caught the people in their fields or at work in the mills. The army contained the Cherokees in concentration camps during the sweltering summer months. A large number fell ill and died there, but they were the lucky ones, for many more were to die in the overland march that fall and winter.

Remembrances of those days have been passed down from generation to generation among the Cherokees of modern-day Oklahoma. They speak of it in Muskogee and Sallisaw, Tahlequah and Okmulgee. It is said that a great wailing of village dogs went up through the valley, and livestock in the pastures lined up at the fencerows, as in a coming storm, to watch the long caravan of wagons carrying the people away.

Some went by flatboat, many in wagons, most of the others on foot. A total of 645 teams pulled the wagons, with the Cherokee people loaded inside like so many cattle, or like Jews in boxcars, nine persons per square meter. The journey was fully a thousand miles to the Mississippi and hundreds beyond to the barren lands of the Oklahoma plains. Nearly five thousand died on the way and thousands more would fall ill in the severe winter ahead. The Cherokee people had never seen the Mississippi River; they had never wanted to see it.

When the deed was done, word was sent to Andrew Jackson in Washington and he was gratified over his last great Indian victory. They were only Indians and they were in the way.

Local tourist guides play up Lincoln's part in the Black Hawk War; their expansive comments ignore what Lincoln wrote about his participation. He said in his scant memoirs that he never saw any "live, fighting Indians" though he had "a good many bloody struggles with the mosquitoes."

We found the marker noting the signing in Prairie du Chien of the peace treaty ending the war. Of all the notable figures fighting against Black Hawk, none finished his life or career happily. It's almost as if this dark episode in our history left a curse on all who took part.

Going upriver in 1882, Twain looked out on the river by Prairie du Chien and noted that massed acres of lumber rafts were being pushed downstream by stern-wheeler riverboats. He wrote that they were "not floating leisurely along, in the old-fashioned way, manned with joyous and reckless crew" but were being propelled "modern fashion, and the crews were quiet, orderly men, of a sedate business aspect, with not a suggestion of romance about them anywhere."

Today Prairie du Chien seems to be the same sedate business town without a hint of romance, or of remorse.

CHAPTER 5

Craps in the Heartland

When I told Canada Bill the game he was playing in was crooked, he said, "I know it is, but it's the only game in town."

—*George Devol*, Forty Years a Gambler on the Mississippi

We crossed the river from Wisconsin over into the corn belt of Iowa, the heartland state where the rich black fields lope off down the Mississippi Valley. Nikita Khrushchev once crossed the river here on a visit to America's breadbasket; what he saw made him so envious that he ranted to the world like a madman.

While the heartland is as rich as ever, it has lately taken on the look of losing its direction. Family farms are going the way of the red barn and the tiled silo. The recessions of the 1970s and the droughts of the 1980s can still be detected in the vistas across the cornfields; many of the great old barns, once the pride of Iowa's farmers, have been abandoned, and new prefab grain elevators have a transient look. The operative term here might be "corporate farming." You can't imagine stopping at a farmhouse to ask for a drink of clean well water.

We were anticipating the old Iowa; we wanted to see Grant Wood scenes and the *American Gothic* picture of the Iowa preacher with his daughter. We found instead that the old picture has been covered with a brochure. At a crossroads convenience store outside Dubuque we talked to a retired farmer who explained.

"The state's going after industry and the tourist dollar in a big way. The shakers and movers in Des Moines stay up nights trying to come up with new promotions and gimmicks. Everybody thinks having a lottery and the new riverboat casinos will bring in big bucks."

He didn't think it would work. He himself had sold out and was living off the interest. The 1980s had been hell on farmers of the Midwest. "The drought had a lot to do with it," he said. "And then came the foreclosures and the bankruptcies. I was lucky to sell out first. Hell, I know of some farmers who killed themselves. It got that bad."

He wasn't exaggerating. Later we read in the *Des Moines Register* that during the 1980s close to a thousand farmers in the Midwest had committed suicide. The most startling headlines were in the farm sections of the newspapers, with news of financial crises, slipping land values and all-time highs in indebtedness.

We felt we had dropped in on a wake. Something was happening in Iowa; the state was in the process of making a big change. We took a side trip off the river to see what was happening, and we saw that the old picture was still there. Up the Iowa River we passed along the Amana Colonies, seven little villages that didn't seem worried about being left behind. The Amanas were established in the nineteenth century by a German pietist sect and they've been producing furniture and woolens and appliances in America for decades—also, in their fine little restaurants they serve the tastiest German food in the heartland.

We came to an Old World Bohemian settlement at Spillville. Here composer Antonin Dvořák lived once, in 1893. He had come like others to see what the New World was all about. While living in Spillville he composed his famous symphony *From the New World;* his rich lyrical tone captured the spirit of the Iowa heartland and is as American as the melting pot itself.

Over in the little town of Nashua we found the original Church in the Wildwood that made the simple, bucolic old song a national hymn. It's still an unpretentious little country church and they still hold services and still sing the old song. While we were there they were getting ready for a wedding. Many young couples use the Church in the Wildwood for their weddings, we were told. Seeing the little chapel set back there in the woods almost made us hear the old hymn. "O come to the church in the wildwood . . . O come to the church in the vale . . ."

We meandered farther around the Iowa map; coming along a state road toward Dubuque, we happened onto a piece of mythology. We saw a small sign off the road that said, FIELD OF DREAMS MOVIE LOCATION 3 MILES AHEAD. We turned off at the little town of Dyersville and went out into the country a couple of miles, up a lane off the blacktop, and saw it, exactly as it was in the movie.

The immaculate ball field, complete with lights all the way around the outfield, does sit in the middle of acres of corn. There's an Iowa farmhouse behind the diamond, a fencerow around freshly plowed ground, a pasture for the livestock. One small souvenir stand sits off the gravel drive; you can buy T-shirts that say, IS THIS HEAVEN . . . NO, IT'S IOWA. An elderly couple live here, grow corn, and run the T-shirt booth. The whole *Field of Dreams* location is void of chamber of commerce come-ons. The old couple won't even charge admission to the grounds and you can walk around the lush sod of the outfield or go out into the cornpatch beyond left field where Shoeless Joe appeared and disappeared. You can, if you wish, deposit a donation for the field's upkeep.

The lady at the souvenir booth told us that a lot of people come to see the field; some of the actors who were in the movie have come back to visit, and some of them want to make a sequel, but that probably won't happen. The attraction is pretty unique. "People keep coming," the farm lady told us. "They want to believe."

Maybe some sort of dream does live here; you can feel it. Just as you want to feel and see Shoeless Joe out there shagging flies. Could he ever cream that pill. Born Joseph Jefferson Jackson on the banks of the Mississippi in Hannibal, Mark Twain's town, and just about five years after Twain last visited his homeplace, Joe had a lifetime batting average of .356—better than DiMaggio's or Musial's, better than Aaron's or Rose's. But Joe was kicked out of baseball in 1919 by pusillanimous old Judge Landis, pretty much because Joe was too naive, too much in love with his game, too much a victim of the slick city world he neither liked nor understood. Shoeless Joe and Huck Finn were innocents, kin. It's likely the real Huck, a young man Twain met out west, wound up getting his spirit burned by life. We do know that Joe Jackson was forced to live an outcast's existence, and when he died in 1951 at the age of sixty-three he had already passed over from folklore into American mythology. The movie may not have been a classic, but it touched us. In the same way this simple plot of ground, stuck out in an Iowa cornfield, will touch you if you ever thought, "Say it ain't so, Joe." The kid in the legend keeps asking the question. Here on the field of dreams, Shoeless Joe gets the chance to answer the kid in all of us.

Driving Iowa back roads, trying to catch the pungency of the old *American Gothic,* we thought we were looking for Iowa's lost image, but when we got to Dubuque we began to understand what was going on. Iowa is saying that it is willing to gamble away its heritage with lotteries, horse and dog tracks, and something the state hopes will be even bigger, riverboat gambling. It's betting on the Mississippi.

Dubuque is an old town that thrived once on coal and lead mining and then on manufacturing. Twain stopped here to visit a big plow factory which exported to the entire world. Dubuque's plow customers have fallen off considerably since 1882; it's not that the town has resisted change, it's that change hasn't seen fit to light here until now. River buffs can learn a lot about the Mississippi in the Woodward Museum and National River Hall of Fame. It's right down on the harbor and it's full of old steamboat mementos, photos and paintings of the *A. L. Shotwell* and the *Robert E. Lee* and the *Natchez.* Not a league away from the riverfront museum stands a new casino frontage flashier than Vegas.

Back in the heyday of riverboat gambling in the middle of the nineteenth century, a special breed of men was attracted to the Mississippi. Riverboat sharks began appearing early in the century, though the first wave brought a tough lot who normally got unceremoniously tossed off onto passing keelboats or stranded on towheads. When the new steamboats hit the river, the gamblers upgraded their style to fit the appearance of the floating palaces. From St. Paul to New Orleans the number of these dapper knights of the Mississippi grew geometrically with the rise of flush times. Their choice of games ranged from rondo, keno, three-card monte and euchre to seven-up, red-and-black, roulette and wheel of fortune. The old stock-in-trade game of poker mostly gave way on the steamboats to an enticement called faro (so named for Pharoah Ramses, who is supposed to be represented by the king of hearts), a banker's game in which players lay bets on the dealer's top card. It looked so beatable that it allowed nimble-fingered sharpers to relieve well-heeled steamboat travelers of thousands of dollars with the flip of one pasteboard. Faro reigned supreme on the boats and in New Orleans, where faro banks by the dozen prospered. The swindler John Law would have been right at home in the Crescent City.

Games of chance did not usually take place as depicted in movies, in spacious casinos complete with orchestras and dancing girls. In fact, the high-stakes games were normally held in the ship's barbershop or in the texas (the upper structure holding the pilot-house and the officers' quarters). Sometimes the first mate or the captain would allow his room to be used for the games. You might think that the corps of cardsharps would have been banned as nuisances by the ships, but that was hardly ever the case. Gamblers were welcomed aboard as friends to the steamboat lines because they were good for business. The gambler established a foothold on the boats by bribing the captains. The presence of known faro dealers was a sign of lively times; many rich travelers wouldn't book passage unless they were guaranteed some action on long trips up and down the river.

The twentieth century would have its share of legendary high rollers: Pittsburgh Phil (the greatest horse player of all time), Jimmy the Greek (the real one), Owney Madden (the very first Godfather). But Phil, Jimmy and Owney could have never stacked up to the likes of King Cole Martin, Posey Jeffers, Canada Bill Jones and Elijah Skaggs in the halcyon days of the riverboat gamblers. From the scarce literature on these sharpers, we can only speculate as to their personalities and character. A few of them left letters and memoirs full of outlandish claims as to the fortunes they won. Others spoke fondly, or meanly, of the grand old days on the Mississippi when a camaraderie existed among the rogues.

George Devol claimed that he never beat a man out of his money until he found out from the ship's clerk if the sucker's passage had been paid. Tom Ellison, reputed to be a gambler turned honest, confessed that a sucker "had no more chance against those fellows than a snowball in a red-hot oven." Still, Ellison spoke affectionately about his companion sharks: "They were good fellows, free with their money as water."

On record are instances where the hustlers risked their lives to help save others when a boiler blew off or a boat hit a snag. For the most part, however, the gamblers were there to apply a single-minded code: skin as many victims as can be accommodated, and take anything of value.

In his book *Forty Years a Gambler on the Mississippi,* Devol tells of the prizes he garnered by skinning the suckers. He won farms, widows' dowries, teams of mules, live alligators and even plantation slaves. He once won a beautiful seventeen-year-old slave girl in a poker game with a grandee. He sold her back to her owner, reluctantly it must be assumed, but not before noting, "I tell you, she was a dandy."

Devol's memoirs, as far as you can trust them, reveal much of the flavor of the era and give the inside dope on the many ways the gamblers cozened their victims. Like many others, Devol sometimes worked with partners in stings, employing such devices as reflector rings, a glass lapboard and honey or molasses on the wires of a wheel of fortune. They worked out elaborate signals and codes with scratching of bodily parts, positioning of walking sticks or puffing of cigars. These techniques were known in the trade as "iteming."

By far the most inventive hustler on the river was an old coot by the name of James Ashley. This guileful curmudgeon always worked with his fiddle and in league with a young country bumpkin. The young man would be losing heavily at the poker table when Ashley entered with his fiddle; he would amuse the players by dancing a jig around the table (getting a good look at each hand) while playing some favorite ditties. "Old Joe Clark," "Turkey in the Straw" and "Wait for the Wagon" were signals for pairs, straights and flushes. The bumpkin began to win one big pot after another. Ashley worked his fiddle scam for years, becoming a fixture on the boats, and the other gamblers never caught on.

Gambling today in Iowa is not a free-lance operation. The state chamber of commerce hypes the show and a cooperative state legislature has spent millions on building and promoting the so-called rebirth of riverboat gambling. To avoid charges of encouraging moral turpitude and, more importantly, to create an auditable tax base, the state of Iowa passed the bill limiting losses to $200 per gambler per cruise. Obviously the state approves of the casinos but disapproves of gambling. Money bets are not allowed in the float-

ing casinos; the punters must purchase $200 worth of official to-
kens to use for betting. This way the state not only knows exactly
what the handle is but can tax it accordingly. Since a service has
been purchased, it's not really gambling; look at it as a charitable
contribution with the state as the chief beneficiary. A long way
from *American Gothic.*

When we walked in, we thought we were entering Caesars Palace, but it turned out that this ostentatiously overbuilt riverfront
façade was merely a ticket office. There were at least twenty bank-
like teller windows selling reservations for lunch and dinner cruises
on the *Casino Belle* at $29.95 a pop. Although the boat can accom-
modate as many as twenty-five hundred customers, our cruise was
far from a sellout. Perhaps the reason for the meager crowd was
that the *Casino Belle* didn't make people think of the old steamboat
days. The idea of bringing back riverboat gambling has a colorful
appeal, but it's not pitched toward the serious gambler, nor does
the new effort have the color of the old days. Despite the expen-
diture on megabuck glitz, the unshakable impression we got was
of a get-rich-quick scheme with a wholesome, sanitized front to
protect the state's official image. Even though the dining hall was
spacious, high-ceilinged and richly appointed, the mood of the
gamblers was petulant; the bathrooms were overcrowded and all
the rooms were tremendously overheated. The cruise was to last
five hours, but it only took a portion of that time for ennui to set
in. We spent the bulk of our allotted cruise time out on the deck
absorbing the wide river vista and wondering what Mark Twain
would have said about all this flapdoodle.

At the end of our gambol, the crowd didn't look nearly as glad
to be aboard as they had at the outset. Most had lost all or most
of their $200 and seemed not at all reluctant to be leaving the
floating casino.

We undertook another boat trip, one not sponsored by the Iowa
chamber of commerce. We rented a powerboat for the purpose of
seeing firsthand what the Quad Cities region, from Dubuque and
Rock Island down through Davenport and Clinton, was actually
like. The environmental watchdog group Greenpeace published
disturbing reports in December 1989, especially a picture of chemical effluents flooding into the Mississippi from the Quantum
Chemical Company in Clinton, Iowa. Greenpeace alleged in its

book, *The Mississippi River and the National Toxics Crisis,* that Quantum "discharges at least 2.2 million pounds per year of toxic chemicals to the environment."

We found the location and witnessed the flow of the effluent, which gushed from a trough six feet wide and immediately began to discolor the already clouded water. The trough was elevated over the river and resembled nothing more than a bizarre waterfall with a frothy foam washing up on the bank and then into the river. Dead fish were a common sight along the riverbanks on our brief tour. Greenpeace didn't single out Quantum; it named Alcoa in Riverdale, Dupont in Fort Madison and Monsanto in Muscatine. Our boat rental cost us considerably less than our casino excursion, but in neither adventure did we emerge as winners.

From Clinton we left Highway 61 to cross the bridge for a short trip to the almost forgotten town of Galena, Illinois, where U.S. Grant had once been so obscure that he was reduced to clerking in his father's leather-goods store. The hard-drinking Grant previously had chopped wood for the army garrison at Jefferson Barracks in St. Louis. But Grant's military career was reborn in Galena when he was commissioned as a captain of local volunteers at the beginning of the Civil War. Within months he was a general fighting on the Mississippi against some of the same officers who had bought wood from him at Jefferson Barracks.

Traveling south again, we came across Black Hawk State Park, in the middle of which stands an outsized statue of the old chief himself. The statue bears a fair resemblance to the old daguerreotypes, except that his stance is all wrong. Frozen here in bronze on his own home soil, Black Hawk looks neither imposing nor defiant; he projects the demeanor of a country gentleman. Black Hawk was never a gentleman; he never had reason to be. He was a wily old hawk who went down fighting like many an American hero.

Just a few miles away on the west bank of the Mississippi near the Wapsipinicon River is the boyhood home of the archetypal American hero, William Frederick Cody, known to boys in two centuries as Buffalo Bill. A museum touting his virtues stands a few miles upriver from Davenport. Browsing through the exhibits, wherein guns are the central feature, we couldn't help thinking of the closing lines of e. e. cummings's portrait:

<blockquote>
Jesus
he was a handsome man
    and what i want to know is
how do you like your blueeyed boy
Mister Death
</blockquote>

Back on Old 61, we approached Davenport, which sits like a sparkling rhinestone on the Mississippi. The city's waterfront was in the process of transforming itself into Casinoville. Where Dubuque has opted for Las Vegas glitz, Davenport has gone in for the theme park effect complete with riverfront mall, piped-in big-band music, streamers, souvenirs. If anything, the lure here is even more elaborate than in Dubuque; players can book an excursion on the *President,* which diesels out about a hundred yards into the Mississippi and drops anchor so the patrons can gamble in sight of their buses over by the docks.

Davenport has more attractions than just the casino boat. Here are several good museums that present art, lore and the history of the river. Here, too, is the first of the really good jazz festivals on the Mississippi. This one is in honor of the great jazz cornetist of the 1920s, Bix Beiderbecke, who came from the area. The festival attracts jazz lovers from all over the country, just as the blues festivals along the lower river pull folks in by the tens of thousands. We caught a night of the show; the crowd was knocked out with the jazz, and Bix was still remembered.

Out of Davenport Old 61 sweeps west following a wide, fifty-mile bend of the Mississippi all the way to Wapello. The Iowa River meets the Mississippi over at Toolesboro, a traditional tribal ground of the Sauk-Fox tribes, just a few miles east of Wapello. The tribes normally built their main settlements at confluences; the fishing was good and the hunting rich. We were drawn to the locale by two conical Indian mounds atop a tall bluff on the Mississippi. In 1673 the French explorers Joliet and Marquette paused here a few days before continuing on what was the first recorded trip down the Mississippi. The Indians here were peaceful, according to Marquette's journal, and the Frenchmen replenished their supplies and enjoyed the freely given Indian hospitality. These tribes prided themselves on their courtesy to visitors, especially to white demigods from far away.

Continuing south from Wapello, Old 61 begins to invade the Mississippi's alluvial plain and then drifts into Fort Madison, a pretty and unpretentious old town that got its beginning as one of the chain of forts demarking the Permanent Indian Territory of the 1820s. The chain stretched from Fort Gibson in Arkansas Territory to Fort Snelling in Minnesota.

The restored Fort Madison along with its barracks sits upon the riverside, and were any soldiers there today, they could walk across to Main Street and have a fine meal at the 1950s-style restaurant called the Parthenon. Here the rich Italian- and Greek-seasoned buffet also includes Southern-style catfish, fried chicken and hush puppies, all at a surprisingly inexpensive price, five dollars a head for all you can eat.

Out the restaurant window we could see one of the incredibly long tow-barges snaking its way downriver. Half an hour later as we continued down Old 61, we saw the same barge at the little town of Montrose. As the barge glided by, we could dimly make out the curious town of Nauvoo across the river on the Illinois shore. In the early 1800s Nauvoo was the largest city in Illinois, with a population of almost 20,000, nearly all of whom were adherents of Joseph Smith and his new Mormon religion. Joseph and his brother Hiram Smith were building an empire on the banks of the Mississippi, complete with their own private army, which had been chartered and authorized by the State of Illinois. After a pitched battle between the Mormons and hostile non-Mormon neighbors at Nauvoo in 1844, a liquored-up lynch mob stormed the jail in Carthage, Illinois, where the brothers were being held, hanged the brothers and mutilated the bodies. Joseph Smith's eccentricities condemned the cult to the martyrdom of being the most persecuted religious group in American history.

We passed through Burlington, which Twain remembers in *Life on the Mississippi* as "a very sober city ... for a most sobering bill was pending; a bill to forbid the manufacture, exportation, importation, purchase, sale, borrowing, lending, stealing, drinking, smelling, or possession, by conquest, inheritance, intent, accident, or otherwise, in the state of Iowa, of each and every deleterious beverage known to the human race except water. This measure was approved by all the rational people in the state; but not by the bench of Judges."

Old 61 takes a curvy, hilly passage from Fort Madison down to Keokuk, where the Des Moines River flows into the Mississippi. Keokok is situated on Iowa's miniature bootheel and at one point was a passing fair river port attracting as many as 116 steamboats to its docks in a single day, according to a free brochure we picked up. Nowadays Keokuk consists of one main drag leading to the bridge over the river into Illinois just down from Lock and Dam No. 19, the longest lock on the upper river.

Mark Twain's first gainful employment was working on his brother's newspaper here in Keokuk. As a young man Twain was more full of dreams than of any work ethic; his youthful desire was to sail up the Amazon. He even figured out how he was going to do it; he had stumbled upon a fifty-dollar bill stuck in the muddy main street of Keokuk, and in his naïveté he imagined it as more than enough to take him around the world.

At the base of the bridge in Keokuk sits an old steamer, the *George M. Verity,* in dry dock. Built in 1926, the boat has long been decommissioned and reduced to the stature of a nickel-and-dime museum. The curator's assistant, or cub, was a scrupulously polite young black man of sixteen who went out of his way to give us a guided tour of the boat. We stood on the texas deck and surveyed the river. We looked beneath the bridge to a prominent sign warning the unwary that the Mississippi was not suitable for swimming.

As we explored the interior of the boat, we asked the young man if his future plans included working on the river. "No, sir, I'm not planning that," he answered. "I'm saving my money to go to college, to study law, maybe." We mentioned to him that Mark Twain had lived and worked in Keokuk as a youngster.

"Is that right? I didn't know. Right here in town, you mean? I've read Mark Twain. Tom Sawyer, Huck Finn. But I sure didn't know he had ever lived here in Keokuk." We related the story of Twain's finding the fifty-dollar bill. The young man was impressed. "I sure wish I could find fifty bucks. I'll be working here all summer and it would sure come in handy."

Twain returned to Keokuk in 1867. His first book, *The Celebrated Jumping Frog of Calaveras County, and Other Sketches,* had been published in the spring of that year to rave reviews and Twain was taking advantage of the publicity by going on a Midwestern lecture tour. He spoke to a paying crowd of some four hundred people at the Chatham Square Methodist Episcopal Church and for his efforts received half the gate at fifty cents a head. The Keokuk *Daily Constitution* called Twain "the most extraordinary delineator of human character in America or upon the continent of Europe." Twain, the Delineator, agreed and pocketed his hundred dollars.

The Mississippi widens below Keokuk and the current sweeps along hurriedly. We crossed the bridge over the Des Moines River and began to quicken our own pace. We felt exhilarated, even a little tense. U.S. 61 was taking us to Hannibal, Twain's childhood home—to where it all had started.

CHAPTER 6

A Mark Twain Dream

"The things about me and before me made me feel like a boy again ... and that I had simply been dreaming an unusually long dream."

—*From* Life on the Mississippi

Road signs are ubiquitous and seldom noticed. But we paid special attention to one as we came into Hannibal. It read: POPULATION 18,811. Road signs should tell you if a place is grand or forgotten. Hannibal hasn't seen much change in the past few decades, so it's hard to know. The town looks as if it should have gone the way of the steamboat, but something's keeping it alive.

The sightseer can cruise all of present-day Hannibal in about ten minutes. We passed the Silver Spur Bar, the American Legion Post, the Down Under Pub, the West End Bar and Grill, the Picadilly Radio Store, the courthouse, an old federal building and a series of sales, supply and service businesses all prefaced with the magic name of Mark Twain. Sam Clemens might be gratified to know that Mark Twain Enterprises, Inc., is alive and well in Hannibal, for Twain's legacy does more than anything else to breathe life into Hannibal today.

Downtown Hannibal's storefront row is rather down at the heels, but along the riverfront the cobblestone streets lend a touch of grace to the drowsy little town. The main attractions for the river traveler are the Clemens family home and the Pilaster House, where the Clemenses first lived in Hannibal after their move from Florida, Missouri, a truly forgotten town. The house across the street where young Sam grew up is a small, two-story cottage almost completely covered with ivy—it's been renovated and contains

*Tom Sawyer and Huck Finn statue
in Hannibal, Missouri.*

some of the original furnishings, including Sam's bed, dresser and bookcase. For a small fee you can tour the house and stand at Sam's window, from which he could look directly across the street to the window of the pretty little girl who would be immortalized as Becky Thatcher. Sam could also look down and see the landing docks, where all the great steamboats stopped for just a few minutes on their way down to St. Louis, Memphis, Natchez and New Orleans.

Tom Sawyer's famous fence still stands along the front of the boyhood home. Local lore attests that the fence is the original, and if you believe it, you'll also believe the old gent down on the courthouse steps who'll tell you he owns the genuine ax that George Washington used to cut down the cherry tree. "It's had ten new blades and two dozen new handles, but it's the same ax."

Next to the Pilaster House stands the law office of Sam's father, J. M. Clemens, justice of the peace and habitual loser in investment schemes. On a nearby corner is Grant's drugstore, where Sam witnessed a man's death in a gunfight. In these two short blocks on a steep hill, the aura of Mark Twain lingers poignantly. Twain told his first biographer, Albert Bigelow Paine, that he was a sickly child, "and lived mainly on allopathic medicines during the first seven years" of his life. Twain asked his mother about this in her eighty-seventh year, wondering, "I suppose that during all that time you were uneasy about me?" The mother replied, "Yes, the whole time." Twain asked, "Afraid I wouldn't live?" His sharp old mother answered, "No—afraid you would."

Down the street from the Becky Thatcher Bookstore stands the harbor, which is disappointing and deserted except for a scaled-down mock-up of a steamboat. The boat is designed to take the tourist dollar; we didn't see too many elbowing their way aboard at ten dollars a head. These wharves once rang with the excited cry, "Steamboat a-coming!" It was the town's only real excitement; now the town has no excitement at all, just memories.

Walking back up the cobblestone Front Street, we passed a lounge called Kelly's Etc. We stopped in and saw one of the finest examples of inlaid hardwood cabinetry you're likely to come across on the river. Above the bar hung a poster supporting the election

Tom Sawyer's famous fence.

of "Thomas F. Eagleton, Democrat for Lieutenant Governor" of the state of Missouri.

Up the street, we found an old metal sign that announced, PLAN-TER'S HOTEL, 1836. Guests at the hotel had included Abraham Lincoln and Thomas Hart Benton. Just below the sign, partially obscured by shrubs, stood a once-proud stone monument to another native son, Joe Beckley, who had been elected to baseball's Hall of Fame. One monument that is missing is a memorial to Shoeless Joe Jackson. No field of dreams here for that Joe.

There's only one more place in Hannibal that a visitor needs to see: Holliday's Hill. When in 1882 Samuel Langhorne Clemens climbed this hill to get a view of the environs, he was moved to write in *Life on the Mississippi:* "The things about me and before me made me feel like a boy again—convinced me that I was a boy again, and that I had simply been dreaming an unusually long dream; but my reflections spoiled all that."

This former steamboat pilot, fortune seeker and dreamer always walked a narrow line between Sam Clemens and Mark Twain. As noted by his Pulitzer prize-winning biographer, Justin Kaplan, "before he slipped into coma his last continuous talking was about . . . Jekyll and Hyde and dual personality." As Clemens he was involved in crazy schemes—a patented steam generator, a self-pasting scrapbook, a perpetual calendar, a history board game, a patented bed clamp, and the phantasmagorical Paige typesetter. Clemens lost three fortuncs on these illusions of wealth and grandeur. The one that got away was Alexander Graham Bell's telephone; Clemens turned Bell down flat and J. P. Morgan got Ma Bell instead. As Mark Twain, he simply was without peer. No greater tribute surpasses what Hemingway said of him: "All modern American literature comes from one book by Mark Twain called *Huckleberry Finn.* American writing comes from that. There was nothing before. There has been nothing as good since."

Standing on the bluff called Holliday's Hill, we saw cloaked in a twilight mist the whole whitewashed town and the great river, all as Twain had seen them. A breeze off the river seemed to conjure up a rough-hewn, ghostly voice:

Hello, strangers, how are you? Damned nice up here, ain't it?

Yes, sir, it surely is.

It's changed a heap but the old river carries itself proud, does it not? I can close my eyes and still see the A.L. Shotwell *streaking past. Hear that steam whistle? Some folks'll be getting on, getting off. Steamboat a-coming!*

You miss your piloting days, then?

Indeed I do. I never should have got out of the river, you see. We can never outlive our childhood memories and desires. I wanted for all the world to live on the river.

Would you give any advice to people today, sir?

Advice? I would not point fools the way to paradise down the paths of curiosity. Eat, drink and be melancholy—that's the price of passage.

And if you could be here today?

No question about that. I'd go right down to that landing, get on a steamboat with a lightning pilot like Captain Bixby and roll on down the river. Y'all best hurry or the boat will leave without you.

Well, we caught a boat out of Hannibal, our own land-yacht. We crossed the bridge to the Illinois shore and passed over the tow-head called Jackson Island out there in the middle of the Mississippi. That's where *Adventures of Huckleberry Finn* started, where Huck first met Jim, the runaway slave. The plan they hatched on the island was to raft down to Cairo and up the Ohio River to get Jim safely out of the slave states. Jim didn't have a choice or a vote in the planning. In the 1840s when the pair's adventure began, blacks weren't safe on either the slave or the free shores of the Mississippi. Iowa and Wisconsin and Illinois were still in the Wild West and declined to give blacks the right to vote. Jim's bittersweet role expressed Twain's vision of life on the Mississippi—a dark shadow reflecting man's inhumanity to man. Con men, killers, lynch mobs, slave hunters, robbers—all schemed around Jim. The bright side of Twain's vision was the relationship between Jim and Huck.

We were driving a two-lane state road and all of a sudden a juggernaut of an eighteen-wheeler whipped out of the line of approaching traffic and right into our lane straight at us. It was sudden panic time, zero at the bone.

It's impossible to measure time and distance in a funk of fear. The truck loomed up in our windshield like a colossus. It missed us by inches. The land-yacht swerved, almost on its own, and transported us off the road, over the shoulder and into a newly plowed field. Time stopped. Then the vituperation began. The trucker had nearly killed us. Was he stopping? No, he was probably so wired that he didn't even know what had happened.

The poor old land-yacht had hurdled a ditch and was now nose down in the soft field. Telltale steam was issuing from under the hood. There was no way we were going to push the heavy car out of the field. We climbed out and stood looking at the furrows we'd made in some Illinois farmer's cornfield. The highway wasn't busy anymore; all we could see was a brown hawk sitting in a tree across the road.

Then an old oil-burner car came along and pulled off onto the shoulder just where we'd crossed it. A banty rooster of a man bounced out, jumped the ditch and came walking toward us, his wispy red hair whipping up in the morning breeze. His smile was as shiny as the tin of Skoal he was dipping into as he walked up.

"If it wasn't for bad luck," he said. He discarded our misfortune with a laugh and before we could say what happened he had popped the hood and examined the engine and relieved the pressure of a busted hose.

"How long since you changed these hoses and belts?" he asked. He didn't let us answer but went on with his automotive checkup, keeping up a steady banter. "Call me Mac," he said. "People laugh at the full name. MacArthur Douglas. That's right. My daddy liked a joke. He was a vet'ran of the big war. You know, in the Pacific. I don't know why he wanted to name me after the general. He hated Dugout Doug. Me, I was one of them boomer babies. I got over to the Pacific too. You know that old Asian war."

The little man turned and jogged back to his car, leaping the ditch like a long-eared jackrabbit. We watched him open his car's truck and a minute later he came back with a brand-new radiator hose still in its box.

"You seem to have a well-stocked trunk," we said. "Do you carry parts for all models?"

"Some but not all. Them Japanese parts are expensive," he said with a yellow-toothed grin. He saw that we were getting on to his game. "Lots of folks break down on the road, you know. Most of the ones I help can't afford Triple A. Gol-durned tow trucks cost you a fortune."

"You stop to help a lot of people?"

"Well, tell you the truth. It's how I make my living. Used to do factory work but that's playing out. Me and the old lady live in Galena, got us a double-wide."

"So you can make enough money at this?"

"Sending my boy to college. First one in my family. He's gonna make a vet. He just loves them animals."

In no time he had the hose replaced and was checking over the car again. "Might as well check the air in your tires. You're under-inflated. I think that fan belt is gonna go on you pretty soon. Tell you a trick. If you got a woman in the car with you, take off her pantyhose and use 'em for a belt. Wrap it around tight and it'll last you till you get to a parts place. Well, we might as well rock this old boat out of his gol-durned cornpatch."

With a couple of two-by-fours he just happened to have in his trunk, Mac pulled us out of the mud like a nut out of its shell. We gave him what we could afford, plus a little more. With the aplomb of one who is used to accepting heartfelt gifts in reward for his efforts, he pocketed the money. He told us that he had no fixed fee, taking the money as he found it; he came clean and told us that some days he made upwards of $200. There are some gener-ous folks on the Mississippi.

While he bore a resemblance to our image of the Dolphin in *Huckleberry Finn,* the con man who teamed up with the Duke in slickering people along the river, Mac seemed to be more than either of these two Twain hucksters. We could tell he was a shell-game artist, but we didn't mind. He had a spark of vitality and ingenuity and was endearingly straightforward at plying his trade. And he was a giver, not a taker—well, at least not completely, in spite of himself. The last we saw of him he was heading back up the road toward his home in Galena. Wherever he is today, we wish this knight of the road the joy of many breakdowns.

CHAPTER 7

Gateways

"The fifth night we passed St. Louis, and it was like the whole world lit up."

—*From Twain's* Adventures of Huckleberry Finn

At Grafton the Illinois River flows into the Mississippi. Modern-day riverboat pilots call the Illinois "the old shit ditch." As we crossed, it looked like a normal river and acted like one, but it's a river in name only. In truth, it is a sewage canal and has been one since just after the turn of the century.

Mark Twain once remarked that the fine folks of Chicago thought they were the best in the world, whereas in his opinion they were merely the most numerous. At the turn of the century a typhoid epidemic struck Chicago and the head count threatened to become a body count. Chicago was drinking its own raw sewage and industrial wastes. Thousands were sick and dying. Something had to be done, and something was done. The city fathers put their engineers to work changing the course of the Chicago and upper Illinois rivers, and this feat was acclaimed as the eighth wonder of the world. Now Chicago's sewage and wastes flowed downstream. Within weeks thousands were sick and dying in St. Louis. The engineering marvel had succeeded only in shifting the epidemic from one city to another. St. Louis survived only by abandoning the Mississippi and turning to the Missouri as its source of drinking water.

Grafton is more important than the local people or casual tourists realize. It was here that La Salle first saw the Mississippi. The historian Francis Parkman paints the most authentic picture in his book *La Salle and the Discovery of the Great West.* Though other French explorers had been on the Mississippi, it was René-Robert Cavelier Sieur de la Salle who is most associated with both the discovery and the exploration of the Mississippi. According to Parkman, La Salle was a haunted, driven young man searching for glory. He was educated by the Jesuits and seemed set upon the course of the priesthood, but he had read the accounts of Champlain in the New World and was determined to exceed the early voyagers. He came to Canada as a fur trader and his early successes inflamed the jealousy of the Jesuit order. He had the complete backing of Louis XIV, but more importantly, he had a way with the Indians that could not be matched by the stern Jesuits.

The seventeenth-century Jesuits were controlled, says Parkman, by but one desire: they wanted to rule every aspect of the New World. According to Parkman, La Salle was the major obstacle in the Jesuits' path: he was their most dangerous rival for control of the West, and "from the first to the last they set themselves against him." With this conflict weighing heavily upon him, he met the Mississippi.

On February 6, 1681, La Salle set out on his journey down the great unknown river. Parkman describes the beginning. The expedition consisted of twenty-three Frenchmen, eighteen Indian scouts, ten of their squaws and three children. La Salle's men were expert handlers of canoes. Among the Frenchmen on the expedition was the "noble Tonty" (more often Tonti), La Salle's most trusted lieutenant. Tonti was called the Iron Hand, having lost one hand in the European wars, and would prove invaluable in this historic voyage, as he was in La Salle's other ventures. Camping at the mouths of the Missouri, Ohio and Arkansas rivers, La Salle made the long rough journey to the Gulf in sixty-two days without losing one member of his party. The epic search for the fabled Vermilion Sea was over.

From present-day Grafton, where the Illinois River joins the Mississippi, the current of the great river carried La Salle past the mouth of the Missouri. Eight years before, Marquette and Joliet had discovered the Missouri and had recorded in their journal: "A torrent of yellow mud rushed furiously athwart the calm blue current of the Mississippi; boiling and surging and sweeping in its course, logs, branches and uprooted trees." The Missouri had scared them to death.

We parked on the bluff at Alton and peered across the Mississippi in search of this turbulent merging. We couldn't find it. The turbulence is gone. Man began taming the Missouri in the 1830s; Robert E. Lee as a West Point engineer was the first to work on the project, using blasting powder to remove the rapids which stalled the massive fur trading industry, whose home base was St. Louis. Today the Missouri is a sluggish, tamed river, a commercial canal. The joining of the two biggest rivers in America comes about without public notice. No historical marker lures the river traveler; we saw no parks, no interpretive center, not even a souvenir stand selling "BIG MUDDY" or "LEWIS AND CLARK WERE HERE" T-shirts. Yet Lewis and Clark struck out from here to begin the most famous American exploration of all time.

Here on the high-bluffed river we found an archaeological dig going on, and in a nearby museum we saw the Piasa Indian pictographs. These primitive etchings are our only links to the ancient river. Marquette and Joliet found the pictographs when they came this way in 1673 and Joliet recorded stories the friendly tribes here told him. The etchings have done more than anything else to bolster the legend of a sphinx-like monster rising out of the river to devour tribesmen foolish enough to try the bad water at the Cahokia confluence. La Salle saw the same pictographs on the high bluffs and actually mistook them for a river monster.

We drove on to Cahokia Mounds State Park just opposite St. Louis. It's a high-tech tourist center surrounded by acres of asphalt parking lots for RVs, school and tour buses and personal automobiles, each in its own segregated area. The center is situated in the middle of a living field of artifacts. Indian mounds cover scores of acres. Some of them are a mere six feet tall; one is several hundred feet tall; the others vary in shape and size.

The interpretive center was full and people were waiting in lines to tour the grounds and to see the canned films in the spacious auditorium. The gift shops were full of monographs, treatises and coffee-table books on what life might have been like here a thousand or more years ago. The most popular account has it that this site was a metropolitan complex housing as many as a hundred thousand Cahokians, and that the mounds themselves had been constructed as places of worship and religious ritual. This explanation follows too closely the theory concerning the Aztec and Mayan civilizations, whose pyramids were supposed by Spanish explorers to have been used for such rites; the riparian civilization at Cahokia must have been far more practical, given its location. The Cahokians were farmers and tied to the soil, dependent upon the goodwill of the Mississippi River. But the river flooded then as now and the mounds, hand-built by years of dedicated terre-pleining, could only have been shelters in trying times. The Cahokians, say the modern experts, were not warlike, and their gentle nature ultimately caused their extinction. While the mounds could keep them safe from flooding waters, they could not protect against raiding parties and migrating warrior tribes. The Cahokians were massacred down to the last child and village dog. No European explorer ever found a tribesman living here. All the history of the mounds and their people comes from artifacts and speculation.

We toured the mounds surrounded by schoolchildren having a good time; for them school was out for the day. Our guide gave us a detailed explanation of the Cahokian way of life and the kids in the background chattered and laughed, as kids will. From the top of the grand "ritual" mound we could see the tail of the river as it flowed past St. Louis; to the east sat a brand-new thoroughbred racetrack, built to replace the old Cahokia Downs that used to be right on the river in East St. Louis.

From Cahokia, we entered, just a mile or so away, a nether place called East St. Louis. It's in another state, Illinois, but East St. Louis is really farther away from St. Louis than the buffalo that used to roam the western shore. Abject poverty has put its stamp on everything here. Street-gang violence, drive-by shootings, drug-related killings have become commonplace. The town is bereft of hope. It has no real constituency to support a tax base; even the racetrack closed because of the encroaching fear of the ghetto. In 1990 the bankrupt city was forced to sell its municipal building. The interstate highways have created blank walls that isolate East St. Louis from the outside. We tried to stop and talk to people, but no one would respond—no one. The town has been like this for as long as we have known it, for decades, and despite repeated federal and state rehabilitation programs, the situation has only become worse.

A river view of the Gateway Arch.

The only ray of hope here is the success of the town's high school sports programs; the reward for the lucky few athletes is escape.

The interstate highways shoot you right over the river into St. Louis virtually in the shadow of the looming arch, styled the Gateway to the West by local boosters. St. Louis used to be dirty and dark and dangerous. In the years after the Great Depression the city let itself become the labyrinth of smoky factories and slums that Tennessee Williams depicted somberly in *The Glass Menagerie.* Frank Lloyd Wright was called in to help plan a rebirth in the 1950s; he took one look and pronounced St. Louis the ugliest city in America.

St. Louis today is as contemporary and banal as all those Budweiser commercials. Downtown has been turned into an enormous shopping mall. The city has lost its identity. Easterners think of it as Western and vice versa; Northerners think of it as Southern and vice versa. They're all right, and all wrong—and that drives official image-makers crazy.

A little above the Arch sits the old courthouse, where young lawyer Lincoln came to argue the railroad-steamboat case. The steamboat companies were claiming that the Rock Island bridge was a menace to shipping; some boats had struck and been destroyed by the first railroad bridge up at Rock Island. Honest Abe's image won the day and the case for the railroads. The court also heard the first arguments in the landmark Dred Scott case, which upheld slavery. And here U. S. Grant stood before a magistrate and freed his one slave.

The Arch doesn't look quite so crass at somber dusk, and the river as a backdrop helps create a different image. Viewing the aluminum shadows the Arch casts, you think about gateways and what they meant to this headland of America. From here the new American nomad had taken different routes, mostly funneling westward out of St. Louis or drifting southward down the long Mississippi Valley.

A heliport sits right on the riverbank close to the Arch; chopper tours show you that the city is a series of gerrymandered villages and districts. St. Louis owes its birth to furs and fur trading; the early French settlers organized the Upper Missouri fur trade but it took true Yankee ingenuity, following the lead of John Jacob Astor, to turn the business run by amateurs into a monopoly piling up huge fortunes. A wave of industrious German immigrants moved into St. Louis as the fur trade was playing out. Instead of being a clearinghouse for furs, the town became a forwarding agent for all the wealth of the whole Mississippi Valley.

From the air you can see the decades of the mid-1800s unfolding. As late as 1840, when the town was in the throes of growth even beyond Astor's expectations, St. Louis had a cosmopolitan air, but what was then a fur trading center for half-breed French voyagers was turning to solid Germanic mediocrity with beer as king. Lightness and gaiety got smothered in viscosity and dourness, Goethe and Schiller triumphing over Rousseau and Voltaire.

Only the growth of jazz and the blues saved St. Louis from this spiritual suppression. The music steamed upriver from New Orleans and Memphis. Self-taught ragtime geniuses known as professors, the brethren of Scott Joplin, played on the Chicago, Kansas City, St. Louis and New Orleans circuit. They were tortured men and their music and lives showed it. They died miserably from alcoholism, drugs and venereal disease. In St. Louis at the turn of the century they played their music in the bistros off the wharf, in the ghetto clubs and even in the livelier joints around old Gaslight Square. No matter what their fame, these black musicians were not allowed in the salons of the city's rich. W. C. Handy, whose "St. Louis Blues" set the standard for all blues artists of the era, couldn't get through the front door.

In St. Louis all roads lead to the baseball stadium just two blocks away from the Mississippi and the Arch. We tuned in radio station KMOX and got a pregame show. Once upon a time KMOX was the flagship station for the largest baseball network in America; its signal reached from St. Paul to New Orleans and from Atlanta to Tucson. Beginning with Dizzy Dean's Gashouse Gang, Cardinals baseball was the king of the river and beyond, making St. Louis the greatest baseball town in the United States.

During the season millions of fans flock here on weekend jaunts; moving along in crosstown traffic, we became part of the ritual. We began to notice from license plates where the people were coming from: Jackson, Tennessee; French Lick, Indiana; Ottumwa, Iowa; Plain Dealing, Louisiana; Paragould, Arkansas; Peoria, Illinois. As youngsters we had taken part in this pilgrimage. Being at the ballpark was the apex of our summers; our bragging rights were firmly established all through the season, for we had been to see major-league teams play and no one could take that away from us. The souvenir scorecard was our ticket to envious looks and affirmed our right to comment astutely on the whole world of baseball, a Klemperer's Rosette, with lesser concerns of the planet revolving around a primary spheroid made of horsehide.

Busch Stadium was comfortably filled by the middle innings of the first game of the doubleheader. We'd bought our tickets outside the stadium right by the statue of Stan Musial, from a group of young people in their late twenties; they'd all grown up in St. Louis and were having a kind of reunion, having flown in from such places as New Jersey, Los Angeles, Dallas and Little Rock. They had a couple of extra tickets and they took a chance on us— we'd have to sit among them for the next few hours.

If you go to a baseball game the right way, it is a picnic, a parade, an old-fashioned tent meeting with dinner on the ground. The game itself is almost incidental and you don't start paying close attention until the fourth or fifth inning. Surveying the crowd from the second deck, we saw the full face of Middle America: German, Irish, Slav, Pole, with a healthy mix of African, Italian, Greek, French. The group we had bought into was fun and lively. They were trim, athletic and smartly dressed, and simply happy to be at the game. They hooted at the umps, cheered hits and great fielding plays and ate with gusto—hot dogs, peanuts, hot pretzels, nachos, pizza. They put a hot spot in our section of the ballpark and it was infectious.

We caught their names from their chatter. They were Mandy and Mary and Joy and Cindy and Robert and Joey, all friends since junior high and serious students of the game. The big crowd in the stadium included a healthy show of young people, and we asked our companions what it was about baseball that appealed to their generation. Amid their intermittent yelling at umps and applauding the players, we gleaned some of the following impressions:

Mandy: "Baseball is unique—it's the only sport where the defense has the ball."

Joey: "It's not like most sports. Like football and basketball or hockey or tennis. They go back and forth, back and forth. The fans get to be part of the action because the field comes way up here or goes way out there to the bleachers. A foul ball is as much a part of the game as a home run."

Mary: "Baseball is the perfect game. If it's played to perfection, it could go on forever. A game could last a million innings."

Robert: "Baseball appeals because it's our game. American. They played baseball right here in St. Louis during the Civil War. It's on record that some form of baseball was being played before the Revolutionary War."

For almost four hours we watched them and listened to their talk. What they were saying, maybe, was that baseball is important because the past is always present. Their folks had brought them to games when they were kids and had told them about all the great players of past generations. Joy's father had brought her to the World Series when she was five years old. It was still one of the tragedies of her father's life that the Redbirds had lost the seventh game to Detroit.

They were a reaffirming circle. These young people were already well into their careers, but they held avid interests in old movies, old furniture, old music, old cars. They were not yet thirtysomething and they hadn't embraced codependency as a creed. Their spontaneity and their wit served them well. Baseball has a way of telling you something about yourself, and this young group taught us one thing at least—the past may be gaining on us. After the game they talked up the watering holes at Laclede's Landing. We decided to check it out.

We dropped into a sports pub and sat at the bar listening to a couple of older gentlemen discussing Cardinals baseball. They had brought their grandkids to the game and were sipping a beer while the kids were up in the Arch with their grandmas. The men couldn't keep from reminiscing about the old days, the war years when not only the Cardinals but the Browns had won pennants. We gathered from their talk that they had been too young to fight in World War II, so all they had to talk about was baseball. They believed Stan the Man Musial deserved all the acclaim he ever got, but their favorites were Enos Country Slaughter and Whitey Kurowski and Terry Moore and Marty Slats Marion.

"I was at the doubleheader when Kurowski filed his bat down flat and slapped all those hits. Damned shame they kicked him out of the game."

"I saw the World Series game where Slaughter scored all the way from first on Harry the Hat's single."

"I don't really care about baseball these days. The only reason I brought the kids is because my granddad brought me. How can you like this stuff today? That artificial grass, every player a big millionaire. Tell you what's ruined the game, all these free agents jumping from one team to another."

"No, that's not it. I'll tell you what started baseball going downhill. Coca-Cola."

"How's that?"

"It was when Coke changed its price from a nickel to a dime. Everybody else doubled their prices overnight. And that's why baseball is the way it is today."

The man was dead serious. We left the granddads going over the only controversy alive in St. Louis today—whether the artificial turf in Busch Stadium should be taken up and replaced with real grass.

We strolled out onto the cobblestone streets of what was once the warehouse and commercial center of riverboat traffic on the

Upper Mississippi. Whether headed north or south, east or west, all riverboats pulled in to Laclede's Landing. America had fallen in love with the river and its gleaming, romantic steamboats. For the monied class the fashionable thing was a cruise to New Orleans. The steamboat lines always catered to first-class travelers, both the affluent merchants of the North and the cotton-rich planters of the South. With money being of no consequence, the luxury boats offered staterooms finer than rooms in New York hotels. The great dining halls were furnished with priceless chandeliers, velvet chairs, thick carpets, statues and oil paintings; grand pianos and even string ensembles entertained the diners. The finest restaurants in America could be found floating on the Big Muddy.

By the end of the 1860s the steam engine that had conquered the Mississippi River was running on tracks and about to root its way through every city and town in the land. Rail lines already had reached the Mississippi (the first railroad across the state of Missouri terminated, ironically, at Hannibal), and long before the Civil War, plans had been laid to build the first bridge over the river at St. Louis. Old steamboat veterans had held to the folly that the railroads coming from the East would stop at the river. But the signs of the times could be read at all the railroad crossings. The same financial interests that had built the magnificent steamboats were rushing to sink money in railroad stock.

In six decades the river had seen perhaps a thousand races, but the race that came off between the *Robert E. Lee* and the *Natchez* in 1870 provided the most fitting tribute and last hurrah for perhaps America's most colorful era. Early in the spring the ballyhoo for the race had already taken on a fervor. Originally conceived as a Fourth of July attraction in St. Louis, the idea of a Great Steamboat Race caught fire and spread across the country and around the world. Newspaper and magazine correspondents came from as far away as New York, London and Paris; the prospects of the race were widely advertised for weeks leading up to the great day. Wagering on the race reached gigantic proportions, as just about every man, woman and child in America sought to get a bet down. Newspapers in New Orleans, St. Louis and New York estimated that millions of dollars were being wagered, and gambling houses speculated that the final sum might climb to an unbelievable one billion dollars. In a very real sense America was showing an explicit side of its national character—it loved sporting events, be they races, prizefights or the new national pastime called baseball, just as long as betting was available. The Great Steamboat Race of 1870 set the pattern for an American compulsion; it was the World Series, Triple Crown and Super Bowl all rolled into one.

The race began at dawn on the first day of July and a throng of thousands lined the docks and the levee to cheer the boats away. The favorite was the *Natchez,* captained by the imposing Thomas Leathers, all six foot four and three hundred pounds of him. For years Leathers had held the record in the run from New Orleans to St. Louis, beating Captain John W. Cannon and the *Robert E. Lee* on two or three other occasions, so revenge was a prime motive in the Great Race, along with a sizable side bet rumored to be in the six-figure range. As the pistol shot rang out to start the race, the two captains, standing on their texas decks in all their regal splendor, refused to look at each other, but Cannon deliberately let the *Natchez* take the lead. A great roar went up from the crowd as the *Robert E. Lee,* stripped of its cargo and fixtures, overtook the *Natchez* before they steamed out of sight up the Mississippi.

Telegraphers were standing by in every port along the river, and thousands of spectators packed the levee along the route. The running times of the two vessels were instantly relayed to St. Louis, then on to New York and the world. A reporter for the New Orleans *Picayune,* on board the *Robert E. Lee,* recorded that the whole countryside seemed alive with excitement expressed "in the waving of handkerchiefs and hats, and running along the shore as if to encourage the panting steamer." Shouts came rolling over the river and were "plainly heard above the roaring of the fires, the clattering of the machinery, the splashing of the water, and the escape of steam."

At Baton Rouge the *Robert E. Lee* was a mile ahead; as it passed Memphis it was leading by an hour. But at Cairo Captain Cannon found trouble; he stopped to celebrate his obvious victory, broke out champagne bottles and entertained his admirers. Getting up a head of steam again, the *Robert E. Lee* began to shake and shudder. It was stuck in that infernal Cairo mud. The ship's pilot worked it free at last, and a good thing, for the *Natchez* had been sighted and was coming on fast.

From Cairo to St. Louis the two boats steamed along in full sight of each other, the crowds along the levees going wild. Night fell, and with it came a thick fog. Fearing disaster, Leathers stopped his boat, thinking that Cannon would do the same. But Cannon, encouraged by his excited passengers, decided to risk the fog. Having stopped, the *Natchez* had settled into a muddy bank and was stuck. The fog lifted after a couple of hours, but it was too late for Captain Leathers. The *Robert E. Lee* was hours ahead and the day was breaking clear and bright.

A great crush jammed the riverbanks in St. Louis; people from all over the region traveled to be there on that Fourth of July in 1870. The *Robert E. Lee* won with a new record time of three days, eighteen hours and fourteen minutes. The *Natchez* came in just three hours and forty-four minutes later; it was given an equally joyous welcome. Captains Leathers and Cannon forgot their mutual bitterness for the moment and saluted each other's stellar crews; they took part in the wild celebration and toasted their dauntless vessels through the night. The legendary General Robert E. Lee may have lost the Civil War, but his namesake steamboat had performed a well-nigh-impossible feat—it had bested the fastest boat that had ever plied the great Father of Waters.

Mark Twain never wrote a word about the Great Race. He wasn't on the river in 1870; he was living Up East, and around the time of the race he was sitting for a portrait by the great photographer Mathew Brady, meeting with U. S. Grant for the first time, and putting together a book called *The Gilded Age.* Twain did have a bet going on the race, but true to form, he backed the loser.

The ultimate winner of the big race would prove to be the iron horse. Rail traffic was faster and cheaper and touched the lives of more people. The trains quite simply put the riverboats out of business, at least until the coming of the long barge about a century later. When the *Robert E. Lee* and the *Natchez* came to port there in St. Louis, they could see the rising stanchions for the first public bridge over the Mississippi. The bridge was being built by James B. Eads, an engineer from Lawrenceburg across the river over in Indiana. Eads had worked with the U.S. Army Corps of Engineers during the Civil War and had designed many of the ironclads that saw service up and down the Mississippi, especially at Vicksburg. He had also consumed himself with the monumental

First public bridge over the Mississippi River.

task of designing the first giant railroad bridge to go over the Mississippi in St. Louis. The first, smaller railroad bridge had been built upriver at Rock Island, but the bridge at St. Louis would connect East directly with West. It would be opened for traffic three years after the Great Race, in 1874, and would stand long after the *Robert E. Lee* and *Natchez* were out of business. The bridge still stands, still carries traffic and still bears Eads's name.

The last irony in the passing of the steamboat was its use by the railroads to transport material up the Missouri River to Omaha to begin the construction of the mighty Union Pacific Railroad—the cause, by the way, of the Crédit Mobilier scandal. But that was an iron horse of a different color.

Perhaps even more than the river, Mark Twain loved the riverboats and the men who commanded them. As a young boy he dreamed only of being on the paddle wheelers. He became a full-fledged river pilot when he was still in his twenties. He idolized Horace Bixby, the man who taught young Sam Clemens everything worth knowing about the Mississippi. Only in his early thirties himself, Bixby had become a legend among pilots all up and down the river; he was famous for his encyclopedic knowledge of the river and his smooth, dexterous handling of boats under treacherous conditions. In *Life on the Mississippi,* Twain composed the most fitting tribute for this pilot of pilots. After watching Bixby handle his run through Plum Point, the most dangerous stretch on the river, Twain recorded another pilot's admiration, uttered in soliloquy and with unction: "By the shadow of death, but he's a lightning pilot!"

We drove by the stadium on our way to connect with Highway 61 again. Driving south alongside the enormous Budweiser brewery, we headed toward Jefferson Barracks; from there we worked our way to a place called Windsor Harbor, where we had an appointment to talk about the Mississippi with a man who had spent his life on the river. His name is Dick Whitehead.

Tall bluffs guard and almost entirely conceal Windsor Harbor; it's not really a town but a row of houses adjacent to the township of Kimiswick. It doesn't lure tourists with boasts of famous people or events. It does have the best vantage point in the area from which to see everything coming along the river. Windsor Harbor is noteworthy in that it seems to exemplify the life and culture of most little ports and landings all up and down the Mississippi.

Dick Whitehead was celebrating his eightieth birthday when we called upon him at his old homeplace here. He was born and raised here, had his family here and spent most of his life following his callings as a civil and design engineer along the Mississippi Valley. His grandfather and his father owned a grain business trading on the old St. Louis Grain Exchange, which used to sit on the riverbank downtown; they'd go up and down the river on steamboats buying grain from the farmers on both the Illinois and Missouri sides of the river, all the way to Cairo.

"Most of the farmers were German," Dick said. "I remember learning to speak some of the language. My father took me along, teaching me the trade. One time we attended a community prayer meeting in a little German church close to the river. They were having a flood prayer, if you can believe it. The German farmers wanted a flood because when the river flooded, the waters refurbished the topsoil. It's the river's way, you see, of keeping the land fertile. After they got their flood, they'd have another prayer meeting and thank the good Lord for the blessing."

Dick showed us a keepsake of that old era, a Winchester scale that he inherited from his grandfather. The scale is a small brass cylinder used back at the turn of the century to make precise measures of grain, and all grain dealers on the Mississippi carried them. "You could stand here on the bluff and see a dozen grain barges at any one time," Dick said. "They still carry grain, only nowadays the barges are much bigger and longer, and I don't know if they're having as much fun."

The river at Windsor Harbor is very wide, more than a mile across to the Illinois side. Dick recalled harrying experiences he had had as a boy on the river. During the winter before the great flood of 1927, he and some high school friends decided to see if they could skate across the river. "The river was frozen solid that winter. None of the boats could move for weeks. Fred and Presley Anheuser used to pal around with us—they didn't live in Windsor Harbor but in one of those big mansion bluffs on up the river— and they came down to see if we'd like to try going across the river on the ice. We slipped and skidded all the way; the ice got a little thinner over the channel and we heard it cracking. It was scary."

Dick told of swimming across the river with the same boys. It was a real feat and strictly taboo, but they had to try it. The current was much stronger than it looked and they were swept about ten miles downstream. The boys' parents never found out about it, or there would have been the dickens to pay.

Dick added a grim note about these river challenges: "One Sunday morning three young men from St. Louis came to Windsor Harbor and climbed up on the bluffs. We saw what they were up to. They were acting like they wanted to dive off. Now there are caves and a terrible undertow along the bluffs, and we yelled at them not to do what they were thinking. But they were smart alecks and wouldn't listen. They went ahead and jumped all at the same time. And they never came up. The undertow got them and nobody ever saw them again."

Before his retirement Dick was an engineer; during World War II he was a tank commander and led the first three American tanks across the Remagen Bridge into Germany. He was wounded but kept on going and was one of the first to see the death camps. He wouldn't talk much about that experience except to say that the camp he helped liberate looked like "a great salt mine with bodies stacked on top of each other. Some were still alive and moving, but there was no way to revive them."

In retirement Dick likes to read history, pamper his cats and have a sip of Southern cordial now and then. His love is art and in the past several of his works were published in the *Saturday Evening Post;* as a volunteer he has been teaching a sixth-grade art class and gets excited about his students' work. Over his mantel he keeps a souvenir of World War II, a German hunting gun. He's never fired it. He hasn't touched a weapon since that war ended.

Dick likes to look at the river, and Windsor Harbor is a good place to do it; the reach is wide and the flow is strong. "Off the point of the bluff there, sometimes you can see the hull of the old gunboat *Windsor,*" he said. "It was sunk in a running battle during the Civil War." When he talks, Dick Whitehead has a curing smile. He was trying to make out the sunken boat down there in the wash of the river. He kind of shrugged and said, "Well, war."

We left Windsor Harbor and drove back past Jefferson Barracks. Just ahead was the splendid estate built by the Busch brewery known as Grant's Farm. Here Grant lived for two years walking on the uppers of his boots (the soles of his last pair had worn out). He was broke, drunk when he could get somebody to spring for it, and only occasionally employed (when old friends felt sorry for him) as a woodchopper for the army at Jefferson Barracks. Grant left St. Louis in April 1860 on a riverboat named *Itasca.* The August Busch clans have long held the estate and have improved it beyond recognition; Grant had christened it "Hardscrabble." Today it is a spa for tourists.

We crossed over the river again to East St. Louis and traveled on Mississippi Avenue to the town of Sauget. Its name used to be Monsanto and it called itself "the Pride of the Gateway City." As you drive into Sauget you pass Monsanto, Pfizer Chemical, Ethel Petroleum Additive, Cerro Copper Products and two separate treatment plants called American Bottoms. Each of these plants contributes to the overall pollution of the Mississippi. Taken together, they have created a situation described by the Illinois EPA in these words: "The water was the most toxic we've ever tested . . . these are some of the most grossly contaminated sites in the state."

Sauget is not really a town now any more than when it was honestly called Monsanto. The company still owns the town. There are some streets and houses and even a mayor; the place still exists to serve the chemical companies, not its few citizens. We stood simply looking and in a few minutes our noses clogged and our eyes began to burn. Even though the companies are finally treating their wastes, the comingled stench of benzene, phosphorus and chlorine was overpowering. We could only guess at what was happening to the river water.

From over on the river we could hear the whistle of a sightseeing boat, perhaps the *Admiral* or the *Tom Sawyer* or the *Huck Finn,* out from Laclede's Landing. Not many people were out and about in Sauget. No interpretive center here, no souvenirs and no T-shirts for sale.

We had planned one last port of call in the Greater St. Louis area: Times Beach, USA. Times Beach is just a holler's echo from the Meramec River. It's down off the highway in a small ravine and it's easy to miss if you're driving more than the speed limit on your way out to Six Flags, the gigantic theme park a few miles to the west. Times Beach used to be a good stop for people coming to St. Louis for weekends of baseball. You'd pull in and fill up the car, stretch your legs, buy some pop and chat with the guys at the station.

That was ten or so years ago. Today Times Beach is America's forbidden city. It used to be a minor resort, and just up the way there's a Daniel Boone Home and a campground. There's no resort here now, nor is there a beach; just some old shells of houses and an ugly sign.

It's not easy getting into the town nowadays. First you have to cross a narrow bridge and then you're stopped by a police trailer. Rising behind the trailer is a billboard-sized yellow sign: DIOXIN CONTAMINATION, STAY IN YOUR CAR, MINIMIZE TRAVEL, KEEP WINDOWS CLOSED, STAY ON PAVEMENT, DRIVE SLOWLY. Most people who reach this point have done so by accident and turn around and leave as fast as they can.

One raging controversy within the chemical industry persists and it concerns the poison dioxin. There's a continuing debate over dioxin; it's a relatively new word and most people don't understand it, can't quite believe it. We learned in conversations with university chemistry professors that dioxin is the ultimate poison— so far. It was concocted in the labs of the country's chemical corporations. These companies themselves don't know exactly how strong the stuff is. Dioxin has been tried out on monkeys with staggering, grotesque results. Some companies have had accidental spills of dioxin and their lab technicians have lived to tell about it, though the long-range effects are anybody's guess. Seemingly because these workers didn't die on the spot from exposure to heavily diluted particles of dioxin, the chemical companies have used this as evidence that "Dioxin may not be as bad as everyone thought." The corporations have even managed some good press out of these observations.

In our own survey of university chemists, we didn't get a consensus; we got a unanimous response: dioxin in its pure form is seventy thousand times stronger than cyanide.

Times Beach is one of forty-two sites in the state that have been quarantined or confined because of dioxin contamination. What happened in Times Beach was that a construction company was contracted to build new roads, and to cut costs the company bought some cheap oil mixed with dioxin waste to be used for dust control. Like Times Beach, several of the other contaminated areas are near streams and rivers that carry the waste sediment downstream.

In the few minutes we were there, we saw the only signs of human habitation in what we thought was surely a deserted town. An old couple who had lived in Times Beach most of their lives were still here. They had chosen to stay in Times Beach and die. Everyone else had left several years ago. There is no electricity in the town, and when twilight came, we thought we saw a light down the street. It was probably a kerosene lamp or candle.

CHAPTER 8

The Confluence of America

"The loneliness of this solemn, stupendous flood is impressive—and depressing. League after league, and still league after league, it pours its chocolate tide along."

—*From* Life on the Mississippi

We are told in the memorials of the early explorers that the Mississippi flowed as a brilliant azure stream from Minnesota to Missouri and that the raging Missouri River translated this placid stream into an ugly and treacherous brown giant. Well, the Missouri no longer rages, but the early explorers had the "brown giant" right. Down the Mississippi basin from St. Louis, the doubled waters run high and, because of the cities' treatment of them, a milky cocoa color.

The river swerves westward for a hundred miles before making straight reaches into the lower basin. Old 61 commits itself now for the long run to Louisiana, falling through pastureland with only occasional fields of corn and soybeans. The decent, orderly, boring landscape is broken only by one little jewel over on the river, the town of Sainte Genevieve. This town got its start as a French trading post but it's a well-heeled place now; we counted about a dozen BMWs and Mercedeses on the chic town square. Sainte Genevieve is a dividing line of sorts—it's the last show of deluxe living before you hit the impoverished delta.

Everything turns Southern at Cape Girardeau (pronounced "Juh ROD Uh"). It's a fine old Missouri town, shaded, with two- and three-story houses set back off the street and with wide porches and front "yards," not lawns. The river bends right in upon Cape Girardeau and, remarkably, you can see some of the concrete levees that the Corps of Engineers began building after the great flood of 1927. Still, the town seems more trapped by the river than it benefits from it now, trapped by the geography of being Mid-western and Southern jointly. A little like St. Louis, Cape waits to claim an identity.

A friend of ours, Bill Seidensticker, used to live in Cape and he told about the time he tried to raft the river from here to New Orleans. He and some friends built the raft in his backyard and "struck out to rediscover" America. What they found, Bill said, were waves of giant mosquitoes, whirlpool undertows that wrecked the raft and "an unsympathetic river patrol who gave us a citation for not having a boat license." They didn't make it to New Orleans but finally got out of the river at Greenville, Mississippi, where they sold the raft to some good old boys for one dollar. "We never found America," Bill said. "I don't think it's something out there, lost or found, but maybe something inside us."

Or maybe it's the feeling you get just floating along with the river, the way Huck and Jim felt when they were safe on their raft.

The land begins to step down as the river moves toward its big-gest confluence. We got the sensation that we were gliding on a naked glacier. We came to the wheelhouse town of Sikeston, a crossroads catchall that turns you toward Cairo. We could also feel ourselves being suddenly swept into the lowest reach of the Ohio.

First called Ouabache (its Iroquois name) by French explorers, this great river, too, could be described as the source of the Mis-sissippi, for it lays a navigable network all the way to Lake Erie as it drains the Appalachian Plateau and the Great Lakes Plains and reaches a major part of the great Midwestern corn belt.

The first organized Indian tribes (the Five Civilized Nations) pa-trolled as far as the upper reaches of the Ohio. A confused La Salle first believed the Ouabache was the Mississippi; he traveled down it as far as Louisville before being stymied by the rapids there. War parties from the Five Civilized Nations canoed the Oua-bache and raided the villages of lesser tribes all the way beyond the upper basin of the Mississippi. But the Five Civilized Nations were less successful in their fight against the encroaching English, Dutch and French, and in the end the tribes could not withstand the seething horde of "Americans" boiling in from the Eastern seaboard and down the Ohio. The march was unstoppable.

A young George Washington first challenged the French and their Indian allies on the Ohio (at the confluence of the Monongahela and Allegheny rivers). Washington built Fort Defiance to oppose Fort Duquesne, but this farce soon ended with Washington's capture and humiliation as he scurried back to his Tidewater plantation. Ever stubborn, he came again to Fort Duquesne, this time with a British army around him (commanded by that dandy of dandies, General Edward Braddock, who insisted his soldiers be proper gentlemen as they marched into this wild frontier). Once again the French and Indians prevailed, cutting Braddock's gentlemen to shreds and sending Washington packing (running like a stung whippet all the way to Philadelphia this time). The tribes could hold out for just a little while longer, but finally the French were vanquished and exiled from North America.

The pattern of defeat and tribal genocide was set. At Point Pleasant in 1774 the tribes lost their lands south of the Ohio, their victories of 1790–91 being brushed aside by Mad Anthony Wayne at Fallen Timbers, 1794. Settlers moved in by the tens of thousands, making fortunes for the Virginia Company's speculators (Thomas Jefferson, following in his father's footsteps, became a big winner). The Ohio basin was rid of Indians even before the nation knew it had inherited the vast Louisiana Territory. William Henry Harrison's victory at Tippecanoe was the last blow to the Indian civilization on the Ohio River. Pontiac, Little Turtle, Black Wolf, Blue Jacket, Shawnee Prophet—not even the magnanimous Tecumseh could turn back the white tide.

A frontier planter with dreams of empire had settled on the Ohio River. Harman Blennerhassett, coming over from England in 1796, set up housekeeping with his young wife on a splendid island in the Ohio; his good, caring wife introduced inoculation against smallpox to the frontier families of the Ohio and Kentucky, saving countless children from a dread, ubiquitous killer. In 1804, after having gunned down Alexander Hamilton, Aaron Burr stopped at Blennerhassett's island and enlisted him in his scheme to establish a Southwestern empire (Louisiana, Texas, Mexico). Blennerhassett yielded to Burr's dream and his powers of persuasion, and both men journeyed down the Mississippi to New Orleans. Both were arrested in Natchez; Burr got off, but Blennerhassett did not, and his island was pillaged, by the fathers of the children whom Mrs.

Blennerhassett had saved; the poor lady lived an impoverished life the rest of her days in America and was shunned along with her dishonored husband.

Andrew Jackson traveled the Ohio often. Abraham Lincoln used it almost like an office. The Ohio was instrumental in the settlement of the West and was the birthplace of the steamboat in Western waters. Today you can see firsthand the richness that lured the early settlers. The river basin is a land of farms and factory towns enriched with Ohio carnations and buckeye trees.

We drove over the high-span bridges and into Cairo. You might expect this famous place to have a population of at least thirty or forty thousand. The sign at the city limits says it's fewer than seven thousand, and that's based on a ten-year-old census. Cairo today is dwindling family by family and block by block. In the first decades of the nineteenth century, when the lower Mississippi basin was beginning to flourish with settlement, Cairo was thought to be a key location for development, attracting speculators and hucksters with grandiose schemes that bilked many people out of huge sums of money. No less a personage than Charles Dickens fell for one of the come-ons.

Dickens came to Cairo in 1842. He and some of his friends had invested heavily in a Cairo bubble, and Dickens traveled all the way from England to this "Mecca on the Mississippi." When his steamboat put to port here, he saw it all firsthand. He recorded his venom in a book he titled *American Notes:* "At the junction of the two rivers, in ground so flat and low and marshy that at certain seasons of the year it is inundated to the house tops, lies a breeding place of fever, ague and death . . . a dismal swamp on which the half-built houses rot away."

Cairo today hasn't got much better, even though it improved a bit when Grant used it for his headquarters on the river; the Navy's headquarters for the western theater of the war was here too, and Cairo for a brief time was a major railhead. Prosperity touched down at Cairo and then flitted away like a whimsical lightning bug. Several fine old Victorian gingerbread houses grace the town's residential areas, and the downtown streets exude a turn-of-the-century air, but they're just old, with no historical restoration going on, no chamber of commerce boosterism.

Main Street presented a grim picture right out of Goldsmith's

The Deserted Village. Most of the storefronts were closed and
boarded up; grass grew in cracks along the sidewalks of the side
streets; only a couple of taverns were open. Going down the next
street over, we met a barricade and had to make a U-turn. A dog
was asleep in the intersection. Only one establishment was doing
good business in town: Mac's, the world-class barbecue place. Many
a time we had stopped at Mac's on our way through Cairo, and we
did so again, for old times' sake; it was still about the best we'd
ever had, but it only gave us a twinge of sadness.

In Cairo we talked to an elderly gentleman named Ernest Shelby,
a veteran of forty-one years on the riverboats. He started his career
in 1933 on the old steam paddle wheelers and worked his way up
until, at his retirement in 1974, he was designing and engineering
the big boats on the river today. Ernie told us he had served on
every kind of river craft, paddle wheelers and diesel tow-barges
that are bigger than ocean liners. And he worked on all the rivers,
the Ohio and Mississippi and Missouri, and up through the Great
Lakes.

"I went through the big flood of 1937," he said. "The one in
twenty-seven was bad but the one in thirty-seven was worse if you
were up the Ohio River. Louisville was about wiped out and everything below it."

He had survived wrecks, hurricanes, floods and fires on the boats.
He had worked on boats named after the states along the river,
Iowa, Illinois, Missouri, Minnesota, and he said the greatest fear
the men had was of fire. "You can ride out a hurricane, but a fire
on the boats, when it gets out of control, will put everybody in a
panic because there's no escape."

Ernie loved his years on the rivers. The boats he was on always
tried to make it to certain ports during special celebrations such
as Mardi Gras and the Veil of Prophets. "We always like to get into
New Orleans at Mardi Gras time. That was the best time you could
have. And St. Louis during the Veil of Prophets was almost as big
a deal as Mardi Gras. When you're on a boat, you don't even think
about being lonely, but when you're ashore, you want crowds, you
want to mix in with a lot of people."

Ernie told us one unique story. Submarines once went down the
Mississippi. Not in the water, of course. During World War II he
and his crew were given the job of moving a whole fleet of sub-

marines down to New Orleans, where they would be launched. "The submarines were built in Wisconsin and were being put into service below New Orleans in the Gulf of Mexico. It wasn't the only time we moved military equipment. We took down tanks and Jeeps and parts of airplanes. But those subs, they were a strange sight floating down the Mississippi."

Ernest Shelby lives in one of Cairo's grand old Victorian houses. He was disturbed and saddened by what was taking place in his home port and admitted that it's all pretty hopeless. He was thinking of moving away to be close to relatives in another state, though we knew he was dreading it because his heart is here on the river.

"We have trouble with break-ins and vandalism in town," he said. "People don't feel safe in their homes. The town's really gone down. There's some talk of putting one of those gambling boats here at Cairo. Maybe that'd put life back in the old town."

After we left Ernie we took a side trip on over to Paducah, Kentucky, where a riverfront festival was going on. At one time the town was a major port on the Ohio and things were on the move, with good growth and big industry coming in. A crowd in the thousands was gathering for the festival; they were having live music and boat races and street dances, all going on for a week. Some of the town's leaders had set up a booth and were collecting names for a petition, a rather curious one. Paducah for years has had an industry that makes nuclear fission components, and the company has been a strong force in Paducah's economy. In the past few years a crowd might have gathered to protest the high-risk industry, but Paducah desperately needs the jobs. The petition asked the state government to subsidize the conversion of the plant to newer methods of production. Jobs come before environmental concerns—we'd seen that attitude all along our trip down the river, and from here on we'd see much more of it.

Coming back to the river, we had to pass through Cairo again. Maybe we thought we could blink and all the depression would vanish. But Cairo's disposition hadn't changed; it was frozen in the glum way the shadows angled across, the way the rusty signs creaked in the wind. As we drove down Main again we heard some low-down funky music coming from the bar on the corner.

A wide boulevard leads back out of town and we were the only ones traveling it. We saw a pretty black woman coming out of a project apartment building; she started to run across the boulevard in front of us. She seemed surprised that a car would be coming along and embarrassed that she'd almost run into us. We waved and she called out, "I'm late. I think there's a party going on ... somewhere."

Not too many parties were going on in Cairo. There was a time when a hundred riverboats were tied up in the harbor; Mark Twain wrote in *Life on the Mississippi* that Cairo was "a good place to get out of the river." In our time we looked forward to seeing friends here and eating Mac's barbecue or maybe stopping at the Texaco station to gab with the funny guys who used to hang out there. We found the Texaco but it was all boarded up and there weren't any hangers-out to see.

We headed for the bridge. In front of us a pickup poked along, pulling a fishing boat. We thought of the advisories that are going into force all down the river. The Ohio can't be excluded either. It brings down its own loads of pollutants, the chief ones being chloroform and methyl chloride and sewage-treatment chemicals that fish in the confluence can't live in. The EPA and other watchdog groups have tested the water of the Ohio and have found that it might even be worse than the Mississippi's. Greenpeace claims there is a significantly higher ratio of cancer mortality in the Kentucky counties along the Ohio than in the Missouri and Tennessee counties around the confluence. Greenpeace says that extremely toxic material is washing down the Ohio from sources in Pittsburgh, Cincinnati and Louisville. We hadn't seen any commercial fishing rigs on our brief trip up the Ohio, but the manager of a marina over there in the green country of Kentucky told us that he serviced several commercial outfits. The region has many lakes and rivers, and fishing is second only to hunting with outdoors people.

A few miles over into Missouri, we found a hustling, tacky place called Boomland. It's an amalgam of cut-rate fireworks stands, convenience stores and gas stations. About a hundred cars and RVs had stopped at Boomland and the whole place was alive with travelers and hustlers. While we stood in line to pay for gas, we noticed a young black woman dawdling by the cashier's counter. Some people in the store were playing the Missouri lottery, scratching off cards in hopes of winning money at a dollar a scratch. The young woman had her eye on every man playing.

"Would you please leave people alone," we heard the cashier say to her, and then to a customer, "She's just scum . . . don't give her anything."

The young woman wasn't listening; she was still studying the lottery players. She went into her routine as each man moved up to the counter. There was an increasing urgency about her and she fidgeted with her blouse as a come-on to the cash customers. She was trying to pass herself off as friendly and appealing, but there was a hard contempt in her eyes.

She came on to us as we got to the counter. "Looking good, man, looking so good," she said. "Give me a lotto, why don't you? You can afford it. I'm nice. I'm real good."

The fellow behind us gave her a ticket, seemingly just to get away from her. She snatched it up and scratched it off and then threw it on the floor. There was never any hope of winning in her eyes, yet as we went out, she was back on the hustle at the counter, where she'd likely stay until they ran her out of the place.

We had already seen the boomland of the early 1800s just back across the Mississippi a few miles up the Ohio, where natural caves occur in the overhanging bluffs along the southern Illinois shore. One such was Rock Cave, a home to Indians and weary travelers before the dawn of the nineteenth century. Folklorists Herbert and Edward Quick, in their book *Mississippi Steamboatin',* wrote that as the traffic of new settlers increased on the Ohio, Rock Cave had been transformed into "Wilson's Liquor Vault and House of Entertainment." When flatboaters and other river travelers pulled in to avail themselves of Wilson's hospitality, the sting occurred. With such lures as games of chance, genuine double-rectified busthead and sporting women, the unwary travelers were easy prey. The Quick Brothers tell the sad tale that when the boatmen were addled with rotgut whiskey and intent on getting the floozies into the back room, Wilson and his cutthroat gang would shoot, knife or just plain bludgeon them to death, and then loot their cargoes. According to the Quick Brothers, the advance of civilization decided Wilson to abandon Rock Cave. He was never caught and died peacefully in his bed. We don't know what happened to his floozies; likely they found a boomland of their own.

The sense of the Mississippi's now unrestrained power was over-whelming as we began our trip into the downward slope of the middle of the continent through the portals of the Confluence of America. Just over there, we envisioned the flood of the Ohio col-liding with the massive force of the Mississippi. We had passed over a tumultuous explosion, seen one of the true vistas of Amer-ica, felt one of the finest sensations.

The collision between the raging strength of the Ohio and the unyielding might of the Father of Waters continues for maybe a hundred miles. Jealous and resisting, the bodies go on warring with each other until all that miraculous energy becomes one. And look-ing at this confluence, you understand why the river is such a big, mean force in the life of the lower basin—why it is, in Mark Twain's words, "the body of the nation."

CHAPTER 9

Crossing the Irony Line

"At least I can get them something and that's better than nothing."

—A welfare daddy at Portageville, Missouri

On the Achilles tendon of the Missouri bootheel, the well-known little town of New Madrid sits on the river and waits for a second coming. It's not as pretty a river town as Sainte Genevieve and it's not anywhere as ugly or grubby as many port towns farther down the Mississippi. In December 1990 New Madrid felt a spark of world interest when newspaper reporters and TV crews came to this fly-speck on the map because it was the expected epicenter of another earthquake on the New Madrid Fault; the intent of the reporters was to await a quake of mammoth proportions like the one of 1811–12.

The New Madrid Fault radiates from this town to Marked Tree, Arkansas, and up the Ohio River Valley past Louisville. The potential corridor of destruction extends about 500 miles (when the San Andreas Fault ruptured in 1906, the fissure covered some 290 miles). The New Madrid could affect St. Louis, Memphis, Louisville and even Cincinnati and Pittsburgh, with major damage as far south as Baton Rouge.

One man convinced a lot of people that it was going to happen; he also told them the day when it was going to take place, almost to the very hour. This quake fever amounted to another Mississippi Bubble, the perpetrator this time one Dr. Iben Browning, who should have added "Snake Oil Salesman" to his official titles. Browning declared that the New Madrid Fault would rupture about

December 4, and his doomsday prediction brought some notoriety and a whole lot of fear to towns and places along the lower river. This Dr. Browning, it should be noted, was the former NASA employee who tried to get the first moon launch scrubbed by predicting that the spacecraft would sink in 150 feet of moon dust. Browning got himself into the spotlight and earned some money selling a videocassette on earthquakes, and he brought about an insurance boom in the region. Mostly what he did was scare people half to death and get kids out of school for a day. It's not too surprising that so many people fell for Browning's bubble; most of the Mississippi Valley was first settled by those duped by John Law and his "Mississippi Company" way back in the 1720s. Browning died at seventy-three in 1991, in seclusion in his New Mexico home, and in disgrace.

We arrived in New Madrid some months after the quake fever had broken. Most people we saw were glad the hysteria had gone away. Some missed the attention and the money the media people spent. When we stepped inside Hap's Bar the place wasn't rocking

New Madrid, Missouri, town on the fault line.

with newspeople, but the owner and cook served up a tangy batch of gumbo for us. Like most all river towns from this point on down the Mississippi, New Madrid has its daily economic depression to worry about. Now and then some of the people wander over to the levee and down to the banks of the river. They watch for sand boils and sniff for sulphur, the signs of an earthquake.

When the quake hit in 1811, New Madrid was not just another small landing where keelboats stopped for wood before pushing on down to Natchez; it was the most important landing on the upper river. On December 15 the town had some hundred and fifty boats, all laden with goods, tied up at her docks. The quake erupted at 2 A.M. and jolted up all those boats from their moorings. Many among the crews perished, but some miraculously saved themselves; a few of these survivors recorded their thoughts, among them John Bradbury, a Scottish naturalist who had stopped that night in New Madrid after a two-year expedition up the Missouri River. Bradbury wrote in his journal that he was awakened by a roar and a violent tossing of his boat; he clung to his boat and witnessed "the river's banks collapsing, the forest caving in, the screeches of wild animals, the river turning red and boiling with geysers." Through the night Bradbury counted twenty-seven severe aftershocks and at dawn he saw many boats that had been at New Madrid "now passing in the flooding current, none of them with signs of life."

Others left similar eyewitness accounts. Captain John Davis of Ohio had brought a full fleet of forty boats and barges down the Ohio and they were docked at New Madrid. Davis reported later that he counted fifty aftershocks. He and his crew survived but battled the river for eight straight days. Another riverboat captain recounted the scene he found at New Madrid a few days after the earthquake. He told of utter desolation: the village of New Madrid was reduced to rubble, the people still in shock. The river was jammed with floating trees. The aftershocks would continue into the new year, with another violent quake erupting in early February. The people of the small port of New Madrid believed that Judgment Day had come.

Only about eight hundred people were living in New Madrid in 1811–12, and according to existing accounts, most or all of them survived. The damage wrought was another matter. Great fissures opened the earth, geysers shot mud and rocks hundreds of feet into the air, new hills and ridges heaved up out of the ground. The river itself ran red with brimstone and sulphur. Whole islands in the river disappeared, the forests went under, the tall oaks snapped like twigs. Violent winds tore the landscape and tossed bundles of fallen timbers. Deafening thunder rang to the heavens. Animals went crazy; thousands of birds hovered and screamed and thousands of squirrels plunged into the river. A thousand acres went down. The river rushed back upon itself.

Brimstone and fire, a river running red in an upheaval of Old Testament proportions—and yet what those few hundred souls at New Madrid witnessed next might have truly convinced them that the Day of Reckoning had dawned. Coming down the boiling river on that day was a sight to further flay the senses: a huge boat, belching smoke and powered by fire. Some may have thought it was a heavenly chariot sent for their deliverance. It passed within yards of the riverbanks where the people were weeping and wailing. And it went on out of sight down the river without saving one of them.

That boat was the *New Orleans,* the first steamboat in Western waters, making its maiden voyage down the Mississippi. The captain of the *New Orleans* was Nicholas J. Roosevelt (great-grand-uncle of Theodore Roosevelt). He had engineered and built the boat in Pittsburgh and he and his partners, the inventor Robert Fulton and Robert Livingston (the chancellor whom Jefferson sent to negotiate the Louisiana Purchase), were launching a steamboat enterprise they hoped would make them the richest men in America. The boat was a floating palace. Painted a sleek gray, it had luxurious accommodations including elegant furniture, baths, a dining hall and staterooms. On board with Captain Roosevelt and his crew were his young wife, Lydia, and their new baby, born while they stopped for a month in Louisville. Mrs. Roosevelt had even brought along her Newfoundland dog to keep her company.

Accounts of the journey tell a story of high adventure rivaling the voyages of Sinbad. Lydia Roosevelt, a former debutante and daughter of a Pittsburgh financier, proved to be one of the truly courageous ladies of the Mississippi. She was eight months pregnant when the *New Orleans* left Pittsburgh and yet insisted on taking part in this historic event. In *The Amazing Voyage of the New*

Orleans, Judith St. George focuses on Lydia Roosevelt, telling how she braved first the birth of her child in primitive conditions and then the earthquake on the deck of the boat with the infant in her arms. When the *New Orleans* passed New Madrid during the first aftershocks, the young mother witnessed the scene of desolation and pleaded with her husband to help those on the riverbank.

But Roosevelt couldn't help. On his boat his own people were terrified; they had experienced the quake as they came down the Ohio River early that morning, had been jolted and tossed like puppets and were now in a panic. All Roosevelt could do was keep up steam and try to save his own.

The *New Orleans* made it to its namesake port a few days later, on January 12, 1812. It had traveled two thousand miles in ten days of actual cruising time. It came to its berth at the French Quarter docks and delivered a load of cotton it had picked up during a brief stop in Natchez—the first steamboat commerce on the Mississippi. The high water of the river had saved the *New Orleans;* its deep-draw paddle wheel was unsuited to the Mississippi (in the near future steamboats would be designed with shallow drafts), and it would not be able to get upriver past Natchez again. The boat would come through the Battle of New Orleans only to hit a snag and sink while carrying another load of Natchez cotton; in the end it would seem that what a devastating earthquake could not do, the river could. It ultimately rejected attempts to tame it in the continuing struggle of man versus the river.

After the second major quake in February, every living hour must have been a torment to those eight hundred first settlers of New Madrid. Today residents still feel quakes in the area; it's a way of life here as it is along the San Andreas Fault of California.

"There's no such thing as getting used to it," a clerk in the New Madrid post office told us. "But watching for sand boils and sniffing for sulphur is as normal as taking the kids on a picnic over to Reelfoot Lake."

Reelfoot is a pretty recreational area just over in Kentucky. The deep, clear lake was created when those thousand acres sank during the quake of 1811.

Driving through the area gave us the feeling that the river and the faultline are one, or at least have some kinship. We also felt the pitch of the land starting to change; a wide alluvial plain was beginning and we felt we were driving onto something like a sub-continent. The Mason-Dixon line was once a convenient cliché for dividing North and South; the line was established by two English astronomers to settle a property dispute in the 1760s and came to be the boundary between free and slave states. A new line probably needs to be drawn, one showing where the progressive, industrious and rather dull Midwest leaves off and the hardheaded, tortured and colorful South begins. For want of accurate geographical borders, the new way should be measured along the path of the senses and could be called the Irony Line.

We drove over the Irony Line in Portageville, Missouri, and at a truck-stop convenience store we met a cool dude who seemed to be the embodiment of what the new line straddles. He was driving a new Cadillac and wearing a thousand-dollar suit, Rolex watch and gold chains. He was open and easy to talk to; he called himself the Welfare Daddy and saw nothing wrong with the way he got the money for his grand life-style.

We had first noticed him standing at the trunk of his Cad peeling out of tattered old clothes and clodhoppers. As we passed by, we got a glimpse inside the trunk; lying there in a pile were several Social Security cards and driver's licenses. The dude took a fat roll of Ben Franklins out of a sock and stuffed them in his Brooks Brothers suit pocket. He took out a bottle of Jack Daniel's, gulped down two big swallows, and said, "Ahhh, sheeit."

He was tall and thin and his skin was the color of the sun. He grinned proudly at us and asked if we were headed for Chicago, his town. When we told him we were going the other way, he puffed out his chest, chuckled and said, "I'm from down there too. Sheeit, yeah, I'm from down there." He was so cocksure that he didn't try to hide anything, and it wasn't hard to draw him out.

"That's quite a collection of IDs you have."

"Aw, now, sheeit. That's easy."

"You collect baseball cards too?"

"I collect money, man."

He laughed and strutted in place as he slipped on his suit coat and adjusted his Ralph Lauren tie. We saw him take a wedding band off his finger and toss it on the seat of the Cad. "Married, man," he sang. "Mah reed."

He was traveling alone and maybe he needed someone to talk

to and brag about his exploits. Once he got started, he told all. He was working a welfare scheme down South; he said he operated in and around Memphis, down in the state of Mississippi, and over in Tennessee and Arkansas. He collected government checks for fifteen different wives and their dependent children, and he had the correct identification to claim all those dependents.

"All I do is show up once a month at the government offices and take the money. I have to wear those old clothes. I keep them in the trunk so they'll stay smelly. Gag a maggot."

He never had any trouble. He said the government people didn't even look at him and were just interested in getting him out of the way. We asked if he didn't feel bad keeping all the money.

"Phew, now. The government, it don't care nothing about them people down there. I the one take care of them. Something go wrong, they call me. Somebody not treating them right, I put it straight. It stay straight, man. Hey, they don't get nothing without me. They don't qualify, know what I mean? I give 'em the food stamps. Hey, what chew mean? I bring them down stuff all the time. It's hard work, man. I get the kids shoes. I brought them some candy and the government sho' don't let them have candy."

He began to act nervous all of a sudden, as if he had spoken too freely. He stepped to his car and then turned to say more. Maybe he was just paranoid; he definitely had a lot on his mind and at the moment he needed an audience. He seemed to want approval.

"Hey, now," he said at last, "it's the risk I take. What's yo risk? I get caught, I go behind the walls. Lawyer, he expensive and I keep me one. I got bills, I got bidness to look after. Them people, man, they wouldn't have nothing without me. At least I can get them something and that's better than nothing. Hey, I got to go. I see you dudes in Chi Town."

He backed the Cad out and drove by us, giving us a hip wave with his jeweled hand. A program from the greyhound racetrack in West Memphis lay on the dash, with a pile of uncashed tickets. He got his stereo blasting rap; we could hear it as he turned out onto the highway. He was heading up to the interstate at Cairo. He'd be swinging back this way in another month.

Not five miles downriver from Cairo is the little town of Wickliffe, Kentucky, and the Welfare Daddy would have felt right at home there. In the early days of the steamboats, Wickliffe was the major port at the confluence of the Ohio. It was also the stomping grounds of Mike Fink, the prototype for Mark Twain's "Child of Calamity." The legendary Fink is in the finest tradition of American folk mythology—half man, half alligator. The blustery yarns about Fink are wonderful exaggerations of master storytellers. He was a crack shot, could drink any five men under the table and "could eat the rear end out of a bear while it was running." Fink commanded keelboats on the Ohio and the Mississippi. Whenever his boat put in to the ports along the way, he assumed the mantle of an anointed king. If local justices of the peace were smart, they'd load up their saddlebags and get out of town as soon as Fink and his tough river rat crew landed.

Fink also became famous up and down the rivers as an old-fashioned cocksman. Quite literally, he had girls and wives in every port. It was this he-man attribute that was the cause of his downfall, according to legend. One version has Fink being killed in a gambling brawl, but the more likely story is that he was shot down by a man he had cuckolded.

As we moved on toward the delta, we couldn't help thinking of Fink's harem and the Welfare Daddy at the same time. The burden of keeping up with all those women would require much more than just a half-man, half-alligator.

CHAPTER 10

Delta Tribes

"I always wished I coulda got me some of them free Nazi cotton-pickers."

—*An old delta farmer*

The river takes exaggerated loops as it pushes down into the wide sunken plain of the Arkansas delta. Old 61 has a hard time staying with the river because the channel seems to need either to eat up the little ports along the way or to cut them off completely.

We entered a flat, horizonless world. It once was the domain of red men and black men and white men. The Chickasaw tribes held this river embayment for millennia, and we could see some of their mounds out on the flatland, solitary humps all grown over with thickets and scrub and left in the middle of newly scored cottonfields. The tribes of the delta had already vanished by the time of the Relocation of the 1830s; this land was a swampy jungle then and what few white settlers came this way brought diseases that wasted the tribes before they ever had to be conquered and relocated.

The Mississippi turns mean and begins to swell. Emotions change, a wildness sets in. Twain found the lower river disturbing and enigmatic. On his last voyage in *Life on the Mississippi*, he was seized with a mood of melancholy here, so much so that he saw the confluent waters as a symbol of eternity. It's no odd circumstance of geography that the little town of Armorel, Arkansas, is a manifestation of the delta. We stood on the high porch of the old general store and could see off across the flatland, a vista which offered nothing more than wearying fields of cotton trussed up with lowland bayous full of water moccasins and gar and butcher-birds.

The delta as a homogeneous region starts here and extends through more than a hundred counties and parishes until it reaches the Gulf of Mexico and has done since Reconstruction. We were about to go down it. We had known some of that world before; it was a crazy-quilt land that in the past had taken to its bosom a peculiar fraternal order: the good old boy, the jerkleg preacher and what Wilbur Cash in *The Mind of the South* called the seer-sucker demagogue. Often they had been interchangeable; they made a salmagundi sight in their banker's vests, puckered suits and flashy Jehovah robes. In the little towns from Armorel to Fat City they mustered up lusty throngs with their pig-iron voices that mimed the Kingfish or aped the apologues of Jesus of Galilee. They strutted the towns with some free election-year barbecue, flapped the revival tents, rolled the whiskey wagons and voted the graveyard one more time. They were the latter-day Caesars or su-perannuated popes of the New South prating against a common enemy, the Yankee one-worlders and "nigger-loving" agitators. On the delta, where men loved revivaling and politicking and land-grabbing as much as they loved sour-mash whiskey and hunting dogs, the brotherhood came to stand for more than champion and messiah—they were the true and final evocation of the South un-der siege.

The writing was always there on the wall waiting for the broth-erhood to come along and decipher it and preach its dark message to all the hardtack, humorous delta men and grainy-frail delta women—until they bled them dry, and until the monied Yankee came down South looking for cheap labor and tax holidays follow-ing WWII; then a new kind of agrarian reform came about in which the brotherhood went into partnership with the reformers and learned to sing a new kind of four-part harmony.

The Mississippi delta is recognized today as perhaps the most economically depressed landmass in America. The delta is dying right before everybody's eyes. Per capita income in town after town has sunk so low that state and federal officials are embarrassed to publish the figures. A national delta commission made up mostly of governors and other politicians along the Mississippi is doing a lot of deploring and brow-furrowing. You suspect that the result

Shotgun shacks on the delta today.

will be a kind of retread WPA; some millions will be spent on the delta, which for all intents has already given up the ghost.

The delta commission keeps reviewing the gloom that has come upon the river's lands without ever looking into the inherent causes. The problem has existed since the Civil War: a closed good-old-boy system has ruled the delta, the South. The landowners and absentee landlords, together with their bankers and lawyers, evolving out of that same old brotherhood, have made sure the South stayed down while playing on emotional hopes that a New South will rise again. They have ensured that it won't by keeping the region poor and easy for the taking. No equitable tax structure has ever existed in the delta. The people are not valued and they remain uneducated, untrained and unhealthy.

Ironically, the delta is as fertile as ever. It is ripe with millions of acres of money crops. Cotton is again king. Yet there is little pride in Dixie, for these are corporate fields whose owners share little, if any, of the yield with the locals. What is happening up in bankrupt East St. Louis might be a microcosm of what's happening down the delta. The only difference is that the delta sold its city hall a long time ago.

Old 61 runs at field level into the first delta town, Blytheville, Arkansas. We came in on a street called Chickasawba and saw another Indian mound off in a field that borders a closed-down textile factory called Rice-Stix. Up in the residential section of the main street we passed a row of kingly planter homes in disrepair. Around town we saw a smoky mill, a Jewish temple, a couple of holy roller churches, a complex of fat grain elevators. Neon lights hawked beer and barbecue and burial plots. The town has a community college that is solar-powered; that idea seemed a good one twenty years ago, but now it's just a curiosity.

We pulled in at the courthouse, a hulking WPA structure that looked about used up. We struck up some talk with three old men on the lawn by a World War II monument. Their names, they said, were Fant and Dewey and Bunk; they had been cotton farmers and were now retired school-bus drivers. They told us a story. During World War II German prisoners of war were kept in camps here; many of the local people thought that half of Rommel's desert legions had come to the delta just to work for the big landowners, and the Army did hire out the prisoners to chop and pick cotton. After the war the Germans were replaced by thousands of Mexicans; they were brought up through Texas by caravans of transport trucks and they lived thirty to a shotgun shack, never thinking that they were latter-day Aztecs come north to get back a little of the conquistadors gold.

"Them Mexicans sure were treated bad ... worse than the Germans."

"The Germans were treated good. A few tried to escape. Not to get back to Germany, but so they could hide out and stay in this country."

"Some did, too."

"I always wished I coulda got me some of them free Nazi cotton-pickers."

Blytheville shows the sum of the delta. It's dying by degrees. An Air Force base used to keep the town going but it's been closed down and the town leaders are scurrying around to find anything they can to replace it, a steel mill, Japanese investors, even dreaming that Federal Express will take over the huge old air base. Like most little towns of the delta, Blytheville used to have two main streets, one for blacks, the other for whites. The livelier streets were black, of course. Old-timers here talk of the days of the Frolic Club on Ash Street, where jazz bands up from Memphis used to rock the Saturday nights away. Ash Street today is boarded up and locked tight, nothing more than a one-way street that leads to the interstate.

Blytheville used to put on a national cotton-picking contest, but now about all it boasts of is a tasty barbecue item called a pig sandwich. We stopped off and had one; it's chopped pork served with a sprinkle of very hot sauce and garnished with cole slaw to cool it down. It rivals the barbecue at Mac's in Cairo.

Several years ago they turned Main Street into a mall; we drove down it and saw hardly anyone shopping. We saw a sign, PASTIME POOLHALL, and went in to take a look. An elderly gentleman, a retired barber, had told us at the barbecue place that the poolhall used to see a lot of action, with high-stakes pool games and crap-shooters in the back room fading bets with thousand dollar rolls of the dice. Hank Williams used to come into the place, the retired barber said, and Ernest Tubb and Jim Reeves, the country-western stars. The poolhall had been turned into a recreational center, and in it were four high school kids playing eight-ball and listening to George Strait on the jukebox.

Main Street was deserted by the time we drove back down it. We drove out to the river at Barfield Landing. Steamboats once stopped here for wood and occasional cargo. Long tow-barges tie up here daily now, taking on loads of fertilizer produced by a plant which sits on the other side of the second levee. The ground and sodded levees were coated with a dusty white film. We drove through a picnic area where guys were out waxing their cars. We saw a boat ramp down on the riverbank and one of the fellows told us you could go water-skiing if the current stayed calm. The river was calm but there were no takers on skiing. We caught sight of the fertilizer plant's wastewater pipe down the way. Nothing was coming out of it at the time, but there were plenty of signs along the bank that foul stuff pours into the Mississippi here: a stagnant pond, dead brush, a few dead fish and turtles.

Not a mile from Barfield hunkers the little place called Tomato. Getting there is a big chore. There's no road down the levee and you have to drive a series of packed dirt, gravel and rubble roads, all within a long-jump of the river. When the Mississippi is running high and threatening to flood, the town of Tomato becomes an island with access only by powerboat. Because the river constantly changes its channel, it wants Tomato to be on the Tennessee side, and sometimes it is. The two states have wrangled over Tomato in the past; in better times the place was almost a town and had a couple of stores and several houses. Now it is a wretched spot; the two or three residents hold on for the sake of holding on.

We got to Tomato by driving field roads and section lines until we swung within yards of the river's shore. There's no levee along this stretch, but we saw that some people think it's a good place to put garbage and waste. We came upon dumps of oil drums, old tires, car batteries. Farther along, we found a few clapboard houses, a gutted village and more old shotgun shacks on the fringe of cotton and soybean fields. The houses had been poor excuses for shelter, often with but three or four hundred square feet of living space that you know served families of eight or ten. All these places were abandoned now, we thought. Until we came upon our river rats.

Facing the river and set back in a thicket of overhanging trees sat two dilapidated dog-run houses, side by side, in the midst of unbelievable junk and trash. We had been stopping as we went along to look through the deserted shacks and these two drew us on. The first house was built high on cinder blocks; we picked our way up the rotting front steps. The old door was standing ajar and hanging off its hinges. We were just about to step inside when we heard a wrathy growl. Some people were actually living here and we were trespassing. A short, scarlet-faced fat man charged at us. He was carrying a shotgun and cocking the hammer.

"Whur the hale you thank yore going?" he yelled. We froze. We needed to explain and we tried to beg his pardon for the intrusion, but he came on at us, waving the shotgun in our faces. Our mouths got a little dry and we learned how cotton tastes. We tried to edge back down the steps while avoiding any sudden move. We were trapped and guilty as sin. And at his mercy.

"Yore own my place, sonsabitches. I could kill ye."

He leveled the shotgun once and we thought we'd bought it. He was not making an idle threat, for he had that feral look in his eye.

He had no teeth, and his garbled speech was all the more menac-
ing as he wheezed out words that shook in the air. We made one
of the steps and then another until we were staring up the bead
of his gun. Somehow we managed to get back on level ground.

"We ask your pardon. We didn't mean—"

"I don't keer whut chew you mean. Come on my place trying to
steal?"

We asked his pardon again and he growled, the killing look in
his eyes a little softer maybe. He wouldn't mind killing, we could
read that message in his face. The river was right there, waiting for
our bodies. We'd get a good look at the Mississippi.

We moved one foot at a time toward our car. He'd like to have
that too, a vintage land-yacht he could put up in his yard and look
at until it became like the rest of his keepsakes.

"Don't you come back around here, sonsabitches. You git off my
property, git away from this river."

We got back in the car and drove very slowly. It wasn't until we
were bouncing along the field roads again that we got our hearts
started. When we'd first been planning this trip down the river,
we'd wondered if we might come across river rats; we had wished
we would. But then, we'd never thought the movie *Deliverance* was
a true depiction.

River ratting has a tradition on the Mississippi dating back to
the eighteenth century. The river rats used to live on boats, not
very elegant boats, for sure, but large enough to accommodate
their broods. The rats traveled up and down the Mississippi and
various tributaries and agreed to work only as a last resort, their
normal vocations being petty theft, burglary, bootlegging and minor piracy. Over the years the river rats have been forced inland
by boat licenses and regulations. We weren't a bit proud that we
had become a part of the river rat tradition.

The towhead area called Tomato is on the reach of the river
where "bad water" has long been suspected. In 1865 the steamboat
Sultana blew up and sank in this bend of the river. The war had
just ended and the *Sultana* was loaded down with twenty-five hundred Union soldiers headed for St. Louis for mustering out. When
the *Sultana* went down, it took seventeen hundred of the soldiers
with it. It was in this location, too, that a travel writer in a small
boat experienced bad water; he felt a strange surge of the current

and a dizzying loss of equilibrium. A man in a country store told us that three men on a hunting trip had disappeared a few years ago; they boated over to the Tennessee bottoms and no one has seen them since.

Coming back out to the main road, we passed through a community called Promised Land. We didn't fail to detect a sense of irony. We'd had our own episode, and, if nothing else, it taught us again that the river's mysteries are approached at your own risk.

A new, wide bypass swings around the old plantation town of Armorel not far from the Barfield landing. The bypass, we found, accommodated the big fertilizer plant on the river, but we wanted to look at the plantation town, since it was the first, or last, on the river. Armorel has all the markings of the postbellum South. It has a town square, post office, public schools and a big general store, but at one time it was completely owned by a land baron and his heirs, before everything went corporate.

CHAPTER 11

"The River Was Dyed with Blood"

"We the law here and we do what we want."

—*Gang leader in Turrell, Arkansas*

The next sizable town on the delta after Blytheville calls itself "the biggest little city on the Mississippi." Its actual name is Osceola, Arkansas, and its high school football team is known as the Seminoles. The real Seminoles lived in Florida and it's hard to see why a town on the Mississippi would take them on as a mascot, but little towns sometimes need myths to give reason to their existence.

Law-abiding citizens would find it impossible to view the river from the levee at Osceola because it's fenced off and posted with No Trespassing signs. We drove into a poverty pocket right on the fence line and asked an old black gentleman how to get to the river. "Just drive on up the levee road there," he said. "Nobody gonna stop you. Ain't many around here anyway." We were determined to see the river from this exact vantage point.

We stood on the levee and gazed a long time across to the Tennessee shore at the restored remnants of old Fort Pillow. Built in 1861 by the South to defend Memphis, the fort fell to the first Union attack in 1862 without firing a shot. In 1864 Fort Pillow became the site of the worst atrocity of the Civil War, the massacre of seven hundred blacks, soldiers and women and children, by the cavalry of Nathan Bedford Forrest, major general of the Confederate States of America. The black soldiers were here because Lincoln had wanted to raise an army of a hundred thousand former slaves from the Mississippi River Valley. Forrest, the only winning general the South had in the West, came here with his "Critter Company" to teach Lincoln and the North a lesson about arming slaves and sending them against their former masters.

On the rainy morning of April 12, 1864, Forrest's fifteen hundred veteran troops, victors on innumerable battlefields, came out of nowhere through the mist and quickly sealed off the fort. Faced with overwhelming odds and under heavy fire, the white Union officers within the fort decided their only chance was to hold out as long as they could to give a gunboat time to come up and drive the Rebs away. The gunboat arrived but retreated when Forrest fired shots at it with his light artillery. By afternoon steamboats from Memphis, crowded with hundreds of reinforcements, arrived but Forrest's guns sent them running back to Memphis. The Union general on the steamboats obviously didn't think the fort with its three hundred black soldiers and only a hundred white Tennessee Volunteers was worth a fight with the much-feared Forrest.

Forrest's troops closed in and kept the fort under a heavy fire. The Union commander of the fort, Major William Bradford, could no longer defend it and ran up a white flag of surrender. Forrest's "critters" charged through the open gate and scaled the walls, crying, "No quarter!"

The first gray-clad horsemen into the fort sabered down the blacks at the gate. More Rebs poured in and began shooting and hacking down the black soldiers still standing in formation along a row of stacked arms. The killing had just begun. Black soldiers were lynched and mutilated. The women and children had run to hide in the sheds by the water battery. Forrest's men stacked hay against the crude shelters and burned them alive. The lesson was over and Forrest left.

Word of the Fort Pillow atrocities reached Washington the next day by telegraph. Washington couldn't believe what was being reported. Two days later the *New York Herald*'s Horace Greeley printed the story under the headline "The Fort Pillow Massacre." A full-blown congressional inquiry was convened immediately at Cairo, Illinois. Hundreds of pages of eyewitness testimony were taken and a report issued on every aspect of the atrocity less than a month later. Forty thousand copies of the report were issued to a shocked public. But after the war, Forrest was never brought to trial for his war crimes.

In *Life on the Mississippi* Mark Twain recorded his views on Fort Pillow: "We glided unchallenged by what was once the formidable Fort Pillow, memorable because of the massacre perpetrated there during the war. Massacres are sprinkled with some frequency through the histories of several Christian nations, but this is almost the only one that can be found in American history; perhaps it is the only one which rises to a size correspondent to that huge and somber title ... we must bunch Anglo-Saxon history together to find the fellow to the Fort Pillow tragedy."

In his memoirs U. S. Grant quoted Forrest's first unsanitized dispatch verbatim: "The river was dyed with the blood of the slaughtered for two hundred yards." Perhaps the most damning evidence of all against Forrest comes from his own journal. Hodding Carter, one of the South's best journalists during the Jim Crow era, quotes Forrest's first reaction to the massacre, written in Forrest's own crude, semiliterate hand: "My men are a-cilling 'em."

Fort Pillow today is a state park and you can get to it by going through Memphis and up the other side of the river. For some reason the Fort has been preserved as if it were as important as Gettysburg. Tennessee has spent millions on the renovations and the tourist-oriented hiking trails, the picnic grounds, the picturesque lake, and the inevitable interpretive center, with video theater. The attendants are ill at ease about the massacre and fall back on the version favored by Southern historians, that tales of the massacre were just a piece of wartime propaganda. Even historian Bruce Catton confirmed the massacre in *A Stillness at Appomattox:* "After the surrender some of Forrest's tough troopers got out of hand and turned the occasion into something like a lynching bee."

Had the martyred black soldiers of Fort Pillow lived to join the ranks of ex-slaves after the war, they could only have stared in dumb shock as they realized the extent of the war's futility. Blacks were to be tied to the land, the same old plantation life as before but without even a modicum of decency or virtue.

We drove off the forbidden levee in Osceola and wound down Old 61 again. The roll call of delta towns is augmented by the names of the rich and powerful families that ruled here like medieval barons: Leachville, Monette, Burdette, Wilson. The town of Wilson is a special case; it is still an empire intact, controlling perhaps the greatest tracts of land in the entire river basin. Drive into Wilson today and you'll behold Elizabethan England. The renaissance architecture is strikingly accurate until you see it's all a façade just like a Hollywood movie set.

The Wilson legend still lives on the delta. Novels have been written about the clan, and sociological monographs have appeared in journals. Local people say that the elder Wilson ruled with an iron hand and ran his plantation in the antebellum way. His offspring mellowed somewhat; one of them attended an Ivy League school and picked up the sport of polo. He later laid out a polo field on the spacious front lawn of his mansion and kept a stable of ponies for matches, assembling his teams from polo enthusiasts in Memphis and back East. It was all a grand show, people around here said. Hundreds would gather for the matches; formally attired stable boys and house servants came out to replace the divots after each chukker.

Try as he might, Wilson couldn't disguise or control the poverty that surrounded his splendid little pocket of paradise. South of Wilson, off Highway 61 a few miles, the delta traveler can find a more hopeful look in a scene from the Great Depression. Called Dyess, it was a colony in the 1930s for beleaguered delta families; it was one of those rare progressive projects of the New Deal and people learned they could come here and the colony would see to it that they didn't starve. Many a down-and-out family pulled into Dyess and found sustenance and the will to keep going. Devotees of the John Ford film of *The Grapes of Wrath* would recognize scenes from the movie, though there was no make-believe here.

Rather than being abandoned or left to decay, the colony's buildings are still being used by the few residents of the little town of Dyess, so even in default the experiment is helping people. The country singer Johnny Cash lived in Dyess back in the mid-1930s; his folks came here to get in out of the Depression. Cash sang songs about this area; his memorable "How High's the Water, Mama" is a tribute to the people of Dyess who braved the river's biggest flood. The colony centers around an American flag, a fountain and a plaque to its founder, W. R. Dyess. The whole place is painted white and the grass is neatly clipped, a pointed contrast to the litter in the ditches we saw coming into Dyess.

The remaining miles of Old 61 down the New Madrid Fault to Memphis are an unrelieved landscape of one-stoplight towns laboring through unremitting poverty—Delpro, Barrett, Joiner, Frenchman's Bayou, Jericho, Turrell. Of these, Turrell has achieved a point of notoriety: the town was the site of open gun battles between rival drug-dealing gangs. In 1989 a stray bullet hit and killed a three-year-old girl playing in her yard a block away from a fight. The shooting made front-page headlines in the region for a short time, but conditions remained out of control for nearly a year. Turrell had become the private turf of three brothers who had been members of gangs in Detroit, Chicago and Los Angeles. Arkansas county and state law officers couldn't stop the violence or the drug traffic. One of the brothers laughed in the face of a sheriff's deputy who came to patrol the streets. "We the law here," the brother told a reporter, "and we do what we want."

Turrell quickly earned the reputation for being the easiest dope drop between Memphis and St. Louis because the brothers had the connections and the supply. When other dealers tried to move in, a news account in the *Arkansas Gazette* reported, "the brothers simply stepped out in the street and opened fire." Hardly a weekend went by without the sound of gunfire. "Sometimes the brothers shot their guns off just to let the town know they were still in business."

When we passed through Turrell an uneasy quiet had settled on the town. Never a booming place, it had seen most of its stores closed after blatant vandalism. We asked in the one store that was open and were told the brothers might have left town. "Their business dropped way off."

We found a young woman to talk to about Turrell. Her name is Stephanie Beard and she was then a nineteen-year-old college honor student; she grew up just outside Turrell. She told us she attended the Methodist church in Turrell while she was growing up, and she had several good friends in town.

"We used to have a lot of fun in Turrell. We'd have church parties and hold rummage sales down by the bank. I knew all the people in Turrell's stores, Mengarelli's and Catalina's. The people of Turrell were nice and friendly, good people, but it amazes me now that anyone stays there."

She said that all the trouble in Turrell began because the former law officer was a drug dealer himself. "When he was arrested on drug charges in 1989, that opened up the town. There used to be a lot of kids in Turrell. When that little girl died, the town died with it. Now there are only a few old, old people left and they hide behind their blinds."

Driving around the empty town, we thought that maybe Turrell was not completely beyond saving. The area has the Wapanocca Indian Wildlife Refuge, one of the best of its kind, and is a haven for migrating ducks along the Mississippi flyway and a hunter's paradise. A large antebellum plantation remains in the area, by the river; the slave quarters are still standing. Indian mounds pock the landscape around Turrell. But tourist bureaus are still scared to look Turrell's way.

"What Turrell needs," Stephanie said, "is a basic course in health and safety."

From Turrell, battered and cracked Old 61 takes aim at the prominent Chickasaw Bluffs of Memphis. In twilight the delta looked like a settling shawl of pitch, but as the lights began to come on the empurpled horizon began a lazy, dreamy dance. Off to the west rises a chain of loess-built hills extending over a hundred miles, a peculiar land formation known as Crowley's Ridge, the likes of which can only be found here and in the Himalayas. On the ridge sits the town of Forrest City, named for the wild and warped Nathan Bedford Forrest. After slave trading before the Civil War and marauding during it, Forrest turned to land developing over here in the jungles of Arkansas, and went broke doing it.

Anticipating Memphis, we were picking up the land-yacht's pace when we passed an old country church, African, Methodist Episcopal, off the highway. People were gathering for a midweek service, and we decided to see if we could take in a prayer meeting. The black worshipers were shocked to see us coming in the back, but we were welcomed right in.

The singing was as good as you'd hope and the preacher was, well, the word is rousing. Afterward, we stood out in the churchyard talking and the topic came around to old times, for the congregation was mostly elderly. They got into lively arguments, did a lot of laughing, and tossed old remembrances off like spirited hymns.

"Oldest thing I can remember, smelling the ice cream parlor, that double dip of strawberry and tutti-frutti."

A delta church.

"The sting of raw cotton in your eye—up in a cotton wagon, that was stifling."

"The taste of salt on ice when your mama was making home-made ice cream."

"Nothing tasted better than crackling bread and hot tamales."

"Collard greens and poke sallet fried with hog brains."

"Whippoorwill peas and side meat."

"Squirrel stew and buttermilk biscuits."

"Never could stomach chitlins."

They told us more of their lives than they knew. When we got back on the road, the delta was cooling. Shadows danced out there, ghosts maybe, red men and black men and blues men. There was nothing to see but a ceaseless flat world and thousands of lightning bugs and country roads that at night looked like white scars cut across the belly of some bloated river creature. We neared the river and caught its odor, the sticky, scaly, fishy smell of the Mississippi.

Coming in sight of Memphis over the river, we thought about the blues, and as we rode along we heard the sound of Old 61. We could imagine we heard in it some sad voices that made us want to lift ours. What was the color of the blues? we asked each other. Was it black or red or dappled? A lot of misery had lived on the delta, and we had only just started looking. Those windy ghosts out there just laughed at us as we were carried along on our sweet ride.

CHAPTER 12

Ramses
and Rock and Roll

"Elvis—I just love that poor old dead thing."

—Voice on a call-in radio show

Moody Memphis broods on its fabled Chickasaw Bluffs. People coming over the bridges can't miss the graceless and vulgar pyramid that looms over the riverfront. You have to wonder what Memphis had in its mind when it adopted the image of Ramses II, known to Egyptologists as a bellicose pharaoh who took some thirty daughters for wives. Memphis could have chosen Amenhotep, a peaceful pharaoh, as its symbolic ruler. Memphis can't seem to stay away from schemes and hucksters selling a bill of goods.

Memphis has an impeccable record. Every ruler who ever tried his hand here was a consummate failure. Going on two hundred years ago, the pompous Chickasaw chieftains stood on the bluff, saw the first steamboat coming down their river and sent out warriors to kill the growling demon, though all they could do was loose a few harmless arrows. Andrew Jackson came here dreaming of riches that a bounteous port at Memphis might bring him, yet he died a pauper. For a time Jackson's Memphis had some heavy competition from the towns of Fort Pickering and Fulton, also on the Chickasaw Bluffs. Memphis grew and the others died, though Jackson took a beating on his land schemes here. Most of Fulton caved in and slid into the river, and what was Fort Pickering, right on the bluff in what today is downtown Memphis, is part of a land development project; actress Cybill Shepherd has a mansion site right on Fort Pickering with Memphis's best view of the river.

Nathan Bedford Forrest was a native son of the city of Memphis. Before the Civil War he had been a successful slave dealer; he plowed the profits of slave auctions into the cause of the South by raising his own regiment, his "critters." After the war Forrest returned to Memphis, tried to be a civic leader, but found his talents more suited to creating and leading the secret army, the Ku Klux Klan. He gave the South a legacy it would find impossible to live down; in the years after the war, the Klan gained upwards of five million members, and the deeds they committed throughout the New South grew so terrifying that Forrest on his deathbed asked the Klan leaders to disband. Journalist Hodding Carter wrote that Forrest "took his vendetta against the black to his grave." Forrest died in the 1870s, the same decade that saw Memphis almost destroyed by yellow fever epidemics, a gift from the city of New Orleans (a steamboat carrying bananas set the plague in motion).

The first thing we saw in Memphis as we looked for Beale Street was a historical marker denoting the house where Forrest died. It was his brother's house, just a block off Beale. In 1991 Memphis elected a black mayor for the first time in its ragged history. For half a century a boss named Crump had Memphis in his claw and made it bow to his will; his legacy left the town mired in mediocrity. One king with a dream of the mountaintop was gunned down here, while another crooned and pelvised his way to such an immense popularity that neither his ignorance nor his innocence could save him.

Memphis keeps trying. It made outdoor malls of downtown streets, but nobody came there. It rebuilt Beale Street at a cost in the millions, trying to make storied old Beale something it wasn't— and the tourists stayed away. It converted a boggy little towhead in the Mississippi into what was supposed to be a major attraction, but Mud Island stays mostly deserted, give or take a rock concert or two, and is certainly not the stuff you build Disney World dreams on. Memphis would dearly love its own major-league team, but it's being passed over.

Maybe if Memphis would quit trying so hard, it'd be all right. The town has always had good things going for it: good colleges, a good zoo, fine restaurants, Graceland, the Liberty Bowl, excellent hospitals and treatment centers, Federal Express Corporate Headquarters. After Atlanta, Memphis is the major distribution center of the South. The town has tried to rid itself of its terrible racist image, though it has a way to go. In the past few years Orange Mound, once the largest black ghetto in the country, has slowly been disappearing. Out south of the railroad tracks, several ball fields have replaced slums. Whitehaven no longer lives up to its name.

The most elegant thing Memphis has going for it is the grand old Peabody Hotel. Like a lot of things in Memphis, the Peabody had grown dilapidated over the years, but they've revitalized it and now it looks like a magnificent old Italian opera house. The lobby of the Peabody draws a cross section of Mid-South culture. The thing to do in Memphis is sit in the brimming lobby, see and be seen, and talk about the possibility of Elvis's being alive while you wait for the famous ducks to waddle through. We know a medical photographer in Memphis who could end the silly Elvis controversy; he took pictures of Presley's body during the autopsy and he can assure everyone that the King is dead. "If you'd seen what I did," the photographer told us, "you wouldn't want Elvis to be alive."

In the Peabody lobby we met two friends, Maxine Russell and Bonnie Ring, to talk about music and Elvis. They were on their way to Nashville to cut an album with their brother, Jim Ed Brown. Back in the fifties and sixties Jim Ed, Maxine and Bonnie formed a singing group called the Browns and had a solid string of number-one hits, including "The Three Bells," "Scarlet Ribbons" and "The Old Lamplighter." They had grown up on a poor dirt farm in south Arkansas, learned to sing their special close harmony in little country churches and were members of the Grand Ole Opry when it was still country.

When we found them in the busy lobby they were chatting with some old fans who had recognized them. Though Maxine and Bonnie gave up the hard grind of going on the road some years ago, they still record and appear on Nashville TV. We read once that Paul McCartney and John Lennon gave credit to the Browns for most influencing their style of music. Maxine told us they met the Beatles in London way back there when the Browns were on tour. "They hadn't broken through yet; they liked our harmony and wanted to learn it." Later the Browns worked with Elvis Presley on the old Louisiana Hayride in Shreveport. In fact, Elvis started his career there and had second billing to the Browns.

Sitting in the Peabody lobby, Bonnie and Maxine reminisced about some great days and hard times in the music world. Early on, Maxine had written a song, "I Was Looking Back to See," that went on to be a classic in both country and pop music.

"Guy Lombardo covered 'Looking Back' and made a small fortune on it," Maxine said. "We got cheated out of the song by a crooked old coot named Faber Robinson and we never made a dime off the song. He was the same bum who cheated Jim Reeves out of a lot of his songs."

We asked Bonnie and Maxine about Elvis, knowing him and traveling to one-nighters all over Texas and the Southwest. They painted a somewhat different picture of Elvis than the one the public adores and thinks it knows. He was just a green kid, always hungry, and thought he'd be lucky if he made it in gospel singing.

"Gospel was Elvis's first love," Maxine said. "That's all he ever wanted to sing . . . and he'd have been better off if he had stayed with it."

They told us of the many times Elvis and his band came through and stopped off at the Browns' home in Pine Bluff, Arkansas. Their mother had a small restaurant and fed for free just about all the country-music pickers and singers on the road.

"Elvis never had any money," Maxine said. "He'd mooch off Mama and Daddy and sleep on the couch most of the time. He broke down on the road one time and Daddy drove a hundred miles to pick Elvis up, and let him borrow his brand-new car. Elvis didn't bring the car back for six weeks and when he did bring it back, it was a wreck."

In the elegant surroundings of the Peabody Hotel, the Browns told us many funny and tragic stories of being on the road. Close friends died in car wrecks and plane crashes, hateful people made it big and great talents went begging. Still, country music had its own code and a peculiar kind of fidelity that other fields of music could only envy. One of the truly good guys in their industry, Bonnie and Maxine agree, is Tom T. Hall, who sums up the picker's life in a line from one of his songs, "Taking pills and drinking whiskey, picking can be mighty risky."

The birth of the blues.

Bonnie had been very close to Elvis and his death was particularly crushing to her; she hasn't talked about Elvis since his death and she wouldn't say much now, maybe because of all the sleazy stuff that the Elvis Industry keeps putting out. Maxine still writes an occasional song and is at work on a book about "what it's really like to be in this crazy business." Maxine Brown always had a name in the music business for being straightforward and totally honest.

"The truth always hurts," she said. "That's really what country music is about."

Beale Street, just around the block from the Peabody, is at least trying to break in its brand-new pair of shoes. It's clean, lit up, friendly, open for business. Occasionally a few tourists wander through, listen to a little music and maybe even go into one of the cafés for ribs, red beans and rice. Blues plays here a lot of the time and maybe things are starting to pick up. During the "Memphis in May" celebration downtown Memphis was swamped with tens of thousands of visitors, and Beale Street got a good chance to strut its stuff with blues bands from all over the country.

Never doubt that Memphis is the Home of the Blues. Beale Street and clubs in surrounding Orange Mound featured the likes of Charlie Robinson, a trumpet artist admired by the great Louis Armstrong. One of the hot spots was Mitchell's Domino Lounge, featuring the Brown Skin Models, who played to standing-room-only crowds. Larger venues such as the Palace Theatre and its altruistic master of ceremonies, Rufus Thomas, spotlighted new talent, paying the players a dollar or two for weekly appearances. Premier bluesman B. B. King came up from the Mississippi delta and got his start at the Palace, thanks to Rufus Thomas.

William Christopher Handy was born here in 1873. Handy was a poet who never wrote a bad line. As a child in the Memphis ghetto he endured a complete lack of education and near starvation through the dark days of Reconstruction. He was a bandleader before he was twenty, playing all the black clubs up and down the Mississippi. He lost his sight in his thirties but kept playing and writing songs. In 1912 he finally got a song published; it was called "Memphis Blues" and marked the blues' birth. His most famous song, of course, was "St. Louis Blues," published two years later. The song became a standard across the country and was played in the most stylish salons and music halls, even though its composer was denied entry to them because of his color.

Handy and Boss Crump are studies in contrast, though their lives ran on parallel courses. Both were born poor and rose to high stature in the same town at the same time. Both came to mean something extraordinary to the people, black and white. Handy had to endure the incontestably demeaning existence that Crump stood for. Crump prevailed, as bosses must, but Handy created his own legend, and right here on Beale Street—where his statue now stands. Boss Crump ended his years a sour man, they say in Memphis—a sour man in a sour time.

Although Memphis elected its first black mayor in 1991, Boss Crump's influence is still alive in the city. The system of municipal government that he installed has long suppressed black political representation in the city and Shelby County. In February 1991 the U.S. Justice Department set aside the entire electoral system for Memphis, saying that the system was designed to "scatter the

black vote so widely as to deny proper black representation." Of
the sixteen City Council members in 1990, only three were black,
thirteen white. The ratio was far out of balance; of the some 307,000
registered voters in Memphis, more than 50 percent were black. In
Memphis only two black candidates have won a citywide election
since 1951. The overview is that Crump's old repressive form of
government has been challenged, its inequities exposed to the light
of day, and change is finally on the way. Memphis is probably the
last stronghold of Dixie. It's mostly a young person's town now, as
witness the yuppie opulence along Riverside Drive right on the
Mississippi. If this new generation is going to be any part of a
mainstream, it can't allow the puffy, cigar-chomping old bosses to
rule its lives.

Just off Beale Street stands an impressive edifice that looks for
all the world like a spanking-new building. In actuality it is the old
Lorraine Motel, gutted and with a $10-million new face and in-
nards. For years after the murder of Martin Luther King at the
motel in April 1968, the curious drove past the seedy place and
didn't risk stopping, for it was a flophouse and den for dope dealers and prostitutes. The City of Memphis and other agencies put
up the money to turn the old Lorraine into the National Museum
for Civil Rights, and the museum was officially opened on the
Fourth of July, 1991.

The day of the opening was muggy and uncomfortable and the
mood was somber, though there was an attempt to make the affair
a media happening, with Hollywood getting in on the act. Cybill
Shepherd officiated at the ceremonies; two other actors, Morgan
Freeman and Blair Underwood, put in appearances. Jesse Jackson,
who got his big jump into national prominence by being at King's
side here in 1968, was on hand to make a speech. But the day
clearly belonged to two stellar women of the civil rights movement—Rosa Parks and Daisy Bates. Parks had set off the movement
back in 1955 by refusing to give up her seat on a Montgomery,
Alabama, city bus; Bates had served as tutor for the black students
who integrated Central High School in Little Rock, Arkansas, in
1957, and had accompanied the students to school each day
through the redneck rabble on the high school steps.

D'Army Bailey, a Memphis judge who led the difficult drive to
build the museum, escorted a tour of the many exhibits, including

Vigil at the Lorriane Motel in Memphis.

a statue of Martin and one of Rosa Parks sitting in her seat on the bus. In the museum, too, is a bust of former Arkansas governor Orval Faubus. Faubus was not in attendance at the museum's opening, and when we asked D'Army Bailey if Faubus had been given an invitation, the judge only smiled.

We spoke briefly with a fifteen-year-old who was working as a volunteer in the museum. He was a bright, serious young man who told us he wanted to study law someday; he was happy to have this experience and thought the museum was "pure, prime." He reminded us a lot of another young man we'd met on our journey, that riverboat museum cub up in Keokuk. They were about the same age and their outlooks were refreshingly similar. And we had the thought that somehow there needn't be such a difference between North and South.

One person who had had a vital interest here was noticeably absent from the ceremonies. Jacqueline Smith, a thirty-eight-year-old Memphis black woman, had lived and worked as the desk clerk in the motel for more than ten years. When the state ordered the building vacated, the last few residents left, all except Jacky. She refused to go, taking up residence in King's room on the second floor, and later had to be carried out by sheriff's deputies. She took up a new vigil in a tent on the sidewalk across the street, and there she stayed, for five hundred days, a thousand, and, when we visited, still counting.

We talked with Jacky on two occasions, the first in the fall and the second the following spring. Her protest was not a personal one, she said. She deplored the local government's spending millions of dollars on "another shrine" while so many needy people weren't being helped. "They are just trying to build another tourist attraction," she said, "another pyramid and Graceland. If they wanted to really honor Dr. King, they'd help people, black and white, with better places to live."

Jacky Smith didn't go without supporters for the many months she held out across from the old Lorraine. Friends brought her food and clothing, and people across the country began letter campaigns in support of her stand.

She wasn't at the grand opening of the civil rights museum. We searched for her and inquired of several bystanders, to no avail. Evidently somebody had got to her and finally talked her into going along with the plan. It's for sure Jacqueline Smith wasn't paid off—the city tried that with her more than once. Coretta King, Dr. King's widow, had vocally opposed the whole concept of a museum, but she attended the opening. Jacky stuck it out far longer than her opponents had feared and with the stubborn will that had once gladdened the ranks of King's followers. In a very real way we felt that the quiet events of this ironic Fourth of July marked the end of an era.

Driving out Elvis Presley Boulevard with Fourth of July rockets starting to burst over the river, we tried to put Memphis into perspective, but it wouldn't clarify. We had always thought that it was our town and somewhere along the way it had got away from us. A sentimental stop at Graceland didn't hold much hope of arresting some disorders and early sorrows. How absurd to even think of writing some graceful words about Graceland.

The last tour of Elvis's mansion was over for the day and some visitors were lingering in the souvenir and T-shirt stalls across the street. We hadn't thought of touring the place anyway; we just wanted to look at it all again. A nice lady named June, who had toured the mansion that day, came back to get her kids some Elvis mementos.

"You're a big Elvis fan?" we asked her.

"Why, *yes.*"

"How do you like Graceland?"

"It's ... sad. It's the most unhappy house I've ever seen."

June was a very attractive lady, tastefully dressed and well-spoken. She was driving a Lincoln Continental and her husband, she told us, was a successful building contractor. She had grown children and grandchildren, yet she was an unabashed Elvis worshiper. She had toured that house across the street half a dozen times and knew everything on display there, the long white couch in the living room, the poolroom downstairs, the Harleys, the jungle room, all the gold records, the King's flashy costumes.

"Sad," she said again.

We guessed that, in a way, we can't keep from loving that poor old dead thing ourselves, and in the same way we can't keep from loving this town of Memphis. As we had done in Cairo, we drove back over the bridge just so we could get another angle. And there it was again, moody Memphis brooding on its bluff.

CHAPTER 13

A Modern-day Captain Bixby

"The river is my home . . . that's how all people on the boats today look upon the Mississippi."

—Dominic Desiderio, riverboat pilot

High on the bluff in Memphis, the Pier Restaurant yields a sweeping view of the river coursing along the city. The Pier is a smart restaurant with good seafood and is properly trimmed in the maritime mode like one of those old inns of Nantucket. River people gather here, captains and pilots and boilermen and deckhands. The bond of the river brings them here and it's a good place to sit over coffee or brandy and spin yarns about the big river while it flows just below them.

In the Pier we sat with a young tow-barge pilot already a dozen years on the long boats but wise beyond his age about the riverways of the country. You could mistake Dominic Desiderio for a movie swashbuckler; he's six-four, strong as a keelboatman, with dark features that point to his Italian ancestry.

His home port is Memphis and has been since he first signed on as a deckhand right out of high school. He's worked his way up the order of rank from deckhand to second mate, tankerman, first mate, steersman, boiler operator, troubleshooter, pilot and captain. Most of the traditions of steamboat days have remained in place. As in Mark Twain's time, the most admired officer on the boats is the pilot, not the captain.

"The pilot is in control of the vessel during the most crucial times," Dominic said. "I'd rather be a pilot than a captain."

The sizes of today's boats range from 1,800 horsepower (considered small) to the jumbo boats of 5,400 horsepower. The average tow-barge carries 20,000 tons of goods. The largest barge in the world is in Shanghai; the second biggest in America, the *Mid South,* is based in Baton Rouge; and the biggest one, the *America,* is kept up near St. Louis on the Wood River. "The *America,*" Dominic said, "is bigger than a battleship and hasn't been in commission for a long time."

Top pay for a modern riverboat captain is about $70,000 a year. Some of the bigger companies are Ingram, Georgia Gulf and the Ohio Barge Line (which is owned by U.S. Steel, heavily into river transport).

"Ohio Barge runs a tough company," Dominic said. "It will not tolerate strikes by workers. They bring in strikebreakers and some union-bashing goes on."

While he talked, Dominic leaned forward now and then to look out at the river. Long barges were docked at the wharves down there, and he scanned them keenly, out of habit. He pointed and said, "The river—it's going to be changed by the time we go up it again. It's in a constant state of change, you know. The buoys won't be in the same position when you make the return trip ... they might change as much as fifteen or twenty feet from one trip to the next." He stopped and we could tell he was thinking about piloting those huge boats. "The best pilot I ever saw was a man named Joe Desmond. He's a legend to all riverboat people. He's saved many a boat from doom. No telling how many lives over the years. Joe Desmond *knows* the river and he works *without* maps. You use him as a go-by, the one you hope you can be as good as someday."

A big part of Dominic's job is the charting of the river with maps and it's done the same way now as Horace Bixby learned and taught it a century and a half ago. Boat crews are responsible for keeping accurate maps, and upriver pilots give the data to their fellow pilots coming downriver. If the river is changing, the pilot is the first to notice—lives, boats and cargoes depend on it. "The Coast Guard runs tough checks on all boats for seaworthiness," Dominic said. "And cleanliness. You've got to have a clean ship and the codes are strictly enforced. Still, there are many, many accidents and spills each year."

Ingram, the barge line Dominic used to work for, has an average of forty-nine spills a year. The cleanup cost ranges from hundreds of thousands to millions of dollars. Ingram's spills are not out of line with other companies, Dominic said, and in fact may be lower on the average. "Accidents and spills are going to happen. The way things are run on the river, it's unavoidable."

One of the worst disasters Dominic could think of happened a few years before he went on the boats. In Pittsburgh fifteen gas barges broke loose and went over the dikes, causing a huge spill that oozed down the Ohio. But that incident was dwarfed by what happened in Baton Rouge at Christmas of 1989.

"The whole Exxon refinery blew up," Dominic recalled, "and I was right in the middle of it. It happened during a hurricane and I was standing on the pier at the Exxon refinery. I was blown twenty feet into the air."

The explosion in Baton Rouge knocked the needle off the Richter scale. All around the city homes were shattered, power lines felled, windows broken, foundations cracked. Damage to the refinery and surrounding areas ran into the billions. Dominic spent time in the hospital and was slow to recuperate from his injuries. He blames Exxon itself for causing the accident and the resultant massive spill into the river.

"Exxon had a volatile situation on its hands and they tried to handle it themselves instead of calling in experts. And then Exxon covered up their fiasco. A lot of the newspeople went along with the coverup. It wasn't the first time. People on the barge lines scoff at the big refinery companies and their boats. Many of them aren't seaworthy. They're dangerous. There are nicknames for them, Shake and Bake and Old Burn Again."

Dominic stopped himself, sighed and scanned the waterfront. An extra-long tow-barge was making headway downriver. He nodded, pointed and said, "Asphalt. I know some of the men on that tow. The asphalt is so hot it'll melt your boots. Some loads are transported at four hundred fifty degrees. I think that one's got fancy asphalt on it. Fancy can run to six hundred degrees. They use it for fuel in the plants and refineries down the river. You can imagine what an asphalt spill would do to the river."

He was constantly studying the river as he talked. Years of watching the Big Muddy had sharpened his instincts and he could see what we and others could not. His regard for the river had grown with each journey; talk of spills and explosions kindled his thoughts, we could tell. He would sit rigidly until he caught himself, and then he would ease back again.

"The river is my home," he said evenly. "You have a wife and kids and a place, but the river is your real home. That's how all people on the boats today look upon the Mississippi."

He hadn't touched his drink and now he picked up the glass and took a big swallow, leaned forward and said in a more relaxed tone, "Then I'll tell you some things I know about the boats and the river . . ."

The barge he had been watching was now alongside Mud Island, passing the amphitheater and the scale model of the river that runs for a quarter of a mile on the island—a microcosm of his world.

"People see the long barges on the river and they think they're not boats, but they are. It's come full circle. The old keelboats two hundred years ago floated cargo the way we do. Hundreds of boats are on the river now. The *Clipper,* the *Charger,* the *Patriot,* the *Leader.* And the steersman runs the show. The first mate takes care of everything, supplies, logs, the wheelhouse, anything to keep the captain happy. But the steersman is in charge, the master of the vessel. He's either got the best job on the boat . . . or the worst."

He leaned back and said, "Oh, there's gambling on the boats today. It used to be big time when I first went on the boats, but they've curtailed it some. The boats would pull off together and the crews would get together and gamble. The company almost encouraged it. They'd keep large petty cash on board that the crew could draw on from their wages. There were some sharpers on the boats, just like the old riverboat gambler days. You're on the boats for thirty days at a time. Thirty on, thirty off . . . and the river can get monotonous."

Dominic stared at the river below for a moment and went on, "Floods, I've been in bad ones. Floods are a way of life for the people along the river. You get to know them and understand that they can't let floods change their way of life. People adjust. Those who can afford it buy insurance, but many don't. They'd rather put their money in marble. Marble floors and treated wood that won't warp. And they buy old furniture, junk stuff, old TVs. They live by a code of *let it ride.*

"Most on the boats are superstitious. You don't ever throw a pair of worn-out boots over the side, you just don't, for it will bring bad luck. You don't take a leak off the front of the boat, no matter how calm a day or night is. And you never bring peanuts on board. Any crew member bringing even a small package of peanuts on board, if discovered, will suffer the wrath of the captain, the pilot and all the crew.

"The first year I was on the boats we were in a big storm down on the Gulf. The winds had pushed up to sixty or seventy miles an hour and when they died down some, a pitch-black night set in with fog as thick as blood. A fog stops a boat dead in the water, but we were in trouble where we were and stuck in a thick logjam that could paralyze us. I climbed out on the front of the boat with a pole to see if I could unclog the jam and debris. I pushed the pole into the jam and all of a sudden the pole snapped in half. I'd hit an alligator, a monster about fifteen feet long. He flipped around in the jam and made a pass at me and, brother, I backed off. The gator had helped unclog the jam, and after that I didn't walk out on too many logjams."

He paused and laughed. "The best job on the boats today is the cook. About ninety percent of the cooks on the riverboats today are women, and they're treated with special respect and favor. If the cook is not on board when the boat is ready to cast off, the crew will just flat walk off the job. Food on the boats is always good, never failing. Or else that cook will be put off at the next port.

"And the ports. Upstream, the last riverboat stop is at Pine Bend, about seventy miles above Minneapolis. Downstream, the last stop is at Pascagoula, a good little port with good seafood, Cajun-style. Pilottown used to be the last stop on the river and it's still there but it isn't a port anymore. The ports up and down the river are fun and then not fun. Sometimes you don't even want to get off when you make port. You work with men so long, twenty-four hours a day, and put up with drunks, fights, sometimes drugs, that you just want to get away to yourself.

"Alton, Illinois, is a good place to get off by yourself. Alton is an old, old river town and it's pretty. It has bars down on the riverfront with stuff from the river for decorations. The town looks like a Norman Rockwell picture . . . churches, old colonial homes, white buildings everywhere. I went into an Alton bar a few trips back. It was run by a salty, good-natured old lady. She's had men on the river for years, sons and husbands and grandsons. Towboaters hang out in her bar and she told me she could always tell them from others—they would be wearing three-hundred-dollar boots and carrying a fifty-cent travel bag."

Dominic's tone brightened here; good memories came flooding back. "The best people to my mind are the Cajuns down in Louisiana. In Baton Rouge, a place called Catfish Alley used to be a lively strip, full of the best Cajun places and food in the world. Baton Rouge has a good many Cajuns and you have to love them. They're funny people who can make you feel good just being around them. They're good people and most trustworthy. If you're a friend, the Cajuns will take you in for life. They'll give you anything they have. They only speak their Cajun French if they don't like you or the way you're acting and know they can't trust you. Then they talk that redneck French just to confuse you."

His tone of voice modulated and he became earnest. "I felt an earthquake once on the New Madrid Fault. We were up the Ohio River near Paducah. The crew didn't feel the quake; I was in the wheelhouse, though, and I saw something. I looked out and saw the water begin to shimmer, like big splattering raindrops hitting the surface of the water. And I saw that the current was moving backward. I had a friendly argument with the mate over it. 'You're crazy,' he said. We got a piece of wood and tossed it over the side, and sure enough the piece of wood got in the current and began to flow upstream."

He just sat smiling and shaking his head. It was getting late and the Pier was emptying out. The river had gone quite dark, until the moon rolled over it, and then the stretch of water along the Chickasaw Bluffs turned as silver as a seam of precious metal. We were about to get up and move toward the door when Dominic, something fresh in his mind, leaned forward again and asked, "Have you heard of a dead pool on the boats?" He began to tell us of the perilous place called the dead pool—the area where barges are coupled together. The dead pool is the most feared area on the boats; if a man happens to fall into a dead pool, it is certain death, for the barges will ram and batter and chop to pieces anything that happens to fall into it.

"We had a bad captain on the boats one time," Dominic said.

"Call him Captain Candle. Usually the esprit de corps is high on the boats and most of the captains are good men, but sometimes a bad one gets into power and makes life miserable for the crew. I had been assigned as pilot for Captain Candle's boat, the *Southstar*. I was only going to be on the *Southstar* for a month, one run, and I could tell that the captain saw me as an intruder, so I went in blind.

"The *Southstar* had been having problems with theft on the boat and right after I came aboard Captain Candle made me a marked man. Maybe he had convinced the officers and crew that I was part of some theft ring. I was immediately shunned by the crew. Some started throwing accusations that I was taking their possessions. They were convinced to a man, and Captain Candle let it go on and even seemed to encourage the others against me. But one man on board, the steersman, saw what was happening to me. 'They're going to lay it all on you, Desiderio, and they've got the wrong man.' So he and I got together and set a trap; we waited a long time to spring it. And we caught the real thief with the goods. He had a secret hiding place in his quarters and in it he had stashed tapes, radios, cartons of cigarettes, money. Captain Candle didn't want to believe us, even with the evidence, and he branded the steersman and me as troublemakers. The company had to send in some investigators, and the truth came out. They took the captain off the *Southstar* and I went on to other boats. The stigma of the *Southstar* stayed with me for some time but the truth has a way of working itself to the top on the river. I heard that the captain had lost another command and was working as a mate on the upper river.

"A year later I heard a chilling end to the story. I was going on another boat and one of the officers came up to me and asked if I had been on the *Southstar*. 'Did you hear what happened to Captain Candle? He's dead, you know. He fell into a dead pool.' "

CHAPTER 14

Delta Blues

"When the Corps of Engineers sought to drain the wetlands, Miss Lily went after them, hounded them, shamed
them away."

—From the biography of Lily Peter

The best way to get out of Memphis if you're going south is down
Beale Street. You can take the interstate if you like, but you'll miss
the real home of the blues and the chance to catch the greatest
blues guitarist who ever was; B. B. King has opened up a new place
on Beale, and the joint was jumping.

Going out Beale, we stopped to look at W. C. Handy's old shotgun shack, which has been preserved by the City of Memphis at
the upper end of the club and theater part of the strip. As we were
about to get back into our land-yacht, a small-time pusher, your
run-of-the-mill street vendor, offered us our choice from his por-
table pharmacopoeia, a cheap black briefcase. His counter stock
included selections from the product lines of most of the ethical
drug companies of the world, in addition to home-grown and imported herbal products. He specialized in cocaine—coke in powder and crack in rock formats. We passed.

The first county in Mississippi as you come out of Memphis is
also the poorest county in the state, arguably the poorest county
in America. Tunica County is named after the unfortunate Tunica
Indians. Marquette, Joliet and La Salle met this tribe on their journeys downriver and entered their name in the long list of the tribes
in the Mississippi Valley. The Tunicas, along with scores of other
tribes, were gone within years, for when another priest-explorer,
Charlevoix, came this way fifty years later they had vanished, vic-

tims of disease and tribal wars. The Tunicas were the first of America's aboriginals on the Mississippi delta to come in contact with Hernando de Soto, the Spaniard given credit for discovering the Mississippi; the tribe was so ferocious that it forced De Soto into crossing the flooded Mississippi into Arkansas.

Today Tunica County can lay claim to the lowest per capita income in the country. Driving through it on Highway 61 the traveler used to see those stone hearts saying PREPARE TO MEET GOD and billboards demanding, GET US OUT OF THE U.N. The hearts are still there but the signs are gone and so are the people who put them up. One significant message used to greet the traveler entering the river's namesake state: WELCOME TO MISSISSIPPI, HOME OF WILLIAM FAULKNER, WINNER OF THE NOBEL PRIZE FOR LITERATURE. When we drove into the state we saw that the sign had been removed. You never know what the state chamber of commerce will get up to next.

Neither Old 61 nor the river runs through Faulkner's homeplace in Oxford, but this is Bill Faulkner country, the perimeter of a mythical region where the Tallahatchie, Yazoo and Big Black rivers angle down through cotton land to the Old Man. Faulkner named that region Yoknapatawpha County and used it as the setting for his chronicles of the New South. In *Life on the Mississippi* Twain viewed this land and assessed it as being "exceptionally productive." It still is; the corporate owners are reaping huge profits.

Tunica County establishes the norm for the ills of the lower river and its delta. The population is at least 70 percent black and *Plessy* v. *Ferguson* is still very much alive. Segregated schools are everywhere, with white "Christian" academies standing in the place of public schools. In the town of Tunica we stopped and talked to a store manager who told us, "There won't be any integration here. If white kids can't pay the tuition to the academy, the other whites will put up the money."

We picked up on another story while we were in Tunica that was about as sad as the store manager's opinion on education. We found one of those Christian schools and stopped just to see what it looked like. There were no classes that day and the only person around was a caretaker washing windows. He looked up at a darkening sky and remarked to us that his work would probably be wasted. He told us this was tornado country and twisters come off the river. A slow-talking, deliberate man in his early seventies, he told us a story that took place during the Great Depression when he was a young man living in Tupelo.

A troubled woman and her sharecropper family lived on a forty-acre farm on the edge of the delta. The woman had reasons for despair; in previous years the crops had been destroyed by floods, and she had never got over losing two of her children, who had been killed by a tornado. The new storm season came and the rains never slackened. The creeks and the deep drainage ditches were swollen to overflowing, and the Tombigbee River was beginning to wash over the levee. Late one evening a black wind began to rush along the river and sweep across the delta. The unmistakable, eerie roar shook the farmland. The family could see the funnel hanging in the sky as they ran out of their shotgun shack to the storm cellar. They hunkered down all night in the cellar and the woman raved until she went out of her mind. When morning came, the family finally dared to creep out of the cellar, but the poor woman refused to move. The tornado had ripped through the house and barn but she was oblivious to that now. Try as they might, the family couldn't get her to come up from the dark of the cellar. Days passed, the floodwaters receded, the fields dried out under the punishing delta sun, but the woman stayed in the hell of her own private asylum. Weeks stretched into months and then into years. Her family brought her food each day, lowering big buckets of it down into the earthen dark. She stayed there for seventeen years. Seventeen years in a foul, dank, unlit cellar. They say the pitiful woman grew so obese that when she mercifully died, they couldn't get her huge body out. We'd heard this story before, in another version. It's becoming part of the oral tradition of the river and the delta.

Downtown Tunica differs very little from the other delta towns we'd been passing through. It's hard to believe things could get any worse. The street was deserted and the storefronts were boarded up or long since closed. The windows had been soaped and graffiti spoke of the dreams of far away: GONE TO MEMPHIS AND WON'T BE BACK . . . GO SAINTS . . . SICKLE CELL, THE GREAT WHITE HOPE.

Yet a last hope exists in Tunica County. The State of Mississippi passed a law that will allow riverboat gambling; each county has to decide its own fate. Voters in Tunica County cleared the way for riverboat gambling in 1990, and by 1991 sites on the river were

Crossroads store in blues country.

designated for permanently moored riverboat casinos. Talk is high
of a possible boom in the region, with employment opportunities
in new motels and hotels and perhaps a Vegas-like strip along the
Mississippi. Evidently riverboat gambling is going forward, and
land speculation in the area is on the upswing, with developers on
the scene working from the models already established upriver in
Iowa.

In the meantime, the delta towns welter along. The river-made,
man-cleared plains are only occasionally broken by fingers of stagnant water fed by periodically flooded bayous and drainage canals
from the fields around which cottonwood, scrub oak, mimosa, cypress and cane grown. Occasionally you see old shotgun shacks
and metal sheds along the plantation access roads. In the fall,
trailer-sized blocks of harvested cotton stud the edges of the fields.
Blue vinyl tarps cover the harvested cotton, contributing a touch
of color to the monotonous stretch of flatland.

South of Tunica, the little town of Clarksdale houses the Blues
Museum, which holds one of the finest collections of blues record-

ings and mementos in the country. The town itself is run-down and pretty wretched, but at various times of the year good crowds gather here to hear blues artists coming in from all around the region. It was at Clarksdale that B. B. King began his rise to prom- ise as the Baron of the Blues. The old delta music, as King will attest, began as field hollers and church spirituals, and it's hard to make the distinction between secular and religious themes in the blues. W. C. Handy brought his band to Clarksdale before he played Beale Street, and the blues honor roll here includes Ma Rainey, Bessie Smith and Ida Cox. "Most Americans today are probably more familiar with blues-influenced music than they are with blues itself," writes David Evans in *The Encyclopedia of Southern Culture*. Evans is a professor at Memphis State University and is a blues advocate. Blues is having a phenomenal rise in popularity across the country, especially in port towns along the river. Despite the commercialism that has attached itself, blues music has taken hold, and according to Evans "can be heard today in forms close to the earliest folk blues . . . it's still in touch with its roots."

While journeying down the river, we attended blues festivals in Memphis; Helena, Arkansas; Clarksdale, Mississippi; Little Rock and Pine Bluff, Arkansas; and Greenville, Mississippi. The crowds were large and enthusiastic. Dozens of groups perform at the fes- tivals and they've gone to school to the masters; they manage to make themselves sound as authentic as pone and poke sallet, and some actually are.

Coming out of Memphis, we flipped the radio dial and stopped when we heard a gravel-road voice drawling, "You're like a dresser, baby, someone's been going through your drawers." When we got to Clarksdale we heard a fine blues group, the David Craig Band. They blended the best of blues and jazz in a class act. John Craig has been on the music scene for some years, having played guitar for Ike and Tina Turner, though his first love is the blues. We caught up with the band again—Cecil, Voodoo, Marc, Dorothy C. and John—at the King Biscuit Festival across the river in Helena.

The Coahoma County Bridge between Lula, Mississippi, and He- lena, Arkansas, affords one of the best views of the lower river. From this vantage point, the river's undulating course is most dis- tinct, panoramic. The best view, however, is from the cockpit of one of those daredevil crop duster's planes. Coahoma County has several "aerial applicator" outfits, and after a couple of futile attempts, we found a pilot who'd take us up over the river for a spin. He was a laconic, good-natured fellow named Wilson and at first he too was suspicious of our motives.

"You want a thrill ride?" he asked.

"We just want a look at the river."

"I don't know as how I can do it. I ain't got you insured."

After we convinced him that we had our own personal insurance, he waited a long time, drank two cups of coffee, and then went out to his wide-winged beauty. He motioned with a jerk of his head and said, "Come on if you're coming."

Wilson was not a daredevil. He was a man in his forties and had had enough close calls with high-line wires and steep banks. Once we were aloft he told us he used to be reckless and liked to play— he'd even flown under the big bridge down at Greenville once— but now it was all business, a way of making a living. "Some of that poison we have to lay down is bad for everybody and I wish't they'd quit using it so much. I'm own have to quit one of these days ... but a man's got to make a living and this is what I can do."

The river looked even bigger from the sky. The fields lay in perfect rows for miles. The landscape was not as dreary as it had seemed but was alive with colors ... the green of the treeline on either side of the river, the white scars of field roads, the brown of the river's channels, its shores yellow blending to dark green, almost emerald. Over there we could see the river bending and trying to change its course; over here it leveled and ran calmly, behaving itself again.

The pilot would never have taken us up if we hadn't convinced him we wanted to look at the river. He had grown up here and the river had always been part of his life. We weren't up very long, just fifteen minutes, but we did get an eagle's view of the Mississippi and a high perspective of the surrounding embayment. We offered to pay Wilson for his time and trouble, but he wouldn't take money. We got the feeling that he'd taken us up because he just wanted to play in the clouds.

The bridge in Coahoma County, Mississippi, took us over to Helena, Arkansas. Mark Twain eulogized this town as a bustling river port with a bright future. Unluckily, Helena's future disappeared with the steamboats. The town was established in 1820 but over the years was flooded out with alarming frequency; the population was thinned by cholera and yellow fever more than once.

In downtown Helena the old train depot right at the seawall and harbor has been made into a delta museum and multimillion-dollar cultural center, the focal point of the ever-growing King Biscuit Blues Festival, which takes place in early October each year. Being a small town, Helena cannot accommodate the more than seventy-five-thousand people who pour in for the music, but it's all a roaring time. Singer-actor Levon Helm sat in with a band at this year's King Biscuit. The festival is beginning to rival the bigger one held each year down in Greenville, and many of these thousands take in both. The thick crowd scenes are akin to those at Mardi Gras.

One other noteworthy facet of Helena is the town's library. Built in 1891 and filled with books donated and collected since 1874, the musty, lovable old building takes pride in its first edition of *Life on the Mississippi,* autographed by Twain himself. The elderly librarian and his assistant, a young black man named Lawrence, seemed overjoyed with our interest in the book. Lawrence told us he was working after school and summers saving up so he could go to the university. He wanted to read all of Mark Twain, he said.

Two other points of interest led us a few miles into Arkansas. We stopped in the shady little town of Marvell to pay our respects to a great lady named Lily Peter. Though she didn't really want anybody to know about it, Miss Lily was celebrating her one hundredth birthday; her friend and biographer, Annie Laurie Jaggers, had told us the date and how old Miss Lily was. Miss Lily, amazingly alert for her years, wanted to talk of other things—art and poetry, philosophy and farming.

"I loved the classical forms of poetry," she said. "My education was in the classics and I tried the lyric and the epic. To me they will be the forms to last through the ages."

Lily Peter has published five books of poetry, essays and history. Her father came down the Ohio River in the 1870s and started farming along the bottoms of the Mississippi and White rivers. Lily went to schools up north, Juilliard, Chicago, Johns Hopkins, Columbia. She came home to Arkansas and after her father died, she took over the management of the Peter farmlands. She never married; she told us once that she was married to the land and the river. She had an uncanny understanding of the land she farmed and became, by old-fashioned farming standards, a wealthy person. But she loved poetry, music, the arts. She started the community college in Phillips County. She once brought the Philadelphia Orchestra to Little Rock, paying for the concert out of her own pocket; she brought other orchestras and name performers to Arkansas and footed the bill.

Miss Lily's finest accomplishment, though, was with the land. Many years ago she saw the folly in the overuse and abuse of pesticides and herbicides—she quit using them on her land, setting a standard that owners of vast tracks of land around her could follow profitably. Miss Lily actually raised more crops and made more money by not using the poisons. "When the Corps of Engineers sought to drain the wetlands in eastern Arkansas," her biographer pointed out, "Miss Lily went after them, hounded them, shamed them away."

Miss Lily had a reputation for being an eccentric; actually she was a soft-spoken, smiling barracuda when she knew she was right and something had to be changed. Paul Greenberg, two-time Pulitzer prize-winning columnist for the *Pine Bluff Commercial*, wrote once that Miss Lily was "a one-woman river."

When we visited Lily Peter she was apologetic about feeling poorly; she'd hurt her hip, which infuriated her because she "couldn't get up and walk to the hairdresser's."

Miss Lily died at age 100 in the summer of 1991. Her biographer and friend said that Miss Lily had always had a fortress of energy inside her and when she grew weak it simply put her out, made her mad. "When Lily read Rachel Carson's *Silent Spring*, it changed her life. She took it seriously, straight to her heart, and she was dead serious about doing something about it. The Corps of Engineers was no match for her—she just brushed them aside."

CHAPTER 15

A Place Called Elaine

"Now we are a nation and a tongue. Why should we be cut off?"

—*From the journal of a black delta preacher*

Twenty-five miles south of Helena, the small town of Elaine languishes apace. Out north of town the church at Hoop Spur is long gone. The population of Elaine has been steadily declining and the old town stores look the same as they did back in 1919 when the awful violence broke out.

We stopped on the one main street and strolled around. Folks were friendly; they all spoke or nodded. A grocer, a white man, had just received delivery of a pickup truck of watermelons and had hired two little black kids to help carry the melons into his store. We bought one of the melons and the grocer said, "These are the best melons in Phillips County and if that'un ain't good, I'll give you your money back."

None of the stores in town were doing any business. The branch bank was closing before noon; it had suffered a holdup in 1990 and one of the employees had been brutally murdered, her throat cut with a butcher knife; the robbers were caught shortly after. Elaine can't seem to escape its legacy, but nobody here or in the whole county will talk about what happened back in 1919.

A husky new red brick Baptist Church sits down at the end of the main street, so there's money around here somewhere. Elaine has not thought to erect any memorial to the events of 1919. Neither has the town elected to put up a statue or museum to honor its most famous citizen. Richard Wright, who likely should have won the Nobel Prize, lived most of his childhood in Elaine. Wright's father was a mill worker in Helena before he abandoned his wife and children, and Wright's mother brought her kids here to live. From Wright's stories and personal accounts, you can draw a picture of the poor woman—she was intelligent, tortured and persevering; she was a teacher and held her classes in those old clapboard churches out on the delta. The fact that someone, anyone, wanted to teach black kids of the delta to read and write is a remarkable story in itself. Wright had just turned eleven that fall in 1919 when the violence broke out. The scenes of mob bloodletting go a long way toward explaining the anger in his work.

We stopped at a house a mile out of town. Some little black kids were playing in the yard and a couple of elderly black men were sitting on the porch. They were friendly and had no habitual look of distrust in their eyes. We were asking directions and they were obliging, so we thought to ask, "Do y'all know a family named Wright around?"

"Wright? Don't think so."

"Might have been some Wrights around a long time ago," the other man said. "Lot of Lefts, though. Whole lot of them. They done left."

Back in 1919 that's what they did; they left by the thousands. They left because of the violence that exploded on the first day of the cotton harvest, October 1, 1919.

There are mysteries and congruities on the Mississippi, and sometimes the two combine. The little towns of Prairie du Chien in Wisconsin, Fort Pillow in Tennessee and Elaine in Arkansas, all three related though separated by hundreds of miles—all three the scenes of mass murder.

Though the Civil War had been over for more than half a century, the blacks of Elaine were living in poorer conditions than their slave forebears. A railroad line ran though the town, but Elaine had always been isolated because it was hemmed in. To the west and south lay a dense swamp known as the White River Bottoms, while only a mile or so to the east flowed the broad Mississippi. Few changes at all had come to that far-flung part of the world in the past century. One change, however, proved to be pivotal.

A few young black men from the county had gone off to fight

in World War I. They returned with a rudimentary knowledge of the outside world; of course they shared this knowledge with their families and friends in the all-black community. The very fact that "niggers" were benefiting from knowledge of any kind was a direct threat to the whites of the county, who were outnumbered three to one by the blacks.

The white people of the delta had always lived with the self-imposed dilemma that stemmed from their domination of the blacks. On that first day of harvest in 1919, the twelve thousand whites of the county were suffering from the paranoid belief that the thirty-three thousand blacks would somehow throw off white supremacy. Rumors had flown among the whites that some young black men had been marching with guns in military formation and talking big talk about higher wages for their work on plantations. The *Arkansas Gazette* reported that "blacks had formed a union to strike against the landowners." The blacks wanted a guarantee of fifty cents a day, to be paid in cash money, not in chit at the company store. Dangerous talk. The thought of any guarantee whatsoever, even the derisive amount the young blacks were asking, amounted to rebellion. Sooner or later these young toughs would have to be taught a lesson. Folks in Phillips County had heard of communism and knew that bloody revolutions were going on across the waters. Could that scourge be coming to this well-ordered nook of America?

No communist-inspired agitators ever bothered with Arkansas. Even if they had come to Phillips County that fall they would have found no one to listen to them. Having lived through generations of white domination, the blacks had learned to listen to only one voice, that of their preacher. And the preacher for the blacks in and around Elaine was a young black man named Robert L. Hill, a sharecropper himself and the grandson of a slave. Hill had not served in World War I, had never been to Memphis or even twenty miles away from his home. But he did not need to go to France to know that the life he and his fellow blacks were living was unjust.

Astounding as it might be to the whites of Elaine, a man knows instinctively when he is not being treated as a human being. Robert Hill was no city-educated agitator, but he was a leader born for this time and place. A lay preacher, Hill spoke to his people in a language they could believe. He combined an orator's rhetoric with

biblical incantation, a language that all oppressed blacks understood. Hill memorized the Bible and held a hunger for the knowledge in books. He even wrote his own book, and though it was
never published, he spoke in a small, strong voice for millions of
others. In his personal journal he wrote:

"The time is at hand that all men, all nations and all tongues
must receive a just reward . . . I see all nations and tongues coming
up before God. Now we are a nation and a tongue. Why should
we be cut off?"

Hardly the favored phrases of communism. Just the words of a
preacher who knows his flock is not being treated with either dig-
nity or common decency. Hill's black followers elected him president of the "Household Union of America" there in Phillips
County. The union had a membership of fewer than fifty men; it
was a unique concept for the times but doomed from its inception,
as events would prove all too soon. Still, Hill's attempt to organize
the plantation workers in 1919 was perhaps the first effort in
America to raise a union among black peons in the South. It would
be put down by outraged local white mobs, the militia, and forces
of the U.S. Army.

Giving in to their exaggerated fears, the white community in
Helena decided to root out the evil. On the evening of September
30, 1919, a carload of white men set out from Helena to discover
what Hill was up to in his church. At dusk the car pulled up outside
the clapboard church at Hoop Spur, a cluster of shotgun shacks a
few miles north of Elaine. Though it was only Monday and not a
prayer meeting night, coal-oil lanterns were burning inside the
church. In the car the white men's suspicions seemed well founded.

The driver of the car fanned his spotlight across the church windows. One of the men got out and started chucking rocks, breaking
a window. The other men in the car got out with shotguns in hand
to join the taunting. They shouted threats at those in the church,
but no response came. Deciding to flush them out, one of the men
leveled his shotgun and blew a hole through the front door. That
would teach the "uppity niggers" a lesson.

That night it was the whites who received a lesson. The blacks
shot back. Rifle fire rang from inside the church. A white man
screamed, clutched at his chest and fell to the ground. More gunfire came from the church and another white man was hit; he

dropped his shotgun and hobbled toward the car. In total amaze-
ment that the blacks would dare to fight back, the white men
scrambled into their car and beat it home to Helena to spread the
word. The black uprising was at hand. What had started with a
bunch of good old boys going to scare hell out of some young
blacks had ended in death. The carnage was just beginning. In his
book *Union, Reaction, and Riot,* B. Boren McCool describes the scene.

The white people of Helena were stunned at the report from the
scouting party. Helena's officials sent off an urgent message to
Governor William Brough in the state capital at Little Rock; the
message was a wildly exaggerated version of what had happened
down at the Hoop Spur church. Helena reported that a full-scale
uprising was under way and thousands of blacks were on the
march. No white would be left alive.

Through that first night in Helena white mobs formed to put
the black ghetto of the town under siege. Any black person was a
suspect. Six thousand Helena blacks were rousted from their homes
that first night and put under heavy guard in cattle pens and empty
railroad freight cars. That night, too, lynch mobs marched on the
homes of Helena's leading black citizens. Many were beaten and
murdered, their homes looted and burned. By dawn the black section of Helena was a charred inferno. For all to witness, the burned
body of a black man hung from a tree in the city park.

During the same night, a similar scene of bloodletting was taking
place down in Elaine twenty miles away.

Governor Brough responded quickly to the situation by calling
out five hundred federal troops stationed at Camp Pike in the
capital. It was now October 1 and news of burnings, lynchings and
pitched battles spread via the *Arkansas Gazette* and *Memphis Commercial Appeal* to the rest of the nation. But they got the story wrong.
It wasn't blacks causing all the killing and burning, it was the white
mobs. Playing to their white readership, the newspapers slanted
their stories to put blame squarely on the blacks, and especially on
a "communist-inspired" Negro preacher named Robert L. Hill.
Governor Brough's troops were needed to bring the whites back
into line, as proved by the white plantation owners themselves.
When the governor arrived on the scene on October 2, he was met
by a large contingent of Phillips County planters who literally

begged him to restrain the white vigilantes. The planters weren't worrying over the blacks' welfare—they were simply afraid that the vast cottonfields wouldn't be harvested before the rainy season.

The governor was plenty worried, as pictures of him at the time revealed. He had to placate the planters and at the same time keep his popularity with the class of white people who were at that same moment spreading out across the countryside on a "nigger-kill." In several instances the troops that the governor had sent simply stood by while blacks were gunned down.

White gangs from neighboring counties and states chartered special trains, destination Elaine. Others formed caravans of trucks and cars. A new special hunting season had just been opened, with no limit on the number of kills allowed. The regional newspapers carried pictures of truckloads of whites coming to the killing grounds, all armed with shotguns and axes and hunting rifles. Meanwhile the plantation owners were imploring the governor, "Don't let them keep killing my field hands! Who's going to pick all that cotton?" But the killing went on, two days, three days and more.

Newspapers in Little Rock and Memphis printed a photograph of Governor Brough assessing the scene at Elaine. Just moments before the picture was taken, an old black woman had stumbled into the street and had fallen a few paces from the governor. An army officer went over to the woman, knelt, and looked at her bleeding wound. She had been hit with a full blast from a shotgun. The officer came back to the governor and said, "She's just about dead . . . she can't be helped," according to McCool.

Clearly the slaughter had gotten out of hand, for the troops on hand could do nothing but stand around and show themselves. No orders for any action had come for more than a day; nobody seemed to know what to do, and the governor was trapped on the horns of his own political dilemma. At last, as the enraged planters descended upon him again, the governor declared martial law and ordered the confiscation of firearms.

The troops moved into the field; the tide of white hunters receded and only random killings went on down in the river bottoms, where hunters were still tracking their prey. In Elaine and back in Helena the blacks were released from their pens and were hauled directly to the cottonfields. There would be no unions, no guaranteed wages this year—or any other year in the foreseeable future. A warrant for Robert Hill's arrest was issued and a reward was put on his head, but he had slipped out of the countryside through a resurrected underground railroad.

The massacre took place in the first week of October, and less than a month later a special session of the Phillips County Circuit Court was convened, setting the all-time record for swift justice in Arkansas. A total of 122 black people were arraigned and indicted on charges ranging from insurrection to murder. Though perhaps as many as four or five thousand blacks had been killed, not one single white man was accused or brought to trial.

With the *Arkansas Gazette* applauding "due process" with daily editorials, the trials proceeded with the matter-of-fact dispatch of an inquisition. Within the first two days, six young black men were allowed to confess and were convicted and sentenced to death. On the next day five more men were convicted and sentenced to death. Robert Hill was found guilty in absentia. The longest jury deliberation had been four minutes. Each of the convicted men had signed a confession.

"I was frequently whipped and put in an electric chair and shocked," said one of the convicted men in a later appeal. "Once they took me upstairs and put a rope around my neck, had me blindfolded, pulled on the rope, and one of them said, 'Don't knock the trick out yet, we can make him tell.' As they were taking me to the courtroom, they told me if I changed my testimony or did not testify as I had said, when they took me back, they would skin me alive. I testified as they had told me."

According to McCool's study, in addition to 12 men sentenced to death, a total of 110 others were put on trial for lesser crimes ranging from second-degree murder to assault with intent to kill. These received from five to thirty-seven years in prison. Imprisonment for these 110 almost nameless men meant servitude at penal farms or on chain gangs. The remainder of their lives would be hell on earth. No lawyer ever filed an appeal on their behalf. Only the twelve convicted of first-degree murder were to find friends to open up the appeal procedure.

Appeals did come. They began soon after the trials and lasted through 1923. During this waiting time the twelve condemned men were kept in Helena, locked inside a twelve-by-twelve-foot cinder-block dungeon with one door and no window. They were destined to remain in these quarters for four years with food unfit for hogs, no fresh air, no baths, no outside communication. Not one scrap of human decency was proffered, yet they survived with a grace that defies belief.

Some small measure of redemption to the stench of Southern justice came about in June 1923. The Arkansas attorney general, ambitious for the governor's mansion, was determined to execute as many of the "Elaine Twelve" as possible. To bypass the slow appeals procedure, the attorney general ordered six of the defendants to be retried (the verdict of guilty was assured). But the design was foiled by the attorney general's own incompetence; the state failed to bring the six to trial during either of two consecutive terms of court, a monumental foulup. Under the state's own law, and at the insistence of NAACP lawyers, the prisoners must be released, and they were, to the chagrin of the attorney general and the state administration.

The attorney general was a fool in the eyes of everyone in his state; now he became fanatical in his pursuit of the remaining six blacks. He promised the whole state that these foul murderers would not escape a condign justice. In the meantime, the manhunt for Robert Hill continued unabated even after four years. Hill had disappeared during the first night of the massacre, and after four years many thought this leader of the rebellion had met the same fate as hundreds of other black victims, that he had been shot down and thrown into the quicksand tupelos of the river bottoms.

Rumors of Hill's whereabouts kept cropping up, and a young agent of the Treasury Department in Washington decided he'd take a hand. This T-man was none other than J. Edgar Hoover, a fanatical hater of Jews and blacks and communists. Hoover was convinced—or saw the way to make a big name for himself in propounding such a view—that labor and race riots were all inspired by card-carrying, smart-assed blacks and Jewish intellectuals. Hoover personally took up the chase in the 1920s as one of the first of his many causes célèbres. Rumors persisted of Hill's presence in black meeting halls in the Midwest and the North. Hoover never found him, not even with the full resources of his own private army, the new Federal Bureau of Investigation.

Hill never got to preach from another pulpit or write his book or see his dream of "one nation and one tongue" fulfilled. He was forced to live a life on the dodge. To this day he remains an unsung hero, though he provided a blueprint for others to build on. If the civil rights movement can be traced to its inception, its wellsprings might be found on the Mississippi delta at a tiny clapboard church in a place called Hoop Spur.

The last six of the Elaine twelve were transferred from their cinder-block hell to the state prison in Little Rock in January 1924. They had been told that they were going there to die in the state's new electric chair. Their guards took them to the walls of the prison and left. No one from inside came out to get the prisoners. Darkness fell and they realized they were prisoners no longer. They walked away.

CHAPTER 16

Crevasses

"The Mississippi River is a tame and responsible member of American society."

—*The Mississippi River Commission*

We returned to the bridge at Helena and drove back into Coahoma County, Mississippi. You have to get used to bridges like this from here on down to the Gulf; mostly they are beautiful old rickety affairs built during World War II or earlier and patched up over the years. Many are built on a steep arc, a really steep arc, and can be scary.

The tiny, already embalmed hamlet of Lula sits at the base of the bridge. Before the turn of the century Lula was a fairly substantial port supporting several doctors, undertakers and saloons. The men of Lula packed shootin' irons and often called one another out in the street. Memphis's Boss Crump began his career here as a bookkeeper in the 1880s. The main street today consists of rotting, unpainted storefronts. One edifice sparkles, though, a brick-and-glass branch bank built here to relieve the local blacks of their Social Security and welfare checks.

We stopped and poked our heads into the bank and saw two teller windows staffed by two ladies, one white and one black. The ladies were late-middle-aged and very friendly, glad to have a diversion in their day. Somehow the subject of the now-gone savings stamps came up; when a couple of other people came in, we overheard some talk:

"I carried a dime to school every Friday to buy my stamp. I

licked and pasted it into my own savings book. Banks gave out those books. The last one I ever saw was back in the fifties."

As we left, they were talking about how much money they had saved back then. One of those books would hold four dollars in stamps, and they were saying it took them a year to fill it.

As these things go, Lula could have been the point of De Soto's crossing the Mississippi. One small intellectual curiosity still persists. It would be interesting to know if any of the members of the expedition went searching in the misty hours of dawn for water lilies, which grew in abundance along the riverbanks. Reading the diary of the Gentleman of Elvas, we keep hoping that he'll tell us. But he doesn't. The Spanish, like the rest of the civilized world in the sixteenth century, believed that pearls were created from the dew collected in such flowers. The illusion was no more realistic than De Soto's quest for gold.

We were in De Soto country now; just up the way back toward Memphis, the little town of Hernando was named for the explorer. Unlikely as it seems, De Soto's brief touch on this countryside influenced its way of life for centuries. For some three million blacks who lived in the Mississippi River Valley at the close of the Civil War, the Emancipation Proclamation had changed their lives—for the worse. They had been pushed into a morass of peonage worse than slavery. The encomienda that came with the Spanish to the New World was in a very real sense practiced by the plantation society of the Old South.

The economic viability of the Mississippi Valley still depended upon cotton. With the coming of the railroads, the plantation system actually expanded and increased the labor-intensive cotton industry from what it was before. Huge pools of now unemployed blacks were forced to work for subhuman rations. No wages were paid, just enough company store staples to keep body, not soul, together. While they were still slaves, their owners had been obliged to protect their investment by adequately feeding and clothing and housing them. But when the slaves were freed, there was no such obligation.

Surveying the countryside from our land-yacht as we drove along Highway 61, we realized that from here north the old highway had been a black Trail of Tears. The carnage of Elaine had terrified the blacks but had not cowed them as was intended. Blacks in the tens of thousands after 1919 packed their few possessions and fled the delta to the cities of the North. Every forty acres we passed an empty, crumbling shack and now and then one where people were still living in the middle of wrecked cars, old washing machines and broken-down John Deere tractors that would never see the fields again. Rich corporate cottonfields ran right up to the sides of these houses, but there were no paychecks for the inmates here. These dwellings only served to punctuate the nearly deserted little towns we were passing through.

We headed inland toward Yoknapatawpha County proper and the home of Faulkner. They've built a nice divided highway from Batesville over to Oxford, mostly to relieve the weekend traffic coming to Ole Miss football games. Oxford hasn't changed much over the years; it's still the slow-paced, sleepy little Southern town that William Faulkner immortalized in his stories and novels. The residential streets are deeply shaded and meandering, and the houses are old two-storied baroque things, most with yards instead of lawns. You'd almost expect to see Miss Emily Grierson come out of one of those houses on her way uptown to the drugstore to buy some rat poison.

Oxford's town square is as picturesque as a movie set; the handsome old courthouse shudders and settles and seems to glare almost contemptuously at the old codgers loafing on the square. Over on the corner sits an excellent bookstore with a little tearoom upstairs. Oxford is a book town (Sauk Centre, Minnesota, was not); several authors live in Oxford and the Faulkner influence has rubbed off some. Surprisingly, no overt Faulkner Industry exists here—there are no Faulkner campgrounds, souvenir shops, dinner theaters.

On any given day you're likely to run into Faulkner's nephew, Jimmy, on the city square. Jimmy bears an amazing likeness to his uncle; he took care of "Uncle Will" during some trying times, especially the last days before Faulkner's death in 1962. Jimmy is a charming man, engaging and easy to talk to. He takes part occasionally in the seminars and programs they hold on Faulkner out at the university, though he says he'd just as soon be home working in his vegetable garden. Jimmy thinks that sometimes the Faulkner scholars are just beating the subject to death. "Uncle Will was the

Rowan Oak, home of William Faulkner, Oxford, Mississippi.

most even-tempered man in the world," Jimmy says, adding, "mad as hell all the time."

Faulkner's home in Oxford has been turned into a museum and national historical site. It sits on four acres back in a grove not far from the Ole Miss campus. The original house was built back in the 1840s; Faulkner bought it in 1930 for $6,000 and lived and wrote his books here until his death. It's a creaky, musty old two-story house that Faulkner himself said was haunted. Most of Oxford was burned to the ground by Union troops back in 1864, but for some reason this old frame was spared.

Keith Fudge, a graduate student in English at Ole Miss, gave us a special tour. A personable young man, Keith was working on his Ph.D. and studying Southern writers. He seemed to know as much about Faulkner as the biographers and was ardently interested in his job as assistant curator and tour guide. "I can't believe they pay me to do this," he said.

We saw first the room where Faulkner used the walls to outline his novel *A Fable*, much as a Hollywood screenwriter would use a storyboard. We sat down at Faulkner's old Underwood typewriter, left the way it was on the day he died. On the wall in the adjoining room were large portraits of his father and grandfather, and down the hall we found a picture of Robert E. Lee and Nathan Bedford Forrest, who was a hero to Faulkner. There's also a framed copy of Faulkner's famous Nobel Prize acceptance speech.

Faulkner's writing table was an old wobbly plantation desk that he had leveled by standing one of the legs in a shot glass. We looked at the books in his room. His favorite book, Keith said, was A. E. Housman's *A Shropshire Lad,* and a copy was prominent on the shelf. Among the other books were some paperback murder mysteries, *The Negro in History, Elmer Gantry, The African Queen.* Over on the table stood a Jack Daniel's bottle as Faulkner had left it, with one shot left. We also found a well-thumbed Sears, Roebuck catalog and a bottle of Maalox. Back in the kitchen we saw the pans and skillets hanging over the fireplace where Faulkner's black housekeeper and cook, Callie, had placed them. Callie is now a solid fixture in Faulkner lore; he used her as the model for his character Dilsey in *The Sound and the Fury* and she remains one of the enduring characters of American literature.

Outside, we strolled across the pretty grounds amid pungent old cedars that have been here since before the Civil War. We walked in Faulkner's flower garden and along the low brick fence that he put up himself. Out back stood the stables where Faulkner kept his horses. We asked if this was the place where he was thrown from the horse on the day before he died.

"That story is wrong," Keith said. "Faulkner didn't go riding that day. It's just a story that got started and is now part of the Faulkner legend. He was bedridden, drunk and out of his mind."

His funeral was private and the only ones attending besides the family were Faulkner's publisher, Bennett Cerf, and the novelist William Styron, who covered the funeral as a journalist. Faulkner is buried in a cemetery on the other side of town; a marker on the street designates his resting place. Keith took us there later and while we were looking around, he got down and cleaned off the grave and pulled up some weeds. "They'll just let it go if you don't watch them," he said.

"I'll tell you something most people don't know about Faulkner's drinking," he went on. "His reputation was that he was your basic serious juicer. And he was. But he also had a reason. He had a broken back that he lived with for thirty years, caused by falling off a horse. He lived in constant pain and the booze killed the pain for a long time. In his last years, the booze wasn't working."

As we had thought earlier, the Faulkner Industry in Oxford is as mellow and gentle as the town itself. Only three or four thousand people come to visit the Faulkner home each year. That's not at all disappointing to those who run the museum, for the visitors are not your basic tourists; they come out of homage. Among those who had paid their respects in recent months were novelist John Updike, poet James Dickey, Justice Sandra Day O'Connor, playwright Beth Henley, actors Ed Asner and Tommy Lee Jones, film director Calvin Skaggs, and pop icon Jimmy Buffett.

A melancholy hue holds the rolling landscape. As we drove out of Oxford and back toward the river, we could almost feel the overbearing heft of the land, this mythical Yoknapatawpha. The brilliance of a single anguished mind captured this lusterless environ and transfigured it into literature.

The mood of the land lingered for miles. It was so weighty that after a while we wanted to find some way to break it. We thought of our own favorite Faulkner anecdote, which we learned from a veteran delta newspaperman who'd spent time with Faulkner and knew his ways. The story was told by a Lafayette County bootlegger whom Faulkner used to patronize. This particular bootlegger lived down the road from Faulkner's house a couple of miles and Faulkner would walk there, drinking up his last bottle. It was Faulkner's peculiar habit that when he was getting good and drunk he'd start taking off his clothes. By the time he reached the bootlegger's house he had drunk himself into nakedness. All he had on was the top to his pajamas. He knocked on the door and asked the bootlegger for a bottle, and when the startled man came back to hand him the liquor, Faulkner said, "Can't you put this in a sack? I can't be seen walking down the street carrying a bottle."

As we drove back to the river, we thought of other writers who had been drawn to the Mississippi. Dickens tried to recoup his losses from his failed Cairo investment with *Martin Chuzzlewit* and ended up with two flops. Washington Irving was on the Mississippi in the 1830s touring the plains; Herman Melville traveled down the river gathering material for *The Confidence-Man;* George Wash-

ington Cable was a native of New Orleans and based most of his
stories on people living on the river; Richard Wright was born on
a delta plantation and like so many other blacks fled north; Eudora
Welty and Tennessee Williams set their finest works in these surroundings. But of all these, Faulkner wrote the best modern novel
on the river, *Old Man,* an authentic account of the great flood of
1927.

Faulkner was at the river in 1927. He watched as the chain gangs
marched in from Parchman Prison to sandbag the broken levees
and help rescue people and animals being swept helplessly down
the river. Faulkner knew the Mississippi was guileful in its treach-
ery and he likened the river to "a mule that will work for you
patiently for ten years for the privilege of kicking you one time."
The mulish Mississippi was getting ready to deliver the most god-
awful kick in its history. Nothing like it has been seen before, or
since.

The time was mid-April 1927. The past year's summer had been
hot and dry and was followed by heavy rains through the fall. Winter snows up North were being unseasonably melted by the torren-
tial spring rains still falling after nearly eight weeks of downpour
throughout the South and the Midwest. The Mississippi River was
badly swollen, as were its tributaries.

Since early April the Corps of Engineers had been trying to calm
the public with its foursquare reliance on the strength of the levee
system to control the river. Thousands of miles of earthen levees
lined the Mississippi and its massive delta; in many towns and
cities the levees were barely holding back the engorged river, which
was cresting at the top of the giant walls all down the river valley.
Levees along the Red, Arkansas, Ohio and Missouri rivers were
strained to the breaking point.

The drainage basin of the Mississippi River covers 41 percent of
the landmass of America. The volume of water moving through
this gargantuan system at any one time is utterly staggering, and
never had all the major and minor tributaries reached such a peak
simultaneously. At times it seems all the water in the country is
funneled into the Lower Mississippi Valley, into one gigantic river
touching seven states. Before 1927 the Mississippi had known
eleven major floods in sixty-five years. Now the pernicious conditions of heavy winter snows, unseasonable melting and extraordi-

nary spring rains spelled disaster on a scale unknown in recorded history.

As the rains continued and the levees rose hour by hour, the Corps of Engineers began to hedge on its pronouncements of safety. Work to reinforce the levees was stepped up to a fever pitch from Cairo to New Orleans. The National Guard was called out and the jails and prisons were emptied and the inmates sent to join the convict-train laborers in holding back the implacable Mississippi. Schoolchildren, farmers, storekeepers, lawyers and judges—everyone who could wield a shovel or carry a sandbag—were put to work. But they might as well have taken off to high ground.

The first signals that the Mississippi was out of control were the simultaneous breaks in the levees at Mound Landing, Mississippi, and Pendleton, Arkansas. Both towns were washed away, never to be rebuilt. These breaks in the levee were called "crevasses" by the people of the river; folks down the lower basin had experienced crevasses as recently as 1922, but never had they felt such force and devastation as was to come.

The river battered the levees with a force of more than two million feet of water per second. Within the next three days as many as 42 crevasses were opened. About 17 million acres were flooded in 170 counties of 7 states, and 162,000 homes were destroyed. Approximately 42,500 buildings were torn apart. A million people were made homeless. At various points from Arkansas to Louisiana the river was more than 100 miles wide. Crop losses were so catastrophic that the government didn't even try to estimate the dollar value of destruction. Anything of value in the Lower Mississippi Valley was threatened, including personal property, homes, farm equipment and, cruelest of all, the farm animals that perished in the millions.

In 1927 no organization existed, nor was any mandate in force nationally, to secure the safety of the Mississippi. Federal funding for levees was virtually nonexistent. The individual states and the affected counties were primarily responsible for their own stretches of the river. Congress had created the Mississippi River Commission in 1879 as pretty much a civilian arm of the Corps of Engineers; the Commission was charged with the maintenance of "uninterrupted navigation of the river." By 1920 the Commission had announced that as a result of its exhaustive studies of the river's hydrology, "The Mississippi River is a tame and responsible member of American society." The Commission was particularly proud of its working scale model of the river. The Corps used the model often to test schemes and feasibility studies. Congress in 1920 loudly hailed the Commission's work as "a truly significant savings to taxpayers."

Such mutual back-patting was excusable pride, in the absence of real disaster. The sweeping devastation of the 1927 flood began finally to teach Congress and the MRC that the Mississippi was a national river with a continental impact, not just a body of running water that could be controlled with a theoretical scale model like the plumbing of a building. Rain and snow in Montana and Colorado had a serious effect on the Mississippi, as did the same weather in Minnesota, Illinois, Ohio and Pennsylvania. When the weather turned atrocious in all the states at the same time, the MRC and the Corps of Engineers had on their hands the worst flood in history.

As the news of the disaster spread, Americans across the land dug into their pockets and purses and donated millions to help out their neighbors in the South. A few million dollars was a drop in the new hundred-mile-wide ocean. The government in Washington remained oblivious. Calvin Coolidge journeyed by train to the site of the flood, but he came almost as a casual observer; he remained unmoved by the widespread suffering. Doubtless his lack of concern for the South merely reinforced his natural parsimony. Coolidge went on record as saying that natural disasters, even large-scale ones, were the problems of the separate states. The business of America might have been business, but it certainly was not humanitarianism. Had the havoc occurred in the North or Midwest, the story might have been different. The legacy of the Civil War was still alive, at least in official Washington.

Herbert Hoover, then secretary of commerce, was put in de facto charge of such relief efforts as there were. Hoover's main concern, however, was to document his personal effectiveness as a leader, not to materially assist the flood victims. He maintained in each of his numerous public reports that the loss of life during the Mississippi River disaster was six persons. Not six hundred or sixty, but six lives only. The Red Cross, known to keep ultraconservative figures, acknowledged that the number of lives lost was in the high hundreds. Life was so disrupted in the flooded regions that there was no way of knowing how many thousands actually perished— but Coolidge, Hoover and company had already shown that these people didn't matter.

Hoover was a man moving rapidly up the political ladder. He was particularly anxious that everything said or written about his handling of the crisis should be positive and exculpatory. He was unbending toward those who sympathized with the victims in the flood states; his attitude was perhaps best revealed in dealings with Robert R. Moton, president of the Tuskegee Institute and chairman of the Colored Advisory Commission. Moton's commission had been appointed to examine the plight of poor blacks living in desperate peonage on the Mississippi delta. Moton was distraught over the impact of the flood on these blacks and had pleaded with the federal government to make wholesale changes in the soul destroying system of peonage. When Hoover showed up in the flood areas, Moton went to him with what Pete Daniel, author of *Deep'n As It Come,* termed an exciting new plan "to rectify the past miseries of peonage." Since the flood had pretty much wiped out peonage throughout the lower Mississippi basin, now was the time for the government to take immediate steps and come up with some innovative policies "to insure that the brutal system could not be reinstituted."

Daniel wrote in his book that Hoover listened to Moton's plan with feigned interest but promised him substantial federal funding if Moton's commission report would "highlight all of Hoover's good works." Moton was trapped. He had to go along with Hoover's chicanery and pray for the best. Moton wrote his report, which showed Hoover to be a prince among men. No federal relief money was ever given to assuage the pain of peonage on the Mississippi delta.

Most of history lingers on dry statistics, the events and notable people encapsulated within a particular timespan. Life on the Mississippi delta for the great majority of its natives has been an unbroken tale of hardship. During the horrible flood of 1927 man went out of his way to make things still worse. In several of his personal essays, Richard Wright tells of thousands of displaced blacks being rounded up and corralled by authorities to keep them from drifting away to the cities. When the waters receded, the plantation owners came to claim their "niggers" and put them back to work rebuilding after the devastation. In his "The Man Who Saw the Flood," Wright explained the scope of the black tragedy. Wright claimed that of the total of "608,000 homes lost in the flood, 555,000 housed black families."

Some surprising acts of heroism occurred during the flood. Up the White River in Arkansas moonshiners had been using powerboats to evade revenuers. When the flood hit, some of these outlaws turned their boats to fighting the flood currents and saving people and animals. The oral history of the '27 flood is full of similar episodes. Civilians and convicts, blacks and whites, rich and poor joined in acts of courage and sacrifice.

The most spirited and genuine record of those grim days is embodied in the oral tradition and in the songs that were already being sung up and down the river. While the Mississippi was still raging over its banks, Bessie Smith was singing "Backwater Blues" and Blind Lemon Jefferson was moaning out "Rising High Water Blues." Folk singer Vernon Dalhart recorded one of the first country-western songs, "The Mississippi Flood."

There would be plenty of stories to tell, hundreds and thousands of them, before the floodwaters receded, for in the end, songs and tales were about all that the people of the river would have left.

CHAPTER 17

Loyalties along the River

"The Mississippi will always be here, long after man. Nature will catalog it away. It will be only a thin dark line for the relic diggers."

—*Doyne Knight, engineer*

The only way to see the confluence of the Arkansas and Mississippi rivers is from an airplane or the deck of a cruiser out of Memphis or New Orleans. You can't drive to it, though we tried. It's all a marsh of canebrakes, timber and water moccasins. You can get close to it by driving back roads and old hardpan trails. Marquette and Joliet made their last camp here at the confluence in 1673 before giving up and turning back to Canada. La Salle's expedition camped here too and was befriended by the local Kappa Indian tribe.

This is a hard, rough country that inexplicably has excited the imagination of generations of dreamers. Each attempt to build on these dreams, beginning in the seventeenth century, has ended in failure. Yet new waves of visionaries keeping the faith came believing that their dream would work. Their loyalty has always ended in shadow.

We searched the area as best we could for any remnants of the town of Napoleon. In his nostalgic trip downriver in 1882, Twain was looking forward to visiting Napoleon again. It was the roughest, meanest town on the Mississippi, named by French émigrés praying for the emperor's escape from St. Helena. During the heyday of the steamboats, Napoleon was a thriving port on the mouth of the Arkansas River, perched on a low stretch of land where the Arkansas joined the mighty Mississippi. The town supported doz-

ens of saloons, gambling dens and whorehouses. Twain was
shocked and dismayed when he saw that the famous little port had
vanished. The river had washed it away except for the "fag-end of
a shanty and one brick chimney." In writing *Huckleberry Finn* later,
Twain would immortalize Napoleon by using it as the setting for
his scathing "lynching bee" scene and also for his Shakespearian
revival. The ruins of Napoleon now lie beneath the murky waters
of the Big Muddy.

The Arkansas River is, strangely, the home of the last working
steamboat, carrying freight up and down the river. In 1838 this
river served as a conduit for a favored few Indians traveling the
Trail of Tears; they went by steamboat to their exile in Oklahoma—at least they didn't have to walk.

Along the river we saw commercial fishing rigs hard at work. In
spite of federal EPA claims of heavy pollution, the State of Arkansas has refused to ban fishing in the Arkansas River. The argument
is that the Arkansas is cleaner than the Mississippi. But the fish
don't know it and there's no boundary to stop them from swimming out of the Mississippi and into the Arkansas. This fish story
isn't Arkansas's only problem.

We were traveling through timber country; the large paper mills
of Arkansas are known to generate toxic wastes that are a major
contributor to acid rain. There's also a notorious chemical company up the Arkansas River that has created a problem nearly as
bad as that of Times Beach through toxic spills and illegal waste
disposal. Further, the state is permitting a cement company to burn
millions of pounds of hazardous wastes in its huge kilns. The wastes
are shipped in from all parts of the nation where similar practices
are prohibited. It's legal in Arkansas because of a gaping loophole
in federal laws not closed by the state's lawmakers.

From a distance, the little town in south Arkansas where the
burning is taking place looks like a great salt sea. The grounds of
the plant and the surrounding landscape are covered in a dull gray
ash coming from the huge 500-foot-long concrete kilns where the
toxic wastes are burning. Mountainous piles of coal and coke used
for fuel sit beside the highway. The company operating this plant
continues to receive permits to do so from the state, but it's not
just Arkansas that is to blame. The states shipping in substances
banned on their own turf are equally culpable; not only that, the

Grave of a Japanese American, Rohwer, Arkansas.

stuff comes by interstate highways, railroads and the river, and everyone along these routes is endangered.

Our trip through the pine woods along state roads that wound around section corners turned into a conscious search for some monument, some marker, that would recognize all the drifting currents from the history the dreamers had tried to make. We could find none.

So we gave up and drifted back to the Mississippi along a state highway that changed directions at every section corner. We came to a woebegone little place called Rohwer.

We missed the sign because it was obscured by trees and when we turned around and came back we saw that the sign said, RELO-CATION CEMETERY. Railroad tracks run along here, and there's a steep grade, though from the top we saw the graveyard out there in the middle of a cottonfield. It's not a big cemetery at all but has a military look about it, with the uniform headstones in neat rows contained within a quadrangle of whitewashed posts.

The scene is tranquil. Mockingbirds flit about in the oaks and apple trees at the entrance. A car or truck goes by on the state road about every half hour. The Mississippi River hooks along a mile or two or three away. No reason ever for relocation to remote Rohwer.

Yet in September 1942 a long train came along the tracks and stopped to unload eighty-five hundred Japanese-American people here. Many were children, though some were in their seventies and eighties. They were all bone-tired and hungry; the Army had had a devil of a time trying to feed them all during the forced overland train trek from California, and many had gone without food during the entire trip. But they were here now and these cottonfields would be their home for the next three years, two months and twelve days.

During the first days they would live in tents while the Army built barracks for their internment. Over the next three years several of the elderly would die here. No record of mistreatment was ever kept; there was never any need for discipline or punishment—the relocated ones conducted themselves in an exemplary manner, determined to show that they were patriotic and proud to be Americans. They were, of course, full citizens of the United States, but because of their Japanese ancestry they had been uprooted from their homes, their belongings taken away, their property confiscated, not to be returned. They were some of the 112,000 Japanese Americans who were relocated in the country's interior after the attack on Pearl Harbor.

As it had against the "Hun" of World War I, America turned hysterically racist during World War II. Fanatical groups in the country immediately put pressure on President Roosevelt to do something about "all the Japs" living on the West Coast. The ringleader of this reactionary movement was J. Edgar Hoover, who contacted the President daily with "viable evidence" garnered by his agents that proved the Japanese-American community was a threat to the nation's security. In September 1942 Roosevelt signed the order for relocation. Officers from the FBI and other government agencies had already begun the roundup; the first trainload reached the Mississippi River on September 18.

Another train would be coming through shortly. A second internment center was placed down the river a few more miles at the little burg of Jerome, and another seventy-five hundred were relocated. The groups never saw each other, knew little of the other's existence or welfare and had no contact with the outside world. They were prisoners of war.

The relocated ones made do. They were segregated by sex in barracks, they put in their own vegetable gardens, they taught their children and they created a ghetto community. Each day they held flag-raising ceremonies, saluted and sang "My Country 'Tis of Thee." They put on plays and held dances for the young people. Hundreds of the teenaged boys sought to volunteer for the Armed Services; at first they were denied. Over the protests of J. Edgar Hoover, the President finally made the executive decision to create the Nisei Unit—it was clear that the President was trying to save face and sway his detractors on the home propaganda front. The Nisei Unit was outfitted, given "American" commanders and shipped off to take part in the Italian campaign.

The Nisei Unit was part of the bloody fighting at Salerno and Anzio beaches and rescued the famous "lost Texan battalion." Especially adept at manning tanks, the unit became one of the most decorated of the war. It helped make the final push into Rome and went on to serve in France and Germany. The American high command lauded the unit. At the war's end, the families of the unit's members were still being held in the relocation centers.

The tiny place called Rohwer became a rather big town during the war. Today it is no town at all, just one store and three or four plain little houses. One of the houses is an interesting story in itself. It's the place where six remarkable young men grew up: the Jones kids, Oliver, Wilbur, Charles, Melvin, Major and Caldwell, who all starred as basketball players at Albany State and all went on to play professional basketball. The Jones brothers are a close unit too; they come home in the off-season and can be seen sitting out on the front porch, gathered around their mama.

The relocation cemetery sits in what used to be the compound; an old Army guard shack remains to this day, falling over and covered with vines and weeds. In the ruins we found a framed mirror, on the back of which was stamped, PROPERTY OF U.S. GOV'T.

Two tall monuments rise in the middle of the cemetery; the words COURAGE and LOYALTY are imprinted at the top of the mon-

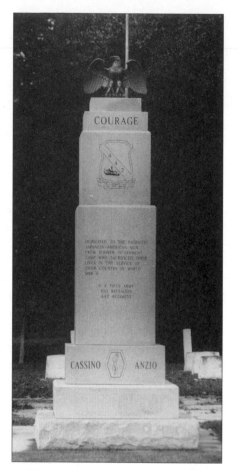

Monuments in Japanese-American
Relocation Center, Rohwer, Arkansas.

uments, and the Japanese-American creed, which in essence says, "We're proud to be Americans, no matter what," is written in full below. We could see all the names, too, of the Nisei Unit soldiers who were killed in action. A concrete replica of an Army tank squats beside one of the monuments but has collapsed under its own weight. The gravestones of the others who died here give the names and dates. One man was eighty-two years old when he died at Rohwer—just the sort of threat Hoover was after.

At the Rohwer store we were told that an old black man is paid

to come over and mow the grounds "when it needs it." Because of some recent interest, the cemetery looked better than it did back in the sixties, when it was all overgrown. "The graveyard gets some attention about every ten years," a man in the store said. "Then it falls off again. Not too many people come to visit."

Something gnawed at us as we started to drive away. It wasn't that ludicrous concrete tank or the shallow words on the monuments, or even the froward mockingbirds. It was those pretty apple trees. How'd they get here? Apple trees do not grow in the middle of cottonfields and they don't sprout wild. They must have been planted by those who lived here. We turned and went back and got a handful of little apples that were just coming ripe. They were sour, even a little bitter, but we got used to the taste and even savored it as we went on down the road.

With the added force of a new river, the Mississippi pushes with broad wings as it runs to Greenville, Mississippi. Levees used to break with regularity along these stretches, and it was here that the river in 1927 spread itself into a hundred-mile conduit of woe. This reach of the river is also a convict corridor, for three of the country's most notorious state prisons lie inside a triangle in the basin—Cummins in Arkansas, Parchman in Mississippi and Angola in Louisiana. It remains one of the ironies of the great flood that inmates from these vintage stockades and not engineers from the Mississippi River Commission were the ones who saved what little there was to be saved during the flood.

For this run of the river to Greenville we were joined by a man whose lifelong interest and calling have focused on the power of water. His name is Doyne Knight and he's an engineer with expertise in electronics and heat fusion. His personal fascination is the study of energy in its relationship to electrical power. His work in recent years took him to Mexico, where he installed dozens of badly needed water wells; once upon a time he put in air-conditioning and refrigeration systems in the biggest hotels and casinos in Las Vegas, but he "got tired of keeping all the high rollers comfortable." Doyne grew up in an orphanage in south Arkansas near the river and ran away and joined the Marines when he was seventeen, putting in two combat years in Korea. He was back home visiting old friends and places when we hooked up with him.

Doyne talked about confluences and why rivers don't like to merge. Each flowing body of water has its own static electrical charge and when two rivers come together, their bodies are unlike each other and they have to, in a sense, neutralize themselves; the process can take miles and miles before the two bodies finally marry into one.

"Rivers used to purify themselves," he said. "People were right in thinking that. If we left the process alone, nature would take care of things—the iron ores, lead, gold, silver—in its own ionization process. But when we pump in the man-made toxic chemicals, we ruin the purification that's been going on in nature. It would take millenniums to bring the river back."

As we drove along state roads, we passed the place called Jerome where another relocation center was built during World War II. The Japanese-Americans here were later shipped out to other centers and replaced with German prisoners of war. Jerome became a camp for an elite corps of German officers and they created something of a sensation with a sophisticated little society, including their own chamber orchestra and art gallery.

"They put an Italian prisoner of war camp near our orphanage in Monticello," Doyne said. "Their camp was something to behold. The grounds were perfectly landscaped and in their flower gardens they had these magnificently sculpted statues that they had made out of white stone. After the war our orphanage got their barracks, had them hauled in. We made feed barns out of them. In those barracks were some of the most beautiful pictures you've ever seen ... done on the sheetrock walls, the infant Jesus and the Virgin Mary and a large mural of the Last Supper. They'd painted them with all kinds of colored chalk and charcoal, and they were absolutely exquisite works of art. We couldn't keep them, save them. We had to tear out the sheetrock to make the feed barns."

Nearing Greenville, we came to the town of Lake Village, Arkansas, along Lake Chicot close to the river. As a boy Doyne had come here with other kids from his orphanage to swim in the lake, which once was the main channel of the Mississippi. In 1927 the flood changed the river, but before that several old paddle wheelers had been moored along the river, wasting away. When the river changed its course after the flood, the Corps of Engineers came in with its concrete levees and sealed off Lake Chicot, leaving the old paddle wheelers marooned near a towhead in the middle of the lake.

"The river and the lake were very wide here," Doyne said. "About five miles across and you could hardly see the other side. We swam out to the island to see those old paddle wheelers. Three or four of their stacks were still sticking up out of the water and we could see the other boats, about fifteen in all. We dived down around those stacks and the water was murky, muddy. It was foolish of us to swim out that far, at least three miles. When we dived down, we

sank in mud up to the neck. But we had to see those old steamboats."

The Greenville bridge was coming up and we pulled off at an
overlook to watch a convoy of tow-barges boiling along in the
deepening water. This obscure reach of the river had been awash
with ghostly old paddle wheelers, prisoners of war, orphans, loyal
sons, lost art. Sometimes we were hard-put to make meaning of it
all, and we could only stand in a stop-time and watch it roll.

"There's a mighty river below this one," Doyne said. "It's the
mother river and it's bigger and way deep. The Mississippi will
always be here, long after man. Nature will catalog it away as if it
never existed. It will be only a thin dark line for the relic diggers."

CHAPTER 18

River Flavors

"The little towns along the river are the only ones that retain some of the Old South flavor. The cities that matter
economically have lost their ways and identity."

—*John Stennis, Jr., Jackson attorney*

Some say the Deep South only truly begins when you cross over
the bridge into Greenville, Mississippi. Louisiana is just a step away
and the delta keeps rolling on toward Natchez, but you feel as you
cross the hoary old antique of a bridge that you're passing over
into something different, something gothic.

At a tourist center just over the bridge we got among a mix of
Mississippians and Northern folk on vacation trips. Everybody
stops in Greenville for a couple of reasons, to get hot tamales at
Doe's or to look at the river and think about the greatest flood of
all time. The river is crazy here; it loops and twists, offshoots and
makes islands. Here in 1927 the river made an ocean that spread
a full hundred miles wide.

"I wasn't alive in the flood of twenty-seven," said a man from
over in Sunflower County, "but we had one about as bad back in
the forties when I was a boy. My daddy was going to take me
fishing the next morning but when I woke up and looked out the
window I could see things just floating by. The house had done
gone into the river and we were sailing along pretty as a boat. It
took us down the river for miles, and I remember Mama and Daddy
and them were up all night trying to chase out all the snakes that
had got in."

Another couple had just walked up and were listening; they'd
come from Arkansas and were on their way to Mobile. The Arkan-

Hot tamales on the River.

sawyer told about growing up over in De Vall's Bluff on Arkansas's White River. The flood of '27 had nearly washed his town away. "Water was seven feet high in the stores downtown and not a house or building was spared. My uncle ran a car dealership for the old Overland model; he had several new Overlands and he had to get them out quick. I was twelve at the time and we thought the flood was the grandest thing we'd ever seen. We got together some old scrap lumber and built ourselves a box boat and paddled all over town playing Tom Sawyer."

We drove into Greenville to Doe's and got lucky: a big lunch crowd hadn't gathered yet. You have no trouble finding Doe's because people for miles around know the place; it's on Nelson Street and the sign over the modest frame building says simply, DOE'S EAT PLACE. One unique thing about Doe's besides the good food is that you enter through the kitchen, where you're greeted by the longtime head cook, Joe Woods. Joe wears a white apron and doesn't miss a lick dishing up steaks and hot tamales, maybe the best in Dixie. Joe will talk to you, show you how he does it, and still make sure everybody's fed on time.

Doe's is owned by the Signa brothers, Doe, Jr., and Charles, sons of the founder. One or both of them will usually be on hand to help out in the kitchen or take care of the overflow crowds, especially on football weekends. The Signa brothers could put themselves in a fancy restaurant with valet parking and maître d's, "But we're not about to do that," Doe told us. "We have a place just like this one in Little Rock and another one in Memphis. We're just plain Doe's and we're staying that way."

A sizable part of their business is walk-in and carry-out. In the evening after the workday, it's a common sight to see people parking their cars a block away and walking along with their hot tamale pails. It's a Greenville ritual.

It also used to be a ritual for the old *Delta-Democrat Times* newspaper office down on the riverfront to be bombed by the Klan. We asked around and found that the newspaper had moved into uptown quarters and changed hands. The *Delta-Democrat* used to be in the hands of Hodding Carter, the tough editor and Pulitzer prize winner who stood up to the likes of Huey Long and Theodore Bilbo, arch-deacons of the Brotherhood.

Carter's paper used to be required reading just about everywhere except Mississippi and Louisiana back in the forties, fifties and sixties. From a base right here in the middle of them, Carter attacked the system of servitude existing in the South. In the end his greatest fight and ultimate triumph was against the KKK. Greenville itself was a KKK hotbed until recent years; the Klan harassed and lynched up into the 1960s with seeming impunity. Now the Klan here and elsewhere appears "brain dead," according to journalist Bob Lancaster. "The Klan is nearly extinct and has become a caricature of its old brutish self—the professional wrestling of contemporary politics." Still, the specter of the Klan haunts this region. Out on delta places as late as five years ago teams of a new variety of Klanners, now wearing survivalist gear, were teaching preteen children how to use assault weapons.

In Greenville we spoke with a nice lady who once worked for Hodding Carter at the *Delta-Democrat*. Retired now, she spends her time gardening and working on her bridge game. "Mr. Carter was not a fearless man," she said. "He was a decent man and he couldn't take people being mistreated and put upon. So I suppose you could say he was fearless. He got used to it, the bomb scares and such. They were just bullies and could be backed off by a good man."

In Greenville we rejoined our fellow traveler Highway 61, which had come down through plantation country. Up at the small town of Cleveland is the purported birthplace of blues music, and they offer a tour there of the original shotgun shacks and crossroads places where the blues originated. The music came out of field hollers, some say, but others claim its moody, low-down quality came from the black delta churches. We turned on the radio in the car and tried to pick up some blues or at least some preaching, but all we got was country and Top Forty. We plugged in a tape of B. B. King and listened to "The Thrill Is Gone" while we rode through this blue land.

Leaving Greenville, we swung close to a loop of the river that Mark Twain called Island 92. It used to be a den for whiskey lockers and bootleggers. We pulled in at a crossroads store and got a conversation going about moonshiners and Prohibition. An elderly man sitting in the store came over and told us about the old "dry" times in Mississippi.

"Back there when it was all dry, you could get a drink if you really wanted it. It was called stump whiskey. You drove out in the country and found some woods and a stump. You left an empty mason jar on the stump with a couple of dollars, and you took a little walk in the woods around. When you came back, the mason jar would be full and your two dollars gone. That was stump whiskey and it was good sour-mash."

These little islands along the river have known their share of misery too. In the early nineteenth century, small colonies of Italian immigrants came to settle in and around the islands. Their hope was to put down theocracies like other colonies that were then coming into the Lower Mississippi Valley. The Italians failed. The river flooded, drowning most of the colonists and washing away their crops and farm animals. The few survivors soon followed the flood victims; they were all struck down by an unknown pestilence caused by the eating of buzzard flesh, the only food left.

While we were in Greenville we scanned the local telephone book and found several Italian names; these were not descendants of the early Italian colonists, who were wiped out, but are likely the offspring of later waves of settlers who came in the middle of the nineteenth century. The story of the Italian colonies can be found in several histories, but none of the sources say whether the Italians were poor fishermen. The lakes and sloughs around Island 92 are known locally as good fishing spots, with plentiful bass and crappie and bream. When we told the story to a man at a bait shop, he said it sure was a pitiful story, all those folks from Italy having to eat buzzard meat when they could have caught themselves a mess of fish. "They probably didn't go after 'em with the right bait."

Great fishermen live in this region of Mississippi. We passed one catfish farm after another that broke the monotony of the cottonfields. Each catfish pond has its own shade of green. The sight is not so much pleasing as it is curious; forest fades to kelly and emerald, mystic and chartreuse to aqua. When a wind or rain whips up, as it did while we passed, the breakers in the ponds lash the dikes like surf.

Folks in county offices in the little towns of the delta are friendly and go out of their way to be helpful. We went by a county agent's office and got filled in on what's going on with agriculture nowadays.

"Yes, most of the land is planted to cotton," the country agent told us. "In Humphreys County they're doing very well with catfish farming. The land used to be under cotton cultivation and sometimes the return of investment is good and sometimes, well, it's bankruptcy for some. So the farmers want to try something different, new crops. There's the big problem."

The county agent told us the farmers who want to change from cotton have to commit their land to money crops, and the money crops require herbicides and pesticides. "If you try to come in and put down new crops, they'll just be killed off by the poisons that are still in the soil. The pesticides and herbicides can stay down in that soil for years."

The agent said that most of the delta is in the same fix. The delta is simply marginal for money crops and is totally committed to the poisons. All this land was drained long ago by canals and ditches, and what is missing is wetlands. The county agent was well

Hard times on the delta.

aware that Congress had passed farm legislation to provide for some return to wetlands. "That process," the agent told us, "will take up to fifty years."

We passed a huge billboard in Humphreys County that claimed it was the catfish capital of the world. Soon we ran out of the catfish ponds, though, and were back in cotton country. All along the highway, we saw tiny crop-duster airports. Some of the planes were up and at it; they looped down right over the highway to get to the fields. But they don't call themselves crop dusters anymore; their signs said, *aerial applicators.*

Old 61 skews inland for the miles to Vicksburg and we turned off to experience some of the infamous Mississippi back roads. They are angular devils indeed, all cut on section lines. We asked an attendant at a service station why the delta roads were so winding, and he answered blandly, as though uttering a law: "You just don't want to build a road too straight down here—it wouldn't be Mississippi."

The pretty town of Yazoo City ends this part of the delta and introduces a Southern phenomenon known as kudzu. Sometimes called foot-a-night vine because it grows so rapidly, kudzu grows in and around Yazoo in lush green volume. More kudzu grows here than in any other place in the world, and that includes Japan, where the vine came from; it was a soil conservation project introduced during the dust bowl years of the Depression, and it was one project that worked profusely.

We zigzagged along Green Mansions State Park Road on a side trip to Jackson, on our way to talk to a man about the state of affairs in this land of great talkers and poor economy. Coming toward Jackson, we saw that the kudzu is a godsend for covering up the poor soil of the loess hills. Near Jackson stands a small petrified forest, not big enough or quite petrified enough to make a going tourist area such as they have in Arizona.

Entering Jackson from the north, we saw old Tougaloo College, put here in 1869 as a token for black students. Tougaloo looks a bit drab and frail today, though it was a hopping place in the 1950s when it served as the center of the civil rights movement for the whole South. Joan Baez used to come to Tougaloo in the 1960s and sing her protest folk songs. A name out of the past jumps into mind: P. O. East, one of the early civil rights leaders.

We drove into semi-busy Jackson with P. O. East's voice buzzing in our heads. *Mississippi, Mississippi.* "We come from where we got the wound," wrote the Southern poet James Whitehead.

We met John Stennis, Jr., of Jackson for iced tea and talk at a restaurant in south Jackson. He's a nice smiling man in his middle fifties and has the look of a scholar about him, but then Jackson lawyers give that impression. John has a wonderful speaking voice and a wit that matches. He's a reticent man or he would have followed his father into the Senate. John strikes us as less ambitious than that, or maybe more intelligent. We thought he looked like pictures we'd seen of Henry Adams, the son and grandson of presidents.

We had to nudge John Stennis into talking about the old saws of politics, the South and its image. Then he got interested and something inbred took over. We asked if the state of Mississippi was going to have more social problems in the future. He answered no, matter-of-factly.

"The reason is that the old order in Mississippi, to the manner born, has just about died off. Now the cotton laws that used to protect the old order are there to protect the corporate farms."

Did he think the cronyism and good-old-boyism of the past were still somehow entrenched? "Maybe, in some isolated cases, like in Louisiana. But it's gone. We've got Harvard graduates as governors, Rhodes scholars as governors. Being a Southerner is not relevant in the 1990s. The places that matter economically have lost their Southern identity. The little towns along the Mississippi River, colorful though they may be, retain some of the Old South flavor, but they are not part of the mainstream now. They abide and slowly fade from the cultural scene."

John talked on and as he warmed up he got into his favorite mode, that of imitating the old Southern filibustering politicians like Vardaman and Bilbo and Barnett. "They were stem-winders from the spread-eagle school and they could mesmerize a crowd and they did about as much good as a hangnail."

He took us for a ride in his daddy's car, "because it needs driving and Daddy can't get out now." We were going to see an interesting Civil War cemetery a little way out in the county; we wound up taking an hour-and-a-half seminar on the South, a charming John Stennis metaphor about Southern penology, garden clubs, whorehouses and the river's capricious way of spoiling the last vestiges of the Old South.

"We had recently a doctor, a psychiatrist, at Parchman Prison," John said. "Now Parchman has as bad a reputation as Angola for evil, and this psychiatrist had a vision that he could change Parchman overnight and make it a national model for penology. He had been appointed to rehabilitate the prisoners and he came up with a plan to hypnotize the convicts and purge all of the bad out of them and leave nothing but good. I suppose he had an Albert Schweitzer complex but he was convinced his plan would revolutionize all the prisons and take a scourge away from society, and never mind that it would be illegal and you'd have all these criminals going around in posthypnotic spells. Anyway, it didn't work and I think the fellow was heartbroken."

We circled around Hinds County looking for the cemetery and John told us about Natchez, his favorite town and the most interesting place, to him, in Mississippi.

"Before the Civil War broke out in 1861, Natchez had more

millionaires per capita than any other single place in America. It was a Whig town and it wholeheartedly supported the Union; it was adamantly against secession and fought against Mississippi's joining the Confederacy. So you've got to expect some eccentric things to happen in Natchez. The strongest force in Natchez is not the landowners and their corporate boards, but the ladies garden club, whose tradition goes back beyond the Natchez-Under-the-Hill days to genteel polish and grace. But the garden club could never get rid of Nellie.

"Nellie's was the most famous whorehouse on the Mississippi River. Nellie ran the place for decades, starting back in the 1920s. She was dark and stunningly beautiful, or so the legend goes. She had turned many a trick over the years with powerful politicians of the South. Nellie's whorehouse in Natchez became a legend. Down on the Gulf and in New Orleans you'd see college boys wearing T-shirts that said, 'Follow Me to Nellie's.'

"They say Nellie was still turning tricks in her eighties, just last year. And then last November a sickening tragedy struck Nellie's place. It burned to the ground—and Nellie died in the fire."

John said that the newspapers in the region gave big coverage to the fire and the stories carried a tinge of sadness. In a way it was funny, like the story of the crazy old woman in the storm cellar or like Faulkner's story "A Rose for Emily," only Nellie would need a peace lily. And you wonder if such happenings in any other state would carry quite the same meaning.

John finally gave up the search for the lost cemetery. It never hurt, he said, to keep a mystery in reserve. The drive around Hinds County had served a good purpose; he had given his daddy's car a workout.

"We're not on the Mississippi in Jackson," he said. "We have the Pearl River and it runs down to the Gulf too and has a lot of good lore behind it. Vicksburg and Natchez are not really on the river, either. They're close but the Mississippi's channel is swinging away from them. Years from now they'll be landlocked and they will lose their special flavor. The Mississippi does give flavor. It takes it away as well."

CHAPTER 19

Siege and Siege Again

"The Mississippi River—too damned muddy to drink, too wet to plow."

—*U. S. Grant*

The road from Jackson to Vicksburg is a romance. In 1863 a prayed-for relief column might have traveled this road to liberate Vicksburg from Grant's death-grip siege. But no relief column came, not from dedicated Robert E. Lee or dashing Nathan Bedford Forrest. Grant's brilliant river campaign sealed Vicksburg's fate. By the Fourth of July in 1863 when the city surrendered, the people of Vicksburg were down to eating rats.

We drove to the Vicksburg Battleground Park first and took the driving tour through it. It lasts for miles and it's stunning. People who keep up with such things say the Vicksburg battlefield with all its monuments is the best in the country, and that includes Gettysburg. The grounds here are immaculately landscaped and manicured. States whose soldiers participated in the siege have erected prodigious monuments, and as we drove along we got the feeling that some sort of contest went on to see which state could out-erect the others, sort of like the floats in the Rose Bowl parade.

Adjacent to the park, a river road winds up and around the bluff overlooking the Mississippi and the best view is here. You can see how the siege developed at the river and up the small Yazoo River, which joins the Mississippi at Vicksburg. Captain James Buchanan Eads, who after the war would go back to complete the first bridge over the Mississippi in St. Louis, was here during the fighting, commanding the gunboats he had designed and built for the Union.

Here too was Horace Bixby, Mark Twain's mentor; the formidable pilot fought for the Union in command of a troopship in these waters.

Other boats passed the besieged town of Vicksburg in 1863; they were not gunboats or troopships or even pleasure cruisers. They were stripped-down steamboats flying the Union colors, all stacked to the texas deck with bales of cotton. Supposedly the South under Confederate president Jefferson Davis had placed an embargo on cotton and had instructed all the cotton plantations to "grow corn, not cotton." Yet if anyone had climbed up this bluff in 1863 he would have seen along the valley wide fields of cotton growing in abundance. Why was the South growing cotton when its market was the textile mills of the Northeast?

The answer leads to one of the incongruities of the Civil War and to the suspicion that self-interest was being served between North and South. Most historians have accepted the South's embargo at face value. The renowned historian Samuel Eliot Morison pretty much summarized the thinking that has prevailed in *The Oxford History of the American People:* "The Southern states, faithful to the old Jefferson embargo theory, withheld cotton, fatuously believing that this would force Europe to break the blockade." Now, in the light of new research, historians have come to believe that the opposite may have been true. The outbreak of the war threatened the very existence of the huge New England textile industry; the mill owners were positively screaming for cotton and didn't care how or where they got it. Soon a plan evolved; Salmon P. Chase, Lincoln's secretary of the treasury, devised a "Licensed Cotton Trader Program" to permit federal agents to go down the Mississippi and buy from the enemy at the going rate. Lincoln approved the program.

In his widely acclaimed, definitive work on the Civil War, *Battle Cry of Freedom,* historian James M. McPherson takes up the issue of contraband cotton on the Mississippi. Some of the movement of cotton to the North was legitimate at first, McPherson says, but when the licensed traders arrived, they began to "bribe Union soldiers to look the other way when cotton was going through the lines." Cotton fever broke out all down the Mississippi, and even Charles A. Dana, the Treasury Department officer in charge of the Licensed Trader Program, was so distressed over what was happening that he wrote to Chase: "The mania for sudden fortunes made in cotton has to an alarming extent corrupted and demoralized the army . . . I had no conception of the extent of this evil until I came and saw for myself."

McPherson writes in *Battle Cry of Freedom* that "the South needed salt, shoes, clothing . . . and canny Confederates sought to flank the blockade by direct trade with the enemy . . . a Chinese wall from Atlanta to the Pacific could not stop this commerce." General Grant was appalled when he saw the licensed traders coming down the river; he protested to Dana and got this reply: "The traders must be allowed to buy what and where they can." Grant and General Sherman tried "to stop the illicit cotton trade through Memphis and western Tennessee," McPherson writes, but their efforts hardly slowed the flow of contraband. "Fortunes were made in New Orleans," McPherson continues. And in the Confederate States, President Davis "looked the other way" as Southerners openly traded with the enemy. During the war, Abraham Lincoln himself wrote in a letter to one of his cabinet members, "at least 900,000 bales of cotton found their way North." And that estimate did not take into account perhaps twice that many bales going south through Texas and into Mexico. Millions of bales were grown down the Mississippi Valley and up the cotton-rich Red River Valley; the textile mills in the East received enough cotton to stay in business. Contraband cotton certainly wasn't the small sideshow that the history books once made it out to be.

The starving soldiers who were dug in along the ridges at Vicksburg in 1863 certainly weren't worrying about cotton. And the people of Vicksburg today aren't thinking about cotton either. They are worried about what's happening to their town. Vicksburg today lives with the depression that grips the delta. The town doesn't thrive but holds itself together by catering to tourists. Besides the splendid battlefield, Vicksburg offers antebellum houses and genteel hospitality. We went by the Balfour House, which was used as headquarters by the Rebels and as a hospital by the Union. You can still see traces of damage from the Union cannonballs.

Vicksburg is also the home base for the Mississippi River Commission and the Corps of Engineers. The MRC was created by Congress in 1879; Congressman James A. Garfield was the guiding force who got the Commission established, and Garfield said back then that the Mississippi River "is one of the grandest of our material national interests." Charter members of the Commission were Benjamin Harrison and Captain James Eads, civil engineers. From that point on, the Mississippi River would be in the hands of the U.S. Army Corps of Engineers.

The Commission's building in Vicksburg is a lovely old Romanesque structure. We walked through it and saw busy people, uniformed officers, titled civilians, all with offices to run. A new commanding general of the Corps had just taken over at the MRC and we went by his office, hardly thinking we'd get a chance to chat. We had a couple of questions we wanted to ask. The Arkansas and Red rivers had flooded during 1990, bringing on a billion dollars in damage, and we wanted to ask what went wrong, since so many dams exist up those rivers. The general's assistant came back to us after a few minutes and said the general couldn't see us; he was getting ready to leave on a tour of the river.

So we went for a Coke. And not to just any place for a Coke, but to the original store where Coke as we know it was born. There's a little museum in Vicksburg that displays the original bottles of Coca-Cola. In 1894 a candy-store owner here named Joseph A. Biedenharn got the idea of bottling a popular fountain beverage known as Coca-Cola. The candy man probably had no idea that his notion would revolutionize marketing principles everywhere and, according to that old codger we overheard up in St. Louis, would upset the world's economy and ruin the game of baseball.

At one time Vicksburg was the largest city in Mississippi and Warren County the most prosperous; nearly all steamboat traffic pulled into port here, and those broad-brimmed Southern grandees boarded at Vicksburg for the "gambling hells" that found easy marks from here to New Orleans.

You have to drive down steep streets to get to the riverfront. We found no barges or pleasure boats in the harbor, though there were some nicer buildings and a few condo-like structures on the north part of the riverfront. We drove along a honeycomb of poverty that made us think of East St. Louis; if anything, conditions looked worse here. The river wasn't fifty yards away, and these shanties barely stood upon their rotting pilings. Trash and litter covered the bare yards and spread into the gutters of the potholed

On the riverfront at Vicksburg.

street. Black people live here in Vicksburg's ghetto. Some children were playing blindman's buff in a vacant lot strewn with garbage. For them, the siege has not been lifted.

Highway 61 runs along the Vicksburg battlefield before taking off toward the famous Natchez Trace. We stopped a few minutes at a store called Jitney Jungle to see if we could find a Southern specialty, a Moon Pie and an R.C. Cola. The Moon Pie is as much a part of Southern culture as corn bread and black-eyed peas. It started in the coal mining country of Appalachia back in the 1930s, and Royal Crown Cola was brought out to accompany the gooey-sweet pastry; an R.C. cost the same as a Coke but gave ten ounces instead of Coke's six.

We were standing outside Jitney Jungle with our R.C.'s and Moon Pies when a frail young woman with stringy red hair came up to us. We judged she was in her twenties, though it was hard to tell because of her tattered dress and slouchy stance. She was tall, maybe five-nine, and so skinny that she probably didn't weigh a hundred pounds. People coming out of the store turned their faces away as they passed.

"Have y'all seen Roy?" she asked. She lisped and we noticed that she didn't have teeth. We could tell she was starved to death. "Roy sent me in there to get him some underwear and socks and this shirt." She dug into her shopping bag and showed us some brightly colored things, and she started crying. She was wearing a wedding band. Once she started crying she couldn't stop.

We had bought a box of the Moon Pies and we gave them to her and went inside to see if anyone knew her. The checkout girl told us she'd been standing out in front of the store for two hours. Evidently her husband had gone off and left her. When we went back outside, she was eating the Moon Pies one after another, gumming and swallowing rapidly. We were offering to drive her home when the store manager came out and said he'd call some church people he knew who helped transients.

As we drove away she was standing there talking to the manager and eating the Moon Pies. Old 61 goes along the slope of the levee for several miles and we didn't have much to say during this stretch. We have to watch ourselves down here sometimes or we start getting mad at things. Mad at Vicksburg for letting its riverfront sink so wretchedly low. Mad at people way back there for selling each other out. But mostly mad at Roy for running away and leaving that poor girl alone and hungry.

Old 61 moves away from the river and comes to Grand Gulf. A nuclear plant sits over there on the river and we turned off and drove close to it. The cooling tower looms over everything. Coming down the river we'd seen enough of these monolithic things to get used to them, but they still put us in mind of something sinister, though the real threat is the reactor sitting off by itself. The tower is what scares people, just the sight of it, like a town bully that everybody crosses the street to keep from meeting.

This nuclear plant has come in for heated criticism in recent years, and it and its sister plant in Arkansas have been singled out for their violations of regulatory standards. Again, the problem is similar to the one at the converted plant we saw up in Genoa, Wisconsin—what to do with all the nuclear waste. We spent a little time in Grand Gulf and on the surface it's a grand town. Life looks prosperous; wages are high and jobs have been easy enough to come by. A man in town told us things are pretty uneasy now and the plant is cutting way back on some shifts. "Vicksburg relies a lot on the plant for jobs," said a park ranger when we stopped by the state park at Grand Gulf. "The plant's pretty new and the jobs ought to last a long time, ten years at least." We kept wondering about this plant's storage of uranium pellets, how many they'd built up by now. Maybe Grand Gulf would get lucky and the life of its reactor would last until the government got its nuclear waste storage location ready.

We were driving through forest country now and it was a relief after the depressing broadness of the delta. Old 61 eased on into the forest and we drove down a logger road not far off the river. It was close to this spot that some French royalty once lighted for a day and took advantage of the game in the woods. Running for their lives, Louis-Philippe, Duke of Chartres, and his brothers, the Counts of Montpensier and Beaujolais, escaped France during the Terror and came to America in exile for three years. They came down the Ohio and onto the Mississippi in a keelboat, their destination New Orleans. Twain referred to them in *Life on the Mississippi* and perhaps used the brothers as models for his Duke and Dolphin characters in *Huckleberry Finn*. The royal brothers were somewhere in this reach of the river in 1799. In their *Mississippi Steamboatin'* the Quick brothers wrote of Louis-Philippe and his brothers and we learn that their cruise was not all luxury. Members of the keelboat crew weren't too impressed with the presence of royalty and even tried to get the brothers to pitch in and help pull the boat off a mud bar: "Hey, you kings! Get up off your lazy arses and help us three spots out!"

In this stretch the river loops in an almost complete circle at Palmyra Lake, a haunt of old-time pirates. The most famous of the Mississippi's buccaneers, John Murrell, was said to have had a lair hidden among the islands here.

We were nearing the Natchez Trace now, and we were ensconced and stifled by the forest as we rolled with Old 61. It's a lonely hurry of a road here and the river is off somewhere by itself. With all our thinking and talking and looking at personal and historical betrayals, we thought we'd just as soon be back on the Big Muddy.

CHAPTER 20

"Follow Me to Nellie's"

"I hereby condemn you to be hanged by the neck until you are dead."

—*An echo of Mississippi redneck jurisprudence*

The town of Port Gibson, Mississippi, isn't a port anymore; it's not on the river, close but not quite. It's one of those ports that the river has decided to landlock and see how the people will take it. It's an old town and was once an important port above Natchez, and it's as solid as the ham and eggs and grits and redeye gravy they serve for breakfast in the little cafés along Main Street. U. S. Grant came through here and decided to spare Port Gibson because he just liked the town's looks. The people of Port Gibson have been so grateful that they've put up a billboard out on the highway: WELCOME TO PORT GIBSON, TOWN TOO PRETTY TO BURN.

The town is all hemmed in by the creeping green lushness of kudzu and is deeply shaded by giant oaks, magnolias and weeping willows. The old courthouse on the square has been plastered over and painted, but it seems to shiver and creak; it sits on the highest ground in town, letting you know it's seen floodwaters. The pace seems deliberately slower in Port Gibson; everybody downtown offered a greeting and was willing to stop and talk. The temperature was climbing into the nineties when we were in town and the businessmen had their coats off, ties loosened. We talked to a lawyer coming out of the courthouse and soon were joined by others; we were standing near a tall statue of the town's Civil War hero and his shadow angled across to give us a little shade. We asked the

A Southern courthouse.

men if people around here were as afraid of hurricanes from the
Gulf as they were of floods.

"We get hurricanes through here," one answered. "Mighty big
ones too. That's nothing against a flood. You go down along the
river and look at what a flood can do. The country around here
was beat down by mean old Camille and afterwards the river decided to get in the act, Lord a mercy. The water marks were seven
feet high on the buildings."

They were sweating and mopping their brows with handkerchiefs but they made no move to leave. A couple of them invited
us to go for coffee in the air-conditioned comfort of a café, "to get
in out of the hot," and one man offered his theory on why the civil

rights stuff finally calmed down back then. "It was air-conditioning," he said. "No telling how long that mess would have gone on if we hadn't all started getting air-conditioning. Everybody got comfortable and cooled off."

These men spoke with the slow resolve of their fathers and grandfathers and their voices, accented with the lyric Mississippi, sounded like old-time music.

Right outside Port Gibson the highway leads you directly to the famous Natchez Trace. For hundreds of years it was a series of Indian trails, and when it was cut and bedded as a road in the early 1800s it saw a host of travelers, haulers, bandits and cut-throats. It was never wider than a sidewalk and impassable in bad

The original Natchez Trace.

A comfort inn on the Natchez Trace.

weather, yet it was the wonder of the age—before the steamboat era made it a mere novelty.

The smooth blacktopped Trace now winds around and down through a thick forest where tree branches close in over you and make you think you're driving through an evergreen tunnel. The Trace extends 450 miles from Natchez to Nashville, and scattered up the trail are comfort stations or "inns" where travelers once stopped for the night.

We stopped at one of those inns and saw what the early Trace travelers had seen: a scrubby outpost, a farmhouse of log and mud mortar set down on the edge of a wilderness where strangers pulled in to rest and often to beg for food. The inns have been carefully preserved but they project the joyless nature of frontier life. One of the truly sad tales of the Trace was of Meriwether Lewis, leader of the expedition that mapped the boundaries of America. Lewis died in 1809 at a remote inn up in Tennessee. It had been just three years since Lewis and Clark had returned as heroes of the greatest American expedition, and Lewis was serving as Jefferson's appointed governor of the new Louisiana, with his headquarters in New Orleans. The histories of the era say that Lewis was distressed over the complex tasks of governing the godforsaken land of swamps, pestilence and backstabbers. He left his offices in the old Spanish Cabildo in the French Quarter to travel up the Trace; he was on his way to the national capital, and perhaps he was going to ask Jefferson to relieve him of his duties. He never made it to Nashville; he was found dead at one of these inns. The circumstances remain vague; all the histories say he either died by his own hand or was murdered by bandits. He was only thirty-five.

The Natchez Trace is a peaceful ride; it's two-lane smooth asphalt and a watchful park ranger makes you hold to fifty miles an hour. It's so quiet on the Trace that a troubled mind like Lewis's could find the setting mesmerizing, or oppressive.

At the end of the Trace, just before the state park becomes Mississippi again, rises Emerald Mound, the last and greatest of the man-made tribal mounds along the river. It was built by the Natchez tribe, perhaps as many as five thousand years ago, and is still by far the most impressive of all the works of man, regardless of color, on the river. For our money, it beats the Gateway Arch all hollow. Emerald Mound overshadows the more noted Cahokia Mounds opposite St. Louis; it is higher and more substantial than any we had seen all the way down the river. Yet no big deal is made of Emerald Mound, no deal at all.

Cahokia attracts big crowds; tens of thousands queue up for guided tours; but here we were the only ones around. There are no attendants, no guides, just a metal-lidded box to hold a fact sheet; the box was empty when we came by. Emerald Mound appears to get only an idle passerby. You can walk all over the mound; footpaths lead up and over the crown. As we stood on its various tiers, higher and higher over the lowlands, we could visualize the times when the Natchez tribesmen huddled up here on the protective heights in sight of the flooding river.

The southern end of the Trace begins on the outskirts of the old territorial capital of Washington, Mississippi. Many eminent people passed this way, presidents-to-be, empire builders, charlatans, rubberneckers. When the steamboats got onto the river for good in the 1820s, the Mississippi began to attract the curious from Europe and America's East. Twain mentions these travelers in *Life on the Mississippi,* singling out the Britons Mrs. Trollope and Captain Basil Hall for their negative views on the emerging American nation, but also for their appreciation and awe of the river. Twain either overlooked or was not aware of two of the more noteworthy river travelers whose books made a strong contribution to the recorded history of the Mississippi. They were Edward King and his *The Great South,* published after the Civil War, and Frederick Law Olmsted and his 1861 *The Cotton Kingdom.*

King was traveling and writing pieces for the old *Scribner's Monthly.* While in New Orleans he met the writer George Washington Cable and was responsible for getting Cable's first works published. Olmsted's book remained obscure for many years but has come to be recognized as an important source book on the nineteenth-century American frontier. Both King and Olmsted found a rough, vulgar way of life on the river and especially here at Washington, though both often enjoyed the friendliness and open hospitality of the people on homesteads. "Step up, stranger, and take some fry," one homesteader greeted Olmsted, and offered a pull on the jug before breakfast. A rigid abolitionist, Olmsted was startled at the manner by which cotton was loaded on steamboats from towns perched on bluffs. He watched as giant bales were heaved down steep ramps and bounced onto the decks of the boats, where Irish laborers caught them and manhandled them into place. What surprised Olmsted was that the bales had been pushed off the bluff by black slaves, while the dirty work fell to the despised Irish immigrants. The explanation he received from the captain of the ship was, "The niggers are worth too much to be risked here; if the paddies are knocked overboard, or get their backs broke, nobody loses anything." After his Mississippi sojourn, King traveled and lived mostly in France; Olmsted went on to become a well-known landscape architect and later, with Calvert Vaux, designed and built Central Park in New York City.

In *The Cotton Kingdom* Olmsted gave his impression of the river as he stood on the bluff at Natchez, and the passage bears quoting: "Through the otherwise unbroken forest, the Father of Waters had opened a passage for himself. Overlooked from such an eminence, the size of the Mississippi can be realized . . . though the fret of a swelling torrent is not wanting, it is perceptible only as the most delicate chasing upon the broad, gleaming expanse of polished steel, which at once shamed all my previous conceptions of the appearance of the greatest of rivers."

At Old Washington we felt we were passing through yet another gateway. A change had come over the pitch of the land and even the curve of the sky. The river was just there, we could feel it, and Natchez-Under-the-Hill was around the next bend. You can feel a different tempo here, a kind of syncopation in the land of dreams.

Our old land-yacht took to Natchez. After the byways and bumpy side trips we'd been on, the car cruised the wide boulevard into Natchez as though it were taking us to a cotillion. It's a storied old river town but it doesn't look or feel like Vicksburg or even Biloxi. Natchez has an abundance of preserved antebellum houses, and that's where all the sightseers were as we rolled through the designated tour. Seeing the splendor of the Old South on display, we didn't doubt that this was a Whig stronghold before the Civil War— and Natchez had given up without much more than a skirmish when the Grant river siege reached here.

Natchez has always been two places, two mind-sets. There was upper Natchez on the hill, with its rich society of cotillions and garden clubs and riding to hounds. Under-the-Hill remained for more than a century a lair for thieves, gamblers, prostitutes and murderers. It is said that during that era, Under-the-Hill was the easiest place in the country to kill someone without fear of punishment.

You get down the hill by very steep streets, and once on the riverfront you drive slowly past nice restaurants, shops and a scenic walk. The garden-clubbers are still up there, make no mistake, and it's this seedy region they abhor, not because it's been slicked up and made to look presentable, but because of what's coming here shortly. In a last stand to save the old order of Natchez, the garden-clubbers fought the supporters of legalized showboat casinos in something of a pitched battle—at the ballot box. They lost. In a local-option election, the city voted to permit the operation of casino boats at the port here.

Businesspeople we talked to along the river mostly agreed that of all the desperate ports along the Mississippi, Natchez may have the best chance of reviving its economy by bringing back the glory days of the steamboat gamblers. "Natchez draws a great many tourists," a financier in Memphis said, "and that's because the people come to stay more than a day. They tour Natchez and the Gulf before they go to New Orleans, and if Natchez plays its cards right, it will attract far more people eventually than the riverboats up-river."

A visitor can take an excursion boat out of Natchez, and we went aboard for a spin, thinking we might capture the feel of the old steamboat days out on these historic waters. Back in 1808, as many as 150 keelboats and flatboats were at port on an average day. Most of the keelboats made a one-way trip and were busted up and used for lumber once they reached New Orleans, but not all were disposed of. According to several sources we came across, some of the keelboats stayed right here in Natchez to become stationary brothels. The prostitutes operated out of the small cargo cubicles, some right on deck with a tarp for cover in bad weather.

The captain of our excursion boat was a young man and he kept up a practiced patter, telling of historical events and even quoting Mark Twain. He could have told more, of course. Steamboats used to pull out of Natchez and make a "hog boat" run up to Memphis and beyond. A hog boat was a floating brothel loaded with prostitutes who practiced their trade in any sizable port, especially during the harvest season when the farmers had money in their pockets. A common call in ports up the way was, "Hog boat a-coming!"

We talked to some of the staff on the excursion boat about the coming revival of gambling here, and they were enthusiastic about it, not for the gambling but for the opportunity to get better jobs at higher wages. "It'd be exciting having it like it was back then, though," one young woman said. "It must have been something special, right?"

Back on shore, we looked out at the river again. It's extremely wide at Natchez and the barges coming along were having to plow deep to make the angling bend in the channel. It was precisely at this spot that Aaron Burr, still sitting as vice president of the country, was caught in the act of his conspiracy to set up an empire for himself on the whole lower basin of the Mississippi.

Where we were standing, Burr had stood and watched his dream of empire being washed down the river, and in a sense what he was after was the river itself, its power and potential. Was the river so mighty that it could inspire a man to delusions of grandeur? Well, the answer is yes, and yet the river was an embattled old thing here before our eyes. Another barge was pushing downriver as we tarried, and we could see another tugging along under the high bridge just at the bluff end of Natchez. Over there across the bridge in the town of Ferriday, Louisiana, we knew of another figure who had inspired poems and literature in his own right. Jerry Lee Lewis, the Killer, had grown up in Ferriday, and you just know that at one time a whole lot of shaking was going on here on the river.

We went back to Natchez Under-the-Hill and started looking around for Nellie's or the ashes of her old pleasure house. Summer was coming and a festival atmosphere had hold of the town, though the rains were starting to set in. We inquired about Nellie's of several people; they knew about the place, everybody in Natchez did, but no one seemed to know where it had been, or at least they wouldn't admit to it. Then we found a young black man, a porter in a big downtown hotel, who knew about Nellie's.

"You're too late," he said. "It's already gone."

We told him we just wanted to see where the famous place was and maybe try to imagine what it looked like. He nodded knowingly. He was as considerate as though he were telling us the directions to the parade of antebellum homes. It turned out he knew Nellie, "Not on a first-name basis, you understand. You couldn't keep from knowing Nellie; she didn't get out much in public but her place was still going strong as of November 1990. Nellie was hanging in," he said. "I believe she was near eighty but those that went around her place said she looked a lot younger and as good as some of the gals. It was a white guy the one started the fire. It wasn't any accident, either. He'd been there that night and musta got in a fuss with some of them at Nellie's. The talk was that he was bad messed up, I don't know, drugs maybe, don't know. He just went crazy and come back and set a fire. Go on see where the house was but there's not nothing left. Nellie's gone like it wasn't even there."

Well, we'd missed one of the legends of the river. We mixed in with other travelers for a time and picked up the well-tuned drawl of Mississippi and Louisiana natives; we wouldn't be getting the savor of Acadia until we were well on down the river, but we did pick up on another touch of tradition in Mississippi, an oral-history anecdote that has become legend hereabouts:

A gent with pretensions of being to the manner born, but without the pedigree, had tried for years to achieve elected office. Finally, well into his sixties, he managed the slot of justice of the peace. He set up offices and waited for his first case. A deputy sheriff brought in a middle-aged black man on the misdemeanor charge of jaywalking, and presented the evidence to the judge. The J.P. sat back and reflected for a moment and then in a deep baritone intoned his sentence. "I hereby condemn you to be hanged by the neck until you are dead."

The wide-eyed deputy coughed and sputtered. "Judge, you can't do that."

"Well, all right then, I sentence him to life in prison at Parchman without parole."

"Uh, judge, your honor, you can't do that either."

"And just why the hell not?"

"You don't have the authority, your honor. You can't sentence this man to one day in jail."

"I can't? Well, then, by God, I resign."

CHAPTER 21

Of Prisons, Floods and Sidewinder Bulls

"See that building over there? See that watermark? Water rose seven, eight feet deep right where we're standing."

—*An old-time riverman at Fort Adams, Mississippi*

From Natchez the great river road can't follow the river because of the rough country along the embayment; Old 61 swings east a few miles into what is called Piney Woods country. It has a rugged, frontier look about it still and the people are not like those of the northern part of the state; they're more like hillfolk, grainy and set in their attitudes and just a little bit suspicious of new faces. The talk is as slow as the pace. Once they've decided you're all right, they let you in on what they're thinking.

"We're just piney woods down here," a pulpwood truck driver told us at the little town of Sibley, Mississippi. "They come down here and go hunting and fishing but they don't know who we are."

We drove along the border of the big Homochitto National Forest, which is full of prime timber and deer and some free-flowing fishing streams, with the old Indian river, the Homochitto, coursing through it before it runs down to join the Mississippi at Old River Lake. The state of Mississippi doesn't have the problem of waste runoff that its neighboring states do; Mississippi just doesn't have much industry to create the waste. It does have some here and there, and we came across a sample down the road a ways.

Old 61 led down to the town of Woodville, a place of a few thousand people with the obligatory fast-food places and branch banks. Out east of Woodville about half an hour on a state road, you come to the smaller town of Centerville. They've got industry here, a rubber company that employs some of the local people and adds a little to the Centerville economy. They've also got a hideous waste disposal problem. For years the rubber company has pumped a thick sludge from its plant out into a kind of swamp. We found the site easily and stopped to look at the mess. It was the blackest lake we'd ever seen, full of slime and gunk that kept bubbling and gurgling. Back in town, we asked about the "lake" and a fellow at a service station said, "Oh, you mean the Valley of the Blobs. That's what people call it around here. Ain't it something."

Coming back toward Woodville through the dense timber country, we dodged in and around a steady caravan of pulpwood haulers. Mississippi may not have a big problem with industrial waste, but paper companies are known to be the biggest cause of acid rain, and all this pine timber being cut and hauled was headed for the processing plants.

In talking to people down here, we found that the prevalent attitude is one of resentment; maybe that's built into the Southern way of thinking. "We've done things this way for years and we've got by, but now you're coming in and telling us we've got to change our ways," a county official told us. Often the reaction takes the form of open, predictable defiance. A few years ago a farmer on the delta used a banned poison on his fields, was caught doing it and was fined $50,000. He was bitter about the matter because he was using a chemical he had been permitted to use in the past. The Southern attitude toward environmental fines is an echo of the siege mentality prevalent since the days of Reconstruction.

In connection with this attitude, some good-old-boyism is still at work in states like Arkansas, Mississippi and Louisiana. A common practice in these states is to reduce fines levied on guilty polluters and to accept "in-kind" services as payment. Typically, the offenders are caught using banned substances or burning hazardous wastes. The states lose almost all the assessed penalties, which run into the hundreds of thousands of dollars, because they are not able to make use of the "in-kind" services. And the states' pollution control agencies are thwarted by big businesses with political connections—they cannot refuse the "in-kind" payment even though they can't make use of the services in any way.

We passed a lot of good old boys driving their pulpwood trucks as we came back to Old 61. We got used to the custom of lifting one finger off the steering wheel to recognize the driver of a passing vehicle; it's a way of saying, "Hidee, you're all right, I accept you, you're a good old boy." Once you get them to lift the one finger, you start feeling more at home.

We pulled in at a truck stop at a junction of Highway 61 and asked how to get over to the river. We met a good-natured man, talkative as a carnival barker. "Y'all know anything about sidewinder bulls?" he started in. He was driving a cattle truck loaded with twenty or thirty heifers and the way he had been striding around his rig, we could tell he was very proud of his livestock. "The damnedest thing you ever saw, them sidewinder bulls." He told us he was on his way to Fort Worth, Texas, to get this truckload of young cows inseminated with serum from the new sidewinder bulls.

The man's name was Gene and he was on his way up to Vicksburg to catch an interstate across to Texas. The sidewinder bull was a revolutionary concept in breeding and Gene was convinced it was about to change everything in the beef business.

"I've seen these bulls," he said. "They have their dicks coming out the side of their belly. Them DNA doctors operate on the bulls when they are little and reroute the dick so it sticks out the side. Makes it easy to milk the serum. See, a bull weighs close to two thousand pounds when he's full-growed and it could do a lot of damage trying to mount these little heifers here. Hey, when these bulls take a piss, the stream comes right out the side."

Standing there beside the highway with a light rain falling, we got an education on the sidewinder bull industry. It's a big thing over in Texas; the breeding farm, Gene said, is owned by a big national manufacturing company out of Fort Worth. One sidewinder bull is worth $50,000. "Them guys are into that stuff heavy and that's where I'm headed. One of them doctors over there told me they could give you a bull with one blue eye and one green eye. Give 'em another year or two and they'll be putting a mule's head on a bull. It's all like tenderloin on the hoof."

Before he took off up Highway 61, Gene climbed into his cattle truck and moved some of the heifers around just right. They were healthy girls, a little sassy with him, and you'd swear he was making this long trip to Texas to spare them the weight of a clumsy bull.

To get to the river from Woodville we stayed on the same state

A 275-year-old church, Fort Adams, Mississippi.

road and drove about twenty-five miles through the forest. It is rugged land but cleanly kept; we passed houses and double-wides and occasionally saw in a clearing an oil well with cricket pump moving ever so slowly. Mississippi didn't get in on the oil boom the way Texas and Louisiana did; here, it's timber.

The state road descends through woods darker than those along Natchez Trace. As we neared the river we began to wonder if historic old Fort Adams existed now. Then we came to a small Catholic church and a meager settlement. A sign at the church told that this was the site of an original mission founded 275 years ago. We'd found Fort Adams.

Fort Adams was one of the first posts on the Mississippi; the Spanish had placed it here in the eighteenth century, had given it up to the French, and the new Americans had inherited it with the Louisiana Purchase. It used to sit right on the river but now the channel was nearly a mile away. We stopped and looked around at what was left of Fort Adams.

Nothing was left except two country stores and a couple of hunt-

Riverman, 80 years on the Mississippi.

ing lodges. Inside the store we found Mr. Bill Martin, a man in his eighties but with a young memory. He spoke in a clear but slow downriver drawl and shared with us some of his experiences.

Bill Martin had lived all his life on the river. He was born and raised in Louisiana but as a young man in 1927 he had come up the river to help in the time of the great flood. And he had stayed. For many years he and his wife, Myrtis, ran the Fort Adams post office and the store. There's no post office at Fort Adams now, so it's not recognized as a town.

"Fort Adams used to be a big place," Bill Martin said. "Back in 1918, 1920. The town had lots of good stores and streets and pretty houses. Had ten saloons at one time and a funeral parlor that got lots of business. There was some pride in the place then. Had a mayor and a fire department. It was just a regular good town on the river."

Bill Martin talked about the flood of 1927. He had got a job working for the Red Cross rescuing people and livestock. "We rounded up a boatload of cattle and people and took them to high ground, and came back for more. Went on all summer and no telling how many people and cattle we pulled out of the flood. There wasn't a channel in the river at all, just a sea as far as the eye could go."

He told of thousands of head of livestock lost in the water. "They'd come floating in a herd, some dead and some still alive. And people too. I couldn't count the number of dead bodies I saw floating down the river."

After the floodwaters receded, he got jobs on big riverboats, and he stayed with that until his retirement years. He had worked on packets hauling freight from Memphis to New Orleans, and he said he made the run so many times that he had the river memorized. "If you let it the river will show you what it's gone do ... if it's gone run dry or if it's gone change its course or if it's gone flood over the levee." He remembered some of the boats he served on, the *Memphis* and the *Tennessee Belle*. All were stern-wheelers; they carried cotton and cattle and grain. It was a good life for him, he said, and we could tell it was true by listening.

Floods helped to kill off Fort Adams. The river has been gradually moving west, though the banks used to stand by the old fort. "Water used to roll right through here," Bill Martin said. "See that building over there? See that watermark? Water rose seven, eight feet deep right where we're standing." People around here are used to high water, he told us; they ride it out. "If you know the river, you can tell when there's gone be another flood. And there may be. Bigger than twenty-seven."

Bill Martin doesn't fear a flood if it comes. He says he'll be out there on the river doing what he did back in 1927. The only thing he seems resentful of is the loss of the small post office at Fort Adams. The post office burned down a few years ago and the government never bothered to replace it. Bill is suspicious that some underhanded dealings went on in the burning. "They burned it down on purpose," he claimed. "I know that. Somebody wanted it gone because they didn't care about the town. So it's not a town now, just a place that once was famous and has now been neglected and forgotten."

Truckloads of people come through Fort Adams during the hunting season, he said. "They have their lodge over there across the road, see? People come to fish in the summer too, and when the deer season is on. It's not a town, just a place to stop and hunt."

We left Bill Martin standing on the front porch of his store in old Fort Adams. He was holding out but after him the town would disappear even before the river got it. We drove the extra mile through the bottoms to the river; there was no levee to stop the water here, and we could see across to a treeline and lake on the Louisiana side. The river was doing what it always does; it was eating its way toward Fort Adams.

A young black man wearing a security guard's uniform had come into the store while we were talking to Bill Martin. When the young man found that we wanted to look at nearby Angola prison, he told us of a shortcut.

By a logging road you pass the state line into Louisiana without knowing it and begin traveling on the upper boundary of the prison farms. We came through what was once known as Pinckneyville, named after Charles Cotesworth Pinckney. The town is gone except for a few deserted shacks and old frames. Pinckney was the man responsible for making the treaty setting the thirty-first parallel, thus defining the lower boundaries of the Louisiana Territory; he also had presidential aspirations at one time and some thought he was assured of the high office, but all he got was this tiny river town named after him, and its only distinction now is that it forms the northern edge of infamous Angola.

Angola. It's a huge place and not one prison but a series of farms spread over thirty-two thousand acres that back up to the Mississippi just as the Red River comes in. We had driven around the Tunica Hills and they are, local people attest, as rough a country as exists in the South. The river and the hills hold Angola in so that any thought of escape is pointless. From the periphery the main prison compound looks well-kept, modernized; white fences border the grounds and flower gardens and green landscaping greets any visitors from the free world. A huge lake sits in the middle of the prison, though we didn't see any boating or fishing going on. One of the guards told us that the children and families of the staff sometimes take boats out.

Conditions have changed some since the bad old days of Angola when it was unsurpassed for institutionalized brutality. Here

Brueghel's grotesque visions of hell and damnation were brought to life. One former inmate compared Angola to the infamous LBJ (Long Binh Jail) in Vietnam—military brutality there reached such levels that a congressional investigation was conducted. Angola has had precious few investigations in its dark history, though the State of Louisiana has taken one or two steps in the right direction.

We talked to a man who comes to Angola once a week to hear inmates' complaints and generally keep his eye on their treatment. He's an appointed magistrate with offices in Baton Rouge; his position is nonpolitical. He makes the arduous drive from Baton Rouge weekly and has been doing it for more than two years, so he's had time to learn what's really going on inside. He assured us that the days of the bullwhip and the electric telephone torture chambers of the past have ended.

"Not that Angola is much easier," the magistrate said. "It's still a maximum-security prison farm and the inmates work long hours at backbreaking labor under the close watch of mounted guards carrying shotguns."

While we were stopped for identification in front of the main compound, we watched a detail of about thirty inmates with machetes and scythes at work clearing a ditch of bramble and briers. Another detail was at work around the main building weeding the flower beds. It was a rainy, muggy, buggy day. Another guard we spoke to said the biggest problem was with mosquitoes. "The inmates learn to work fast enough to keep the mosquitoes from lighting on them."

By federal decree, the old "trusty" system of using prisoners as armed guards has been abolished here, as well as at Parchman in Mississippi and at Cummins in Arkansas. Atrocities in the trusty system were the rule in Southern prisons; the prisons literally became the province of the tough, brutal inmates in partnership with their wardens.

We talked to a man who had served a nineteen-year sentence in the prison and he told us of the numerous times he had been beaten with a bullwhip, "sometimes for not working fast enough or just because the captain liked to use the whip. I saw them kill men, beat them to death, and then put it down as heatstroke."

Angola keeps five thousand prisoners and they all live and work in camps spread out over an area the size of a large city. The camps used to be segregated by race but that's been stopped. The magistrate told us that the prison pays only lip service to vocational retraining, though there's not much call for a machete mechanic in the free world. The prison provides a school for those who want to work on finishing their high school credits. On average, the magistrate said, the prison population has about a sixth-grade education. Of those who finish their time and are set free, about 60 percent will wind up back in prison.

"It's an expensive proposition. It's like the state is paying a full scholarship to college for every inmate at Angola, but every state's in the same situation." The magistrate said he didn't want to sound like an Angola advocate because it's a hard place and depressing. "It is better now. It's a little more civilized."

He said the complaints he hears from inmates are concerned mostly with living conditions, the lack of air-conditioning, the food, things of that nature. "If brutality goes on, it's certainly not out in the open as it used to be. But it'll always be a hard, mean place."

Louisiana's death row is at Angola. In the spring of 1991 the state held its first execution in many years. Other Southern states, led by Florida, have begun putting inmates to death once more. Louisiana has a sizable backlog, so the population of Angola's death row will soon dwindle. We didn't tour death row this time, but we had done it in the past. Those who wait have a few special privileges, color TV and private toilets and guitars to strum away the hours. Before the executions started up again, the room that held the electric chair was used as the prison chapel.

The magistrate did speak with pride about one aspect of life at Angola. The prison's magazine, the *Ango-Light*, has won national awards for being the best prison publication in the country. "The writing is quite good," he said. "Each issue is eagerly awaited by the whole prison population. Angola has many stories to tell and there are some talented writers here."

Indeed there have been talented men here. A well-known country music star served seven years at Angola before going on to fame. And one of the country's top rodeo stars served several years before he was cleared of his crime and set free. But Angola's most famous prisoner was a singer named Huddie Ledbetter, better known as Leadbelly. In the 1930s Ledbetter was serving a life sentence for murder and was the lead man on a chain gang when the folklorists John and Alan Lomax found him and listened to him singing his songs to the other prisoners. Some of those songs were "Good Night, Irene," and "Midnight Special" and "Rock Island Line." The Lomaxes worked to get Leadbelly a pardon and took him to New York, where he became a recording star and the darling of café society.

Inside the main compound at Angola are ball fields and basketball courts, but the passion here is for rodeoing. Every October the prison stages its own big rodeo and an overflow crowd from the outside world turns out for it—it's about the biggest happening in these parts besides a flood. The prison band entertains and the events are as heatedly contested as the championships in Madison Square Garden.

We weren't at Angola this time for the rodeo but a few years ago we attended with friends. The inmate announcer stole the show: "Coming out of the chute is Skeeter Hale, doing two hundred twenty-five years on twenty-one counts of burglary and grand larceny, riding Old Dynamite . . . give that cowboy a good hand! Next out is Sonny Boy Bertucci, doing a hundred sixty years for ten counts of assault with a deadly, riding Widow Maker . . . how about that Sonny Boy!" A special event is the bull-wrestling competition. They tape fifty-dollar bills to the bull's horns and the convict-cowboys try to get the bills off the horns without being gored. Some got cut up pretty good but they never quit trying, and the tradition here is that they always get the money. The Angola cowboys perform almost superhuman feats; the grandstands are filled with pretty girls from outside. There's an expression down South, "as nervous as a virgin at a prison rodeo," and after watching these men throw themselves on a two-thousand-pound bull charging at them, you understand where the expression originated.

We had been looking around Angola in a misty rain, but now a hot sun was coming out again, and before we pulled out we saw the machete detail back out along the ditch. Rain is a happy time at Angola because the men can't work in the muddy fields, at least not as hard. With the sun came the punishing humidity and the mosquitoes. As we glided along in our air-conditioned land-yacht, we were both humming a little Leadbelly. Sometimes you can't keep from singing. "Sometimes I live in the country, sometimes I live in town . . . sometimes I take a great notion to jump into the river and drown."

CHAPTER 22

Old River

"One who knows the Mississippi will promptly aver—not aloud, but to himself—that ten thousand River Commissions cannot tame that lawless stream, cannot curve it, or confine it, cannot say to it, Go here, or Go there, and make it obey."

—*From* Life on the Mississippi

If you're coming down the east bank of the river, you'll miss the Old River Project, and if you want to see this critical juncture of the Mississippi, you'll have to double back and come up the west bank some miles. The confluence of the Red River is at the Old River Project too, so we took the extra trouble.

We hadn't seen a dam on the river since above St. Louis, but we found what surely looked like one across the river at Old River. As we drove along the complex of locks and power plants of the Corps of Engineers' project here, we thought we had simply entered another recreational area. The Red River was lost somewhere in the tangle of concrete viaducts and reroutings. We had to ask a Corps ranger what river we were looking at, and he said, "The Atchafalaya." We'd almost forgot that old Cajun river, and it's easy to lose track in this expansive project.

Coming down the river in 1882, Twain saw the evidence of man's attempt to tame the Mississippi. He noticed the lights that had been installed here and there and thought they were a marvel, but when he noticed the other man-made changes, he grew somber in his prose, perhaps dismayed. To one who had piloted the river for years, the jetties, dams, dikes and wing canals would be monuments to man's folly.

The Old River Project fifty miles above Baton Rouge is modern man's attempt to finally conquer the river. At one place the water was surging against the levee and at another place a canal was almost bone-dry. We talked to a secretary in the Corps' main office who turned out to be very knowledgeable about the internal workings of the project. "Everything from here on down the river depends on this project," she said. "The farmers and the fishermen and the towns have to have the river's water to survive."

What she didn't say, though, was that maybe the Corps was trying to serve too many masters here. A lot of crawfish boats work the Atchafalaya River and if the dam here doesn't control the water level, the fishing industry collapses. Towns down the river depend on the Mississippi for drinking water, and they require a steady flow or they will start coming up short. Yet if the dam lets too much water through, the river may suddenly swell and flood. In short, everything here hinges upon the Corps of Engineers and its ability to make the project keep working. Civilian hydrologists have been warning for years that the Old River Project won't hold—that an inevitable break and flood will come to wipe out lower Louisiana.

The problems at the Old River Project actually begin back up the river at the major confluences—the Missouri, Ohio, Arkansas and Red rivers. In the past the Corps undoubtedly has been guilty of being overzealous with its damage control projects. After 1927 when the Corps began constructing thousands of miles of new concrete and earthen levees, it got carried away and sealed off the potential floodwaters of some tributaries; when the water rose and the floods came, there was no place for the water to go except to thoroughly flood the lands behind the Corps' array of locks, dams and levees protecting the Mississippi. The Corps had to come in and install pumping stations to drain the newly formed lakes; huge pipes funneled the waters from the land side of the levees into the Mississippi, bypassing the dams.

The Mississippi has seen major floods in 1927, 1937 and 1948, with fair-to-middling "minor" floods in between. After the 1948 flood the Corps decided to make a major assault on the river: it constructed a massive "emergency spillway" using the nearly placid little Atchafalaya River as a conduit for floodwaters from both the Mississippi and the Red River. And when the floodwaters came down, the Corps kicked in the spillway. But the Mississippi was no more obliging then than it had been in 1927. Rather than just a portion of the floodwaters going down the spillway, the Mississippi itself changed course completely. The Atchafalaya flooded and left hundreds of miles of concrete levees, put in to control the raging Mississippi, high and dry.

This setback caused the construction of the Old River Project. The Corps is determined to control the river. It's truly ironic that the Corps has built the Project almost exactly on the spot where Captain Henry Miller Shreve tried to change the course of the Mississippi in the 1830s. Shreve had been a worthy pioneer on the river. He had all but invented the steam-powered riverboat, though Nicholas Roosevelt gets proper credit for steaming the river first. Shreve's *Enterprise* was the second steamer to reach New Orleans and the only one that could make it back up the river past Natchez. Shreve had added many innovations—the boilers were above the waterline, as were the passenger cabins and the cargo. Shreve later broke the illegal monopoly that Roosevelt and Fulton had obtained from the City government of New Orleans, thus finally opening the Mississippi for full commerce in the mid-1820s.

Shreve was a master of the river. His riverboat model was copied by all other steamer lines, including Fulton's. Shreve performed an even greater service for steamboat travel; he invented a monstrous-looking snagboat that went up the river and its tributaries clearing the submerged trees, logs and debris that took such a heavy toll on the steamers.

Yet when Shreve tried to change the course of the river by setting crews to digging a canal that would connect loops in the river, he created a devastating flood from here all the way to Baton Rouge.

When we passed through, the land around the Old River Project looked barren, dry, even though there had been rain the past few days. Certainly there were no wetlands in the area, or in the region for that matter. The absence of wetlands came about as a by-product of flood control (as disagreeable and potentially dangerous as it is). What we were about to see next was an intentional act of man, a reprehensible fact of life in corporate Louisiana.

Scattered here and there across the lowland landscape, we saw wells. These were gas wells, but the state of Louisiana has a problem with another kind of well. A total of forty-five hundred wells have been drilled here to dispose of brine wastes from the oil fields. It's been a common practice in Louisiana, Texas and Oklahoma since the days of the wildcatters—they drilled wells right next to the ones that brought up the black gold. The EPA and private environmental groups have tested the water tables in the state and have found seepage from the brine wells; already much of the water table has been spoiled, the agencies say, and the cropland is being ruined.

What's worse, the State of Louisiana has drilled about seventy deep wells to dispose of hazardous wastes. They've been pumping poisoned wastewater as deep as nine thousand feet. Other states refused to adopt this type of disposal after the various state pollution control agents ran tests and found toxins seeping back up; the toxins were found in lakes and streams, and even in drinking water.

We worked our way back toward Highway 61 and came into the pretty town of St. Francisville. Now we were into parishes instead of counties. The Catholic town of St. Francisville was nestled among the hanging gauze of Spanish moss and showed off its remodeled antebellum houses. The old mansions looked different from the ones we'd seen in Natchez, and a local woman told us it was the French Creole influence. We'd be seeing this influence, along with half a dozen other Creole variations, as we passed on down the river.

For fifty cents we took the land-yacht back across the river on a ferry and noticed a distinct change—no antebellum mansions, no Spanish moss dangling like intricate lace. We drove by an Audubon Park that was so misty and green it looked like a jungle, and we stopped in a little town to watch some fellows putting on a hot-tar roof.

We were just standing aside watching and chatting with the foreman of the job; he wanted to know where we'd been and when we told him that among other places we had passed through famous old Angola prison, he said, "Well, you're looking at a bunch of Angola boys up on that roof."

It turns out he'd hired them through a rehabilitation program and they were working as hot-tar roofers, one of the hardest and dirtiest jobs in construction. The smell of the hot pitch was almost unbearable. They were almost down in the stuff and using mops to smooth it. The day was still muggy and when the sun poked out, the humidity became so thick we had to hold our breath at times.

The foreman called them down for a break, telling us, "You can't do this shit more than a few minutes at a time—can't stand the heat off the tar." The Angola boys came bouncing down the ladder, cursing and laughing and slapping the sweat off their foreheads. They were all young, in their twenties, genial but quickly provoked. Their shoes were coated in tar and their faces looked darker than coal miners'. We saw on their arms the homemade tattoos of the "Aryan Brotherhood" with skulls and crossbones. They'd no doubt got the tattoos in prison when they'd joined a club for protection. The foreman said he'd never seen boys eat more cheeseburgers and drink more beer in his life. They all had fat beer bellies and wore jeans that rode way down over their hip bones, and the tar on their flesh made them look like badly made-up natives in a Tarzan movie.

We watched them during their break. They had little-boy attitudes and took delight in taunting each other; we overheard them talking about girls, one who had been "blacktopped" and had clabber between her tits.

"They do a good job for us," the foreman said. "It's not easy to find guys that'll work in tar. Boy, they know how to work. One hell of a job."

As we were leaving we saw the Angola boys still horsing around on their break. They were throwing little jagged pieces of fiberglass at each other's butt-cracks. Their work here was probably harder than what they'd done on the farms of Angola. Somehow we didn't want to sing "Goodnight, Irene" anymore as we drove on.

By the middle of May the lower river basin of Louisiana is a tropical rain forest. Circling on in toward Baton Rouge on back roads, we tuned in the weather station and heard one flash-flood alert after another. The coast was getting its twenty-fifth consecutive day with rain, more than thirty inches of rainfall for the month of May, and almost another week was left on the calendar.

Soaking winds whipped up a gale suddenly. Our old land-yacht had endured the raw bite of Minnesota northers but it couldn't take the Louisiana monsoon; the car began to sputter and cough, then quit on a back road to Baton Rouge. Like one of Faulkner's

Yoknapatawpha mules, it had worked for us nearly ten thousand miles for the privilege of kicking us out in a storm.

We were marooned out in nowhere but we were about to get our first taste of Cajun hospitality. Not five minutes later a car pulled over and a dark-complected man said, "You bought it?" His name was Ramon and he spoke with an unqualified Cajun accent. He was from Baton Rouge, on his way to Jackson, Mississippi, on business and just passing through some old home grounds on back roads he liked to drive. He loaded us into his small car, offered fresh bottled water and coffee; he was listening to classical music on National Public Radio.

"This town here is Amite," he said; he pronounced it "a MEET." "Little place, good people. They will fix you up. You have to break down out in this bad, doggone."

Ramon took us to a service station he knew, a kind of hangout. The station manager was a squat little man, definitely Cajun; he looked like a bandido out of an old Wallace Beery movie and he was very busy; still he took time to call a wrecker for us. Pool shooters congregated in the station; we saw several trophies on the shelf behind the counter, and a poster announcing an upcoming nine-ball tournament. A frail little Cajun man came to talk to us while we waited and we didn't understand a word he said; we could tell he was a pool enthusiast because he kept trying to show us a magazine full of pictures of pool tables.

Our samaritan, Ramon, came in and waited; he leaned sideways toward us and politely translated what the old man was saying: "See this table, hm, to have such a table. That man that called the wrecker for you, he is the champion of these parts but there is a better shooter and he'll be here Friday night—he's been fighting in that Gulf War, you know, and there'll be pool Friday night and you can come see it with me if you want to do such a thing."

Ramon waited until the tow truck arrived; he'd been held up almost an hour but wouldn't leave until he was sure we'd be okay. Thinking of our old general back up in Illinois, we offered to pay Ramon but he shook his head, wouldn't hear of it, and said, "Maybe you'll get a chance to pass it along."

The storm hadn't let up. We rode back to our car in the wrecker; the driver was a black man, quiet and a little shy; he kept looking at the pouring rain and shaking his head. Later we stood out in the storm while he got the old land-yacht hooked up to the wrecker. Some eighteen-wheelers were coming along, drenching us, and we were foolishly standing on the skirt of the blacktop. The driver came around, put his arm around us and pulled us back, shielding us for a minute.

"Better step back," he said. "You have to look out for yourself down here. They don't care about you."

The town of Amite, Louisiana, is a tender place, we thought. At the Chevy dealership in town not one but three mechanics looked at our car. They decided that the land-yacht had an old-fashioned vapor lock; they got us back on the road in less than half an hour. The Chevy dealer himself took the car out for a test run.

"I believe it will run now as far as you want to go," the dealer said. "I don't want you going back on the road worrying. If you have any trouble, just call us and we'll come and get you."

They had towed us in, fussed over the car and tested it out. We were prepared to pay at least $50 for the tow alone, but our total bill came to $15, and the dealer was apologetic about that.

Vegetable farming goes on around Amite. They grow a lot of cucumbers and bell peppers. They say the gumbo is good in this town, and you have to believe the nine-ball shooters can hold their own with any hustler. The town's name, Amite, comes from the French word for friendship, and though these people have their own way of saying it, they take its meaning seriously.

CHAPTER 23

Louisiana Bubble Town

"Every man a king ... For you can be a millionaire."

—*Song by Huey P. Long*

On Old 61 and running with the river again, we entered the last leg of our trip down the river. We were rolling into Baton Rouge. For all practical purposes, this town's founder was John Law, the infamous purveyor of fine blue-chip stocks that weren't worth the few francs it cost to print them up in the thousands. Yet it was Law's stock swindle, the Mississippi Bubble, that tricked gullible Europeans into settling this diseased, godforsaken land. One man's ultimate greed caused generations of heartbreak, and the pattern would be repeated from father to son.

More and more as we drove on, we felt we were entering boundless rain forests. The storm followed us down the drowned highway and what visited our minds was the thought of all those early settlers and the wretched ordeals they went through to hold this land. The rain kept driving down, kept making this green world more lush, and as we moved into it we could almost feel the pulse of the centuries beating out, "Yellow jack, yellow jack."

The first tribes on the lower river had an immunity to the certain death of yellow fever, an immunity that the white settlers and their African slaves would take centuries to acquire. Yellow fever plagues or not, the settlers came, and before it was over this verdant basin would see every race and creed, every walk of life.

We faced some of what those beguiled early settlers found here as we came into the deep-port parishes around Baton Rouge. The drenching winds whipped the land-yacht to and fro and we felt as if we were traveling on the bottom of the river. Baton Rouge, former domain of the Kingfish, Huey Long, is now a tangle of oil refineries. We drove along the river as it runs through the heart of town. Old 61 is by no means the scenic route, but it does give the best perspective. John D. Rockefeller's Standard Oil Company came here in 1909 after the big gusher blew in over at Spindletop in Texas, and though the Texas Railroad Commission kicked Rockefeller out of that state, Louisiana took him in. As you drive along, it's easy enough to see that Exxon owns the better part of this town of the Red Stick.

The Exxon refinery covers block after block and mile after mile along the river at Baton Rouge. We came along at twilight and colossal Exxon was lit up like a million Christmas trees, with all yellow lights. The town may be named Red Stick but its true color is dizzying yellow. We pulled off and looked at the city but the yellow smog of Exxon's emissions was so thick and biting we could barely make out the farcical skyscraper that is Louisiana's state capitol. Walking around in the evening, you find it a labor to breathe; traffic is atrocious and thickens the soupy smog.

We saw no testaments in Baton Rouge to the work of John Law; people here have never heard of the guy. But if Louisiana was settled mostly as the result of a confidence game, the con is still on. Baton Rouge likes to think of itself as a sophisticated city: it's the state capital and has all this megatechnological industry with high-salaried management and lots of jobs; it's also got the intellectual community at Louisiana State University. Yet it's a town that gives the real impression of a place on the make and take. The influence of Huey Long and the Long clans is still in evidence here, for no matter where you are in Baton Rouge you can't escape the sight of the capitol rising to the heavens like a Babylonian tower. The Kingfish also built the lower bridge in Baton Rouge as his own personal vendetta against elitist New Orleans—he didn't want anything to get past Baton Rouge on the river. Huey wrote a song, "Every Man a King," and had it sung to the yahoos and rednecks on the campaign trail; the song is still popular in Louisiana, though they're singing some new verses along the chemical corridor. Some revisionist historians like to speak of Long as a populist and even a socialist, though he was neither. He worked in the same tradition of the good-old-boy brotherhood dating back through the Faubuses, Bilbos and Wallaces all the way to Andrew Jackson. Coming into Baton Rouge, we saw VOTE FOR DUKE signs nailed up everywhere. Louisiana people, especially third- or fourth-generation ones, have come to accept political corruption as part of Louisiana's charm and heritage. It sells to the waves of tourists. Duke was defeated in his bid for the state house of Louisiana but has since turned his sight on the national scene as a George Wallace-type clone.

Elected officials in Louisiana openly admit that the state has made a deal with the devil in exchange for the oil and chemical companies. Nobody has put forth a plan to break the devil's contract. The legislators won't regulate and the people won't vote in enough numbers to even hint of change over the horizon. The current malaise probably got its impetus way back in the fifties when the Tidelands Oil giveaway was made, ensuring Eisenhower's election and giving Louisiana and Texas all the offshore oil. In the offshore bonanza, Eisenhower forfeited national interests to the interests of the major oil companies. Once that deal was struck, the chemical corridor was inevitable.

Mark Twain once wrote about a town like Baton Rouge in a story titled *The Man That Corrupted Hadleyburg.* In the story the town's leaders sell their souls to the devil and are made to change the town's motto to read: "Lead Us Into Temptation." Some time back Baton Rouge and Louisiana hung out the same banner, and if you look close you can still see it. It's faded, greasy and about to rot and blow away in the poisoned wind.

At the top of the river we had gone onto the University of Minnesota campus to chat with students, and here in Baton Rouge we swung down onto the campus of LSU. The spring term was over and most of the students had left. Those we spoke with were going home for the summer or were looking for jobs in Baton Rouge. Their prospects weren't bright, they said, and it looked like "Fast Food City" again. They told us that the big oil and chemical companies didn't like to hire students that much. "They don't want educated people ... they want a mindless mob." The students all spoke with slow Southern accents; most were from around Louisiana.

LSU has a beautiful campus, one of the prettiest in the South, and the Old Creole influence shows itself in the architecture. We saw several funky bumper stickers that said, GEAUX TIGERS. We met a group of students outside the Student Union, relaxing and playing with Frisbees in the misty rain. We asked them what they thought of David Duke, the KKK politician. They just laughed and said, "Only in Louisiana." They did think the chemical corridor was "deplorable" and "unforgivable." One young woman, a graduate student, said, "They should just close them all down and move them back up North where they came from."

Baton Rouge divides itself culturally at the river. The town has the basic nightlife, with singles' watering holes and sports bars. Popular, too, are ritzy country kicker places heavy on the two-step and cottoneyed joe. Seafood restaurants abound and are packed on nights when you can eat all the crawfish you want for a bargain price. Baton Rouge has its own version of New Orleans's Garden District, where the old landed gentry hangs onto its roots. The Cajun section of town is across the river on the west bank, and it is there that you find dark-haired, dark-skinned people speaking with French accents. The nightspots seem livelier and are full of Cajun dancing and singing; it's not pretentiousness when the waitresses call you "cher" and want you to have a good time. One of the best shows in Baton Rouge is the annual parade of the Lawnmower Brigade. All the guys who spend their summers sweating in the subtropical heat and humidity, keeping the town's lawns tidy, get their chance to strut down the streets, and the town turns out.

We went to the suburbs of west Baton Rouge and visited with a lady named Vera Strickland. We'd met her up at tiny Fort Adams in Mississippi at her Uncle Bill Martin's store. She had been helping out, she said, though she lived in retirement here. "West Baton Rouge is the only place to live," she said with a sparkling smile. "All the good folks of Baton Rouge live here." Vera is a very bright, deliberate person; before retiring she had done missionary work in the prison at Jefferson City, Missouri, and she was still active in her church work.

"Baton Rouge is my home," she said. "I couldn't think of living

anywhere else. The cancer corridor starts right here in this neigh-
borhood. I don't like living on the corridor any better than other
people. That sign that says GATEWAY TO THE CANCER CORRIDOR is
just a couple blocks away. We went in on it and put it up, you
know."

The towns from Baton Rouge to New Orleans use the Mississippi
river for drinking, bathing and cooking. "It's too bad," Vera said.
"A lot of people get bottled water, have it delivered, but that can
get expensive for people on fixed incomes. Most people just can't
afford it, so they use what the city provides, running water. People
have to have water."

From the top of the river on down, we had been in areas of high
environmental risk, and in a sense the story of the chemical corridor was no different from the story of Sauget or Paducah or
Grand Gulf. With people who have to live at risk, a psychological
numbness has set in; there is about these people an uneasy willingness to let anything happen. We spoke with a young woman, a
former secretary for one of the major chemical companies, who
talked candidly about what it had been like to live on the inside
of the corridor.

Her name is Angel (pronounced "Ahn-JELL") and she worked
in the head office in downtown Baton Rouge. Angel is in her early
thirties, married and the mother of three children. She has raven-
black hair, is petite and very proud of her French blood. She had
worked for the chemical company for several years and knew as
much about the internal affairs of the business as most executive
officers.

"I worked for a *Fortune* Five Hundred company," Angel said.
"You know how they got to be a *Fortune* Five Hundred? They pay
their employees less. We're good slaves. They hire you if they think
you'll make a good slave. Maybe you've never heard this expression, but it's called the golden glove policy. They handle you with
golden gloves and you belong to them—if you stay for long. They
pay just enough to keep you from hunting a job somewhere else.
They've got you trapped. You can't afford to quit, and it's true with
the secretaries right on up to high management. Those guys at the
top know better but they just can't give up the money. They're
squeezed in the golden glove. The company is proud of their

golden glove ... they talk about it all the time, the rule of the golden glove."

Angel told us of the new policy that has come about inside the chemical industry. "They've hired these public relations people to change the image of the chemical companies. They're putting out all this propaganda about how safe they are now. They're putting up big signs and running stuff on TV guaranteeing the people that they are a safe industry and even environmental. They invite you to come and inspect all their new safety features. It's to laugh. They really haven't changed a thing and they won't as long as they're making big profits."

She told of an incident in her company's so-called safety awareness. Back in the 1980s the company had an explosion in its plant in Pasadena, Texas. "It was bad, very bad, with a lot of environmental damage, leakage and runoff. They were using a certain chemical compound they knew was banned. They knew they were supposed to get rid of that stuff, and yet they were still using it and it caused the explosion.

"There came into our office in Baton Rouge a letter from the Pasadena office. The secretary over there had sent it to the wrong place and hadn't even marked it confidential. We all read it. The letter said right out in the open what had caused the explosion, and it directed all the executives of the company to "keep the matter in-house with no disclosure whatsoever." They were telling everybody to keep their mouths shut about the stuff they'd used. I sneaked a copy of the letter and I've still got it. The leftovers from that explosion were taken out and dumped in the Gulf.

"Some workers were hurt in the explosion and later there was a big lawsuit filed. I think it's still in the courts. The managers in our office acted huffy about it all. They said, 'The very idea that some common laborers think their lives are worth a million dollars.' "

Angel told us of other incidents, all pointing to the notion that public deception is business as usual on the corridor. "The public just takes it," she said. "If you are from Baton Rouge, you try not to think about what's going on because you were raised here and you have family here. If you're not from Baton Rouge, all you do is try to get a transfer and get away from the corridor. It's the damned truth. It's not worth it in the long run. Just driving to work is crazy. It took me two hours sometimes to go thirteen miles."

Angel grew up loving her hometown and its people but she says her eyes are coming open more and more. She doesn't like the people she worked for, she doesn't like what the company does and she detests the way the workers get lorded over. "Most of those guys just have a master's degree in chemistry or physics and they think they're Nobel prizes. They'll do anything for the company . . . they're in the squeeze of the golden glove."

She does like the South and living in Baton Rouge. She and her husband go dancing at the Texas Club in north Baton Rouge and sometimes they dine at good restaurants like Ralph and Kacoo's, where the seafood is excellent. "We like hurricanes too," she said with a nice Cajun laugh. "Not the drink, the storm. The sky gets all spooky and the atmosphere has a strange glow . . . the air feels funny and the clouds look different. It makes you feel kind of strange inside. When the hurricane season comes, we get the special weather maps and track the cells of the storms coming in. Everything is different then . . . the hurricanes have a way of bringing people down here together."

Angel's face was all lit up as she talked about hurricanes. She tried to teach us other facets of the Cajun way of life and even gave us a lesson in the Cajun card game of *bourré,* but we could never get the hang of it. Her children were lively and entertaining and adored their mother, running up to give her hugs and kisses now and then. Her little boy was playing with her key chain and she grabbed it away from him quickly.

"He almost squirted this Mace stick in my face one time," she said. "I carry the Mace on my key chain because I work downtown again and there's a lot of crime down there. All the girls in the office have Mace on their key chains. You get used to it . . . it's a way of life."

We passed through the invisible gateway of the chemical corridor and into the suburbs of Baton Rouge. Near some of the big refineries stood office complexes of the petroleum companies, surrounded by semiaffluent residential areas. In south Baton Rouge we found the home of a young married couple who had invited us to talk. She, too, worked as a secretary and her husband was a chemist in a research lab. This couple was willing to talk because they wanted to get something off their minds.

The Exxon refinery in Baton Rouge blew up at Christmas 1989, causing more than a billion dollars in damage to the area. The catastrophe went without loss of lives, or so the TV and newspapers reported. According to this young chemist, the reports were in error.

"People were killed in the explosion," he said. "I'm not sure exactly how many but the in-house talk was that as many as twelve to fifteen people died in the explosion and fire. They were the homeless people of Baton Rouge. They sneak down into the refineries to get out of the cold, and it was a very cold Christmas. They were sleeping down in the works when the explosions started.

"And Exxon was aware that people were killed. They covered it up because they couldn't stand the bad publicity. It didn't matter. Those were just street people."

The chemist told us that it was anyone's guess what happened to the bodies of the victims. "We heard they were put in body bags and disposed of. They were just the nameless and homeless ones you see in all cities. Their wrongful presence in the refinery was simply a nuisance to Exxon."

The chemist's wife told us that where she worked, a sick joke after the explosion went, "Well, Exxon just reduced some of the homeless problem in Baton Rouge." She added that spills and accidents and explosions were common in the chemical corridor. "There's always a coverup because the safety regulations are a joke, and the government looks the other way."

After we left the young couple we took another tour of Baton Rouge. We'd been told about it, and we found the sign on the lawn of the governor's mansion: NO FISHING. The grounds used to be a popular place for people to bring their kids and teach them to fish in the big clear lake. It's said that the lake was a favorite strolling place for Huey Long. There's no fishing at all now because there are no fish. The problem again is PCBs. The water in Capital Lake has been tested and measured and found polluted to a degree eighteen hundred times worse than the federal water standards.

We drove back to north Baton Rouge and a little beyond the city limits. Here spread the shame of the city. By no means could you call it a sanitary landfill—it's a dump. The municipal airport is nearby, residential areas surround the dumping ground, and beyond them a pastureland begins. Back in the 1980s a herd of

150 cows and calves died near here. They perished from drinking the water in a bayou that backed up to the dump. State and federal authorities measured hydrocarbons in the bayou. The poisons that had been dumped into the bayou were almost pure. They came from the chemical plants that sit on the nearby Mississippi. The dump has been sanitized somewhat since then, but the bayou still holds its poisons.

CHAPTER 24

The Invisible Corridor

COME PARTY

—*A sign at a tavern on the chemical corridor*

Highway 61 widens into a freeway and takes you all the way to New Orleans. The rains didn't let up and we had to feel our way along until we got to a turnoff that would take us to State Highway 44, called here simply the River Road. It's a good blacktop road and it meanders precisely with the river along the edge of the earthen levee. It's a beautiful levee, neatly clipped and as green and soothing as fresh mint, with cattle grazing lazily on the slopes behind a chain-link fence.

Just south of Baton Rouge begins a procession of beautiful old antebellum houses and estates, most open for tours at about five or six dollars a walk-through. We were told at a state tourist center that firms specializing in restoration have taken over most of the old houses and have made them profitable attractions. We stopped and chatted with a group coming out from a tour and one person said she thought it was "really nice for those families who've owned the mansions for ages to open them up for us."

The chemical corridor has actually already begun above Baton Rouge; it runs through the city in an almost uninterrupted line to New Orleans. Before striking out for the levee we had swung over on the west bank to pass by Ethyl Corporation, B. F. Goodrich, American Cynanamid, Dow, Cos-Mar, Copolymer, Fina, Arcadian, BASF, Borden. We were just getting started, for there were others to see down the river: Georgia Gulf, Kaiser, Marathon, Melamine,

Monsanto, Nalco, Triad, Texaco, Exxon again, Union Carbide, Uniroyal, Vulcan, Shell. And we probably missed some.

The charm of the antebellum mansions back in their cupular groves of tall live oaks and Spanish moss suddenly changes as in a movie montage and you're thrown upon an industrial expanse. One minute you're driving along the frontage of Tara, and the next you see an Orwellian phantom—an undressed pile of steel and sheet metal with octopus arms and bulgy pipes and conveyor belts leaning against the river. Here all of America's *Fortune* 500s churn out the products of daily life, from prescription drugs and videotapes to the wax coating on milk cartons.

The sugarcane fields begin just south of Baton Rouge and grow south and west through the land called Acadia, home of the Cajuns. The cane was head-high as we passed through and was sucking up the rain and turning a rich, dark green as it moved off toward the bayous along the river. In the fall the cane will grow as tall as trees and turn amber at harvest. In Twain's time the heavens would have been choked with thick black smoke from the bagasse fires, but now the cane farmers don't burn the cropped cane; they use stalk and all for feed and fertilizer. We passed sugarcane fields planted right up to the walls of the chemical plants; sloughs of stagnant black water seeped into the fields.

The River Road hugs so close to the levee that occasionally we could look out and see the Mississippi. Huge oceangoing ships were in the deep channel and we made out one old red tanker with Russian markings; later we would see Japanese and Norwegian ships. This portion of the Mississippi is international and the big foreign ships can get upriver as far as Baton Rouge; the ones we saw were oil tankers.

All the little towns on the levee seemed oblivious to the fact that they are plugged into the chemical corridor. We stopped in a town called Prairieville after passing other large estates, interspersed among humble little houses. At an old-fashioned corner grocery we listened to some men talking about football, the Saints of New Orleans; the men weren't at all interested in our questions as to how they feel about the chemical companies. "Who cares about 'em?" one young man said. In Prairieville we passed a playground of basketball courts someone had thought to name after baseball great Jackie Robinson. We wondered how Jackie got all the way down to Louisiana; in his era he wouldn't have been allowed to play ball here.

Billows of white smoke rose off the BASF Corporation refinery next along the levee, and around a bend we came to the outsized Borden plant. Now followed Uniroyal, jammed up against the river. As we passed these plants we saw big rusting cast-iron pipes running over the levee to the river, carrying off the wastewater. The plants take in enormous amounts of water and return it to the river, and it is this process that so disturbs the environmentalists. Posted on the levee were NO TRESPASSING signs. Security cars came along the River Road ever so often; it's not a private road but you have to believe it is the province of the companies. We had learned in Baton Rouge that all the big companies on the corridor are extra-sensitive, almost paranoid, about sabotage. We just stopped and asked a security guard about the matter and he said, "It's understandable, with all the explosions they have."

Next came an oddity. The road sign said, GILLIS W. LONG HANSEN'S DISEASE CENTER. A white gravel road led up over the levee; we took it and came down to a ferry landing. Three pickup trucks were waiting to get on the ferry. The sign by the ferry said, CARVILLE. We had come upon what was once called a leper colony, the only one of its kind in America. Leprosy, or Hansen's disease, is not totally a thing of the past. Cases crop up and when they do, those afflicted are brought here for treatment, across the river at Carville. The treatment center sits on a remote little island of its own, among the chemical plants.

We got out and talked to the people waiting in the pickups. One man, who was on his way to work across the river, said he didn't think they allowed visitors at the Hansen center. He was right, and we didn't need to bother those people. In another pickup two men sat reading the morning newspaper; they worked at a plant near Carville. We asked them how they liked their jobs and one said blandly, "The work's hard but okay." The other said, "Sheeit, they pay dog-do."

Rain was coming down harder and through it we proceeded into a kind of surreal fog. We didn't even need to conjure up visions from Kafka; it was vivid enough, like an American gothic turned dark, and there sat a leper colony in the middle of it all.

The levee road winds on past more antebellum estates with

prominent signs announcing guided tours daily. Because it was raining so hard, we didn't see a great many tourists taking in the shows, and somehow we didn't think too many people would be coming to tour chemical plants and refineries. We saw no signs by the plants inviting guests. We did see more cattle grazing on the levee and more rusty pipes going to the river. At the big, rambling BASF plant an extra-tall chain-link fence stretched along the levee. BASF wants no sightseers and puts up NO TRESPASSING signs about every hundred yards. Evidently the companies own, or think they own, the levee. Maybe they hold lifetime leases.

State Road 44 winds on toward New Orleans, and still more pre-Civil War mansions appear. We passed through the town of Donaldsonville, where a high arching bridge connects to the western shore of the river; the sugarcane fields come on again to the levee, thickening like a jungle. The Burnside plant ahead looks as if it will block the highway, and actually it spreads across it, so we drove right through the plant. They were making asphalt and the world around the giant plant was totally blackened. Heavy viscid smoke concealed the sky and did not dissipate even in the stiff wind and steady rain. We passed a honky-tonk at Donaldsonville called Duke's Place, with a sign that said, COME PARTY.

Marinas along this stretch of the corridor offer boats and pirogues for rent and a few pleasure boats were berthed in the little harbors. The estates in the vicinity seemed so affluent that we were reminded of the silk-stocking strip of the upper river. But the look here is a bit deceiving. Nowhere is the contrast more pronounced than in the picturesque little place called Good Hope.

In the early 1980s calamity struck the quiet town of Good Hope. A series of spills at the big Good Hope refinery left the town on the brink of annihilation. Fires broke out one after another until there were so many that the river itself, local people claimed, caught fire. In the end a hundred fires struck the Good Hope plant, and there was so much combustible material pumping out that there was simply no way to stop the inferno. We spoke to one local resident who said the fires kept breaking out for weeks, months. That was back in 1982. In an edition devoted primarily to the chemical corridor's problems, *Newsweek* reported in 1990 that the Good Hope Refinery was ordered shut down and that the company had bought and closed the adjacent public school. *Newsweek* also reported that Georgia Gulf bought out forty families who lived in Reveilletown and settled a class-action suit out of court. Dow Chemical is trying to buy up as many communities as possible, we learned in Baton Rouge.

Something of a buy-out and buy-off mentality seems to be taking hold of the chemical companies along the corridor. "Maybe their thinking is that they will be absolved when they remove all the citizens," a veteran newspaper reporter in Baton Rouge told us. "Some of those boys higher up in the companies think they are now untouchable."

We stopped at the closed elementary school in Good Hope. It's gone a little shoddy because it's just sitting there. Spills, explosions and fires have been so commonplace that any new one hardly rates a headline in the state papers. The town of Good Hope is pretty enough still, and people live here and go about their business. They weren't very talkative or neighborly, and we could understand that after all the fires and the evacuations. With the refinery closed, the town is just about dead too, and in a very real way it reminded us of Times Beach. A few people were hanging around, hanging on. The harbor wasn't doing much business with its pirogue rentals. One fellow told us they were thinking of renaming the town, and that would be a step toward reality.

The rain came harder again and to get in out of it we took a tour of one of the antebellum mansions. The place was called the San Francisco House; it was just down the way from Good Hope and wedged in among Cargill, Marathon and Dow.

The tour guides at the San Francisco House were gracious; there was a fair turnout of tourists despite the rain, and the old plantation proved to be a unique diversion. The house has nothing whatsoever to do with the city of the Golden Gate. Instead, it derived its name from the French slang expression *sans fruscins,* "without a cent." That's what the original owner of the plantation claimed his wife left him after she spent his money furnishing the place. Before the Civil War, the San Francisco plantation was part of several parcels of land dating back to the original French colonies, though the big house itself wasn't built until the mid-1850s—in time for Mark Twain perhaps to notice it during his piloting days. The house sits just a hundred yards off the riverbank. Most of the features in the mansion were designed for ostentation; the owner put down crushed brick in the dining hall to make it look like a rich carpet, and the crown molding of the ceiling was done in polished cypress that has an amazing resemblance to marble.

The plantation owner's name was Edmond Marmillion. His family had owned other estates in the area and his lineage dated to the settlers who came here with Bienville. Marmillion consolidated the smaller estates into one big sugarcane plantation. The slave quarters are still out back and the house itself is a galleried affair in the French Creole style; it has an enormous roof ventilated by a band of louvers at the attic floor. Much of the house is the original work. Marmillion had three daughters, the tour brochure says. Two of them never married, not a surprising fact considering that the Civil War wiped out most of the South's male population.

As we went past the Cargill plant down the road, the second shift was just going on. We saw white men and black men and dark sons of Acadia. They all looked hardy and they didn't hurry to get in out of the rain. Marmillion would have welcomed them in.

The corridor ends without announcement; the levee road curves and takes you back out to Highway 61. We couldn't be sure, of course, but we had the idea that the chemical and oil companies like the presence of all the elegant mansions along the corridor— they lend a needed look of credibility.

The tour of the chemical corridor is not really an unpleasant drive, and we almost found ourselves going emotionally numb. In 1989 when the Greenpeace people toured the river, they were anything but numb. They studied in detail all the companies here and made many shocking accusations and formidable disclosures, using the EPA and other official agencies as sources of data. Greenpeace indicted all the companies for gross water and air pollution. Dow Chemical at Plaquemine, for instance, has a daily wastewater flow, says Greenpeace, of 452 million gallons and the plant generated 98 million pounds of hazardous waste a year and released more than 6 million pounds of hydrocarbons into the air. Dupont at Laplace, Louisiana, had a daily wastewater flow of 57 million gallons and released 1.6 million pounds of toxic waste into the environment. Greenpeace's lists fill a good-sized book and the statistics are so stupefying that they become almost ludicrous. Greenpeace also drew some damning conclusions in its cancer studies along the corridor, and it was over this critical point that Greenpeace became a victim of its own overwhelming statistics. It pin-pointed the corridor as having the highest rate of mortality from cancer and infant death in the Mississippi basin. And the Chemical Association jumped on Greenpeace, saying it had "committed scientific malpractice" because it couldn't prove its claims.

The Association went on record that the chemical companies return water to the river in better shape than when they draw it out. The Association was aided by local public health officials in Louisiana who said that "there might be a cancer problem on the Corridor but it is a small one." Greenpeace had intended its river survey to put the country on alert about the poisoning of the national waterway. The actual result was to alert the chemical industry that it needed to improve its public image.

Before we went on to New Orleans, we took another side trip over on the west bank of the river. We had contacted a man at a fishing camp who agreed to take us up a bayou where there had been a tow-barge spill. The man told us he'd seen big turtles down in the swamp dead from poisoning. "The stuff was such a bad mess the scavengers wouldn't even touch it." We went down the bayou a way but didn't find any dead turtles. Instead, our man showed us some young alligators that had got into some poison somehow and had gone belly up. On the way back up the bayou, we met some folks on their way to fish for their supper.

The sun came out the morning we headed down Old 61 again, but it disappeared by midday and the rain set in hard again. Weather bulletins were coming thick and fast on the radio. Flash floods had hit the suburbs of New Orleans, now just a few miles away, and two lanes of the interstate into the city had been closed. We were thinking that maybe we'd have the threat of a hurricane. Maybe we'd get to the Crescent City in time to see what one of those parties was all about.

CHAPTER 25

Neo Orleans

"The Mississippi River is the most interesting continuous drama in New Orleans."

—*Roy Reed, journalist*

The most celebrated street in New Orleans was not named after a whiskey. Bourbon Street owes its name and style to the succession of courtesan-chasers and wine-bibbers dating back to the House of Bourbon-Orléans in the time of Louis XIV ("Louie the Putrid," as Twain called him in *Life on the Mississippi*). New Orleans lives on myths, thrives on them. A lot of people think New Orleans is at the end of the river, that the Mississippi magically stops at the French Quarter. But then a picayune was never a small cigar or even a newspaper—it was a coin worth about six and a half cents.

The color of New Orleans is red. You see red everywhere you look, from the red beans and rice and Tabasco to the Caribbean red tile on the rooftops. If you go up in one of the oil company skyscrapers downtown, you can look out to see that New Orleans is a patchwork of Caribbean villages nestled along a meandering river. On any given day of the rainy season, New Orleans will get four or five thunderstorms. The sun will blaze out between, burnishing the moldy old Spanish and French buildings and turning the river almost scarlet. At Mardi Gras, the most striking, outrageous costumes are heart-red. Perhaps the most famous red-light district in the country's history belonged to New Orleans. At the turn of the century, a lively, wicked place called Storyville thrived here in the French Quarter; it covered some forty blocks and was alive with brothels, saloons, cabarets and gambling halls.

Window on the River, New Orleans.

Social historian Herbert Asbury has called New Orleans of the Storyville era "the promised land of Harlotry." But perhaps the most enlightening source on the era is Anne M. Butler's book, *Daughters of Joy, Sisters of Misery,* a detailed account of the life and times of the women who made Storyville famous. When the steamboats stopped coming in the 1870s and 1880s, New Orleans turned to the oldest industry by permitting the open procurement of girls into flagrant prostitution.

Butler's book profiles the most successful procuring madams, who put out elaborate brochures describing their girls. These girls commanded top dollars, as much as a thousand dollars each, and some of the madams became so well known that they were considered celebrities here and in ports up the river. Butler tells of Nellie Haley, called the queen of the procuresses, who commanded the highest respect because her girls were of the highest quality. Nellie got tough competition from Louise Murphy, a schoolteacher turned hooker and procurer. But there came dozens of other grand madams, and oversupply drove the prices down to a low of fifty dollars per girl. Nellie had to leave town finally, according to Butler; Nellie tried to set up a procurement business in Chicago but was thrown in jail so many times that she was reduced to the fate of a common streetwalker.

Sidney Story, a New Orleans alderman at the turn of the century, lent his name to the strip by pushing through a law to create a controlled red-light district in 1897. Storyville became the sin capital of America, the home of a new music called jazz, and it lasted nearly through the first two decades of the twentieth century, until the outbreak of World War I.

Long before Storyville, the first true American music to hit these shores landed with the slave ships at New Orleans. The first generations of slaves were savages who hated their captors; the whites didn't even consider them human. The blacks were held in rough pens called barracoons (hence the epithet "coon," although the Dutch can be blamed for the universal indignity "nigger"). The slaves had to be beaten into submission before they could be sold, and the survivors were marched in chains to the auction blocks in New Orleans, moaning and chanting as they were whipped along.

One of the centers for "knocking down the niggers" was called Congo Square, and this scene of tragedy later became a gathering place where black couples entertained themselves with singing and erotic dancing to music made with improvised, handmade instruments: gourd horns, box fiddles, reed flutes, hollow-log drums. From this was born the music we know now as blues and jazz.

The legion of artists who transformed their intense, scorching desperation into the music of today owes much to such greats as Buddy Bolden, who played during Storyville's glory years; Freddy Keppard, cornetist with That Creole Band; Joseph King Oliver, mentor to the great Louis Satchmo Armstrong; Ferdinand Jelly Roll Morton, composer and piano virtuoso; Bessie Smith, the Empress of the Blues; Kid Orrey, trombone innovator; Sidney Bechet, clarinetist and leader of the Southern Syncopated Orchestra; and

Bunk Johnson, jazz cornetist. Within the past few decades, the music of these legendary artists and more has had a rebirth inside Preservation Hall on Bourbon Street.

Federal agents and some rather reluctant military troops swooped in to close old Storyville for good in 1919. New Orleans didn't invent the red-light concept—that distinction belongs to Dodge City, where train crews left their red lanterns hanging outside when they entered the brothels. But Dodge City couldn't hold a lantern to the innovations of the New Orleans girls, who often walked along Bourbon Street carrying their mattresses on their heads.

When people come to New Orleans today and stroll Bourbon Street with their hurricane drinks, they are unknowingly trying to recapture the old flavor of Storyville. The jazz is still here, though it is only a tinny echo of the scrubby street bands that started it all on Congo Square more than a century ago.

Modern sociologists like to think of New Orleans as an international city; in the harbor you'll find ships from around the world. Norwegian, Greek and Russian sailors walk along Decatur Street (the first one off the river), and there's a foreign flavor in the cafés (sometimes you'll see belly dancing in the bars). You'll find German bars and grills, Yugoslavian ones, Chinese, Spanish and of course French.

New Orleans puts up a steady drone of street-band music, but if you wish, you can sit in the courtyard of the Napoleon House (built in case Bonaparte might choose to raise a new rebellion in America). You'll get quieter music there, Bizet and Ravel, and you can look across the street to another bar in a building where slave auctions were held. People sitting around you will probably be speaking French, but they might converse in Spanish or Portuguese. French is no longer the second language of New Orleans, for Spanish is making a comeback; each year new waves of immigrants arrive in New Orleans from Central America.

Down the way a couple of blocks you can look for the blacksmith shop of the famous pirate Lafitte, perhaps the greatest myth of New Orleans. Lafitte was no pirate and in fact probably stood on a ship only twice in his life—once when he sailed here at the turn of the nineteenth century, and once when he sailed away a few years after he helped Andrew Jackson win the Battle of New Orleans. Lafitte was no buccaneer, no murderer or kidnapper. He was a skillful businessman who organized the Gulf Coast's priva-teers and received commissions from several nations doing busi-ness in and around the Gulf's ports. His biographer, Lyle Saxon, relates that Lafitte "never committed an act of piracy in his life." He simply wasn't operating under the rules of the corrupt port authority at New Orleans. When the War of 1812 came, the British tried to get Lafitte to come in on their side, but he refused, saying he would not turn on the nation that had adopted him. Instead, he organized the privateers below New Orleans and helped soundly thrash the British with his buccaneers on the plains of Chalmette.

If La Salle had been able to plant his colony here, New Orleans would now be called St. Louis. It's likely the whole region would have evolved as French-speaking, though what betrayal and star-vation didn't do to La Salle's pathetic venture, yellow fever surely would have. New Orleans could also firmly be called Plague City, for epidemic after epidemic has visited here. One of the worst plagues occurred in 1853, when the town's leaders were confi-dently announcing that "yellow jack" was a thing of the past. Six thousand died in the summer and fall of that year.

New Orleans has known other blights on its history as well. Race and religious riots have broken out periodically, but perhaps the worst scourge to hit New Orleans was the infamous Basin Canal. During the 1830s thousands of Irish and German immigrants gave their lives digging the canal under the most cruel and inhuman conditions. The canal was used as a commercial waterway until the 1950s, when it was at last filled in, creating some fifty acres of new real estate and setting off a greedy land rush whose outcome was only recently settled in the courts.

The city's most recent plague has been the battle over paying its bills and avoiding bankruptcy. The city administration com-plains annually that the state is bleeding it to death and won't help with turnbacks. The mayor of New Orleans has come out for se-cession—he wants to withdraw the city from the state of Louisiana and create a separate city-state. New Orleans has tried this ploy before. In the meantime, education and the city's services continue to suffer, and the town's motto, "The City That Care Forgot," wears on through its lowers and deep into its uppers like U. S. Grant's boots.

New Orleans has got by so far on its charm and surface grace, but the town is facing some critical changes and is still trying at this late date to decide just what kind of place it wants to be. With the progress of riverboat gambling upriver, New Orleans is sure to have casinos, has already laid the groundwork, and everybody in the city is taking the casinos for granted. Store owners in the Quarter are of two minds—they'd like more tourists but they fear gambling will cut into their business, and they're probably right. Given Louisiana's record, you can imagine what an era of new corruption might do to the town. In 1991 the state began to operate its own lottery; that too is a potential deadfall. About a hundred years ago Louisiana tried a lottery and the result was one of the biggest scandals in the state's history.

Yet the city is going to try gambling again. Certainly it was the riverboat gambler's haven in the nineteenth century; all those dandies and dapper knights of the river landed here and lost all trying to beat the faro banks. The New Orleans gamblers were a cavalier bunch—when the city was all but deserted as the Union gunboats closed in, a band of gamblers outfitted themselves as cavalry and at least put up a front of resistance; they were the ones to surrender the city, and soon they went to work running the gambling houses for Union general Ben F. Butler. Butler turned the city into his own private enterprise, looted the banks and opened up all the brothels; he was so greedy that he had to be removed from his command. The New Orleans gamblers practiced their skills through the war and won back some of the loot from Yankee officers occupying the town.

As the last city on the river, New Orleans is the sieve for all the pollution and poison that washes down, not only from the chemical corridor but from all the upriver centers of waste and pollution. The city lives by its restaurants and much of the seafood comes directly from the Gulf. Unlike the upper river, no advisory on fish consumption is in effect in New Orleans. The city has a lifetime cancer risk of 33 percent, according to national health statistics; for the past forty years New Orleans has had the third highest rate of kidney cancer among the country's major cities. The town also has three times the national average number of deaths due to cancer of the mouth. And the water supply of New Orleans is, of course, the Mississippi River.

Jazzmen on the Levee, New Orleans.

On the day we arrived in town we read an editorial in the *Times-Picayune* which put the problems of the city and of Louisiana into grim focus: "The truth is that all too many of Louisiana's legislators are more concerned with protecting the interests of big corporate polluters than they are with protecting the state's environment." The editorial should have added that the day may be coming in Louisiana when there will be very little environment left to protect.

But this city prides itself in never having a care. By the middle of the day the streets are just coming awake with people. The lunch crowd dines on gumbo and rice, crawfish dishes, soft-shell crab, shrimp Creole, oysters, blackened redfish, all delicacies drawn from the Gulf. Nobody worries about cancer, for every day is a festival. Street musicians dominate the Quarter. Little black kids tap-dance on Bourbon Street for dimes and quarters; full bands play on Jackson Square, gathering in dollars from crowds that close in as soon as the music starts. Later other performers, magicians and jugglers, take over the spot and play to the same crowds. Bourbon Street nightclubs are in a huff over these free acts and have asked the

city to bar them, but in New Orleans hardly anything gets barred. The Quarter is a continuing festival, part Araby bazaar and part freak sideshow.

Jackson Square is the heart of the Quarter; it faces the old Jax Brewery, which is now a multilevel shopping mall. The river runs beside the mall and the French market, and there's a boardwalk where a lone sax player blows jazz and gets an open sax case full of bills by midday. The street musicians have got their territory all staked out, sort of like old Storyville, and they don't invade each other. Sightseers stroll the boardwalk and get serenaded by the saxman. Everybody gives him a dollar.

The thing to do is get some warm beignets (doughnuts covered with powdered sugar) and chicory coffee at the side window at the Café du Monde and carry your breakfast up the steps of the levee and sit on a bench looking out on the river. The river runs fairly narrow here—it's only about half a mile over to Algiers. You see the excursion boats paddle-wheeling along and one attraction is to watch the ferry coming from Algiers, dodging between the tour boats and the oceangoing vessels.

The river is actually several feet above the city, and the most crucial work done in New Orleans is the manning of the pumps during the rainy season. From our vantage point we could see the swollen river being churned up by tour boats; we also saw big splotches of gunk coming along and being stirred into the reddish mix. The river had come east from Baton Rouge and it seemed to actually slow down along the Quarter, taking its time and bowing and bending before it rushed on to the Gulf.

As we sat looking at the river, an older man climbed down from the boardwalk and onto the rock breakwater. It was a dangerous thing to do, for the river is very deep here. Sure enough, the man slipped and went partway into the water; some young boys rushed down to help him back up. "I just wanted to touch the Mississippi," we heard him say. The river snaps people up for lesser whims; it kills people in the city every year. Out there at the wheel of those barges, the pilots are tense and ever alert to perils. A few years ago a ferry up the river wandered into the path of a tanker and seventy people died.

Along Pirate Alley the sketch artists were busy drawing children and young couples. We stopped and leaned out and tried to see the room on the second story where William Faulkner lived in 1925 while working on his first novel. Ferns blocked the view. Another major writer lived in New Orleans at about the same time Faulkner was here. Erskine Caldwell, the fine old Southern proletariat writer and author of *Tobacco Road,* had come to New Orleans in the early 1920s and found it "as good a place to starve as Paris or the French Riviera." After the success of his first novels, Caldwell came back to write a book about this land of the lower river with his wife, the photographer Margaret Bourke-White. Their book, *You Have Seen Their Faces,* focused on the widespread poverty of the South and turned out to be one of the more perceptive portraits of the Great Depression. Not long before his death in 1987, we were privileged to spend a day with Caldwell and he spun some wonderful yarns about his career and early times, including a story of how he once spent a week in jail down here in Louisiana:

"The time was in the early 1920s and New Orleans was a wide-open town full of speakeasies and clip joints. Faulkner was here then, hanging around with Sherwood Anderson. But I wasn't in on that. I was still in college, in and out, and I was in New Orleans just looking at life, soaking up the experience. And starving. That's how I got thrown in jail. I answered an ad in the *Picayune* and got a job selling magazine subscriptions. There were ten or fifteen of us selling subscriptions to some kind of mechanics' journal at twenty-five cents a year. I sold my quota for several days and gave the money to the manager of the crew, but the first thing I knew everybody else had cleared out—the crew manager had run off with all the money, so I was stranded in the town of Bogalusa on the other side of Lake Pontchartrain. I was broke except for five cents, a nickel, and two policemen came and put the cuffs on me and took me to jail for not paying my hotel bill.

"There I was in jail I don't know how many days, over a week, and I was in a cell with a very friendly old black man—he was in there for stealing chickens and he and I were the only inhabitants. The jailer brought us a meal twice a day in a bucket, usually fatback and grits and beans, two buckets a day. Finally I found a pencil and the old man gave me a piece of paper and said if I wanted to mail a letter I'd have to smuggle it out. So I climbed up to the top of the cell block and over to a window and sat there all day, until a little black kid came along; he had a stick and he was knocking the heads off of weeds as he walked along. I called him and asked him if he'd mail a letter for me. He said he would and I dropped the letter out the window and it floated down to him. I threw him the nickel I had. He could have kept the nickel, I guess, and I thought he had, but a week later my father in Georgia got the letter and called up somebody, a minister, he knew in New Orleans, and that minister came up to Bogalusa and got me out of jail, gave me a meal and a bath and put me on the train home.

"I never did write a story about it but later, in the *Faces* book, I went back to that same cell I had been in, and I found a young black girl there. Bourke-White took her picture and it got in the book. I asked the girl why she was in jail and she said, 'Just misbehaving.' We put that in the book and nobody knew there was a story behind it."

Around the corner stands a long, shabby building, the old Spanish Cabildo. After the deal with Napoleon for the Louisiana Purchase was sealed, this place would become headquarters for Louisiana. The Cabildo today is about to cave in but a sign said it was being restored and would be open again in 1992. Young Meri-

The Spanish Cabildo—seat of government of the Louisiana Purchase.

wether Lewis had conducted his business as governor of Louisiana here, and from here he had set out on his ill-fated journey up the Natchez Trace.

We went up Chartres Street (pronounced "Charters") and made a circle of streets where many writers and artists once lived. Mark Twain met George Washington Cable here in 1882 and they did a public reading together to pick up a few dollars. Around the corner, we stopped and sat in the courtyard of the Maison de Ville Hotel, where Tennessee Williams used to sit and drink wine and entertain people with his wonderful wit. The rain started again and set a nice *Cat on a Hot Tin Roof* mood. We chatted with a waitress who said she had known Tennessee; he was always a good tipper, she said. It was fine to lounge in his place and think of Blanche and Stanley and Stella and the kindness of strangers.

Bourbon Street is busy in the daytime but at night it shoots itself in the foot and hobbles and howls. For about seven blocks here everybody tries to re-create Storyville. Thousands come out each night to walk the middle of the street, maybe carrying a hurricane in a plastic cup, but mostly looking at the show: strip joints, mud wrestling, female impersonators, sham orgies, jazz joints, dance halls, lounges, famous restaurants. At one end of Bourbon they've got an off-track betting parlor, and at the other end a gay zone with bars and upstairs apartments, and they put on their show for the walkers too.

People come to New Orleans for this, to go a little wild and to get drunk.

We met him in the brasserie of the Monteleone, a stately, elegant old hotel; he was a stately, elegant old gentleman. The Capote family once lived here. Like most buildings of worth in New Orleans, the Monteleone has floors and staircases paved with marble (the only substance that resists mildew in this drenching climate). We ordered *deux cafés restraites et deux Calvas.* The old gentleman leaned over to us from his table.

"Vous parlez français comme les parisiens, mes amis. C'est refraîche-ment ici."

"Nous parlons français, mais comme la vache espagnole." He laughed. We had been honest with him; we didn't speak French all that well. Chatting with him, we knew him to be a gentleman when he referred to his wife as *mon épouse,* not the common *ma femme,* if our college French was still working. He told us he came here each morning for his coffee and rolls rather than disturbing his wife, who was ill. His name was Guy-Michel and he told us he was originally from Normandy. His family had served France for five centuries as soldiers, all the way back to Henri IV. In World War II he had fought with the resistance and had been decorated by De Gaulle.

"Le Grand Charles," he said, partly in respect, partly in derision. He'd even been cashiered, he said, for taking part in the Algerian mutiny in 1958. He was now in exile in New Orleans. Guy-Michel yarned on, ordered another round, and departed with a breezy *"Au revoir, mecs, bonne chance, hein,"* leaving us with the bill.

There are all kinds of ways of cadging a free drink in New Orleans.

Bourbon Street is actually a secondary part of the New Orleans experience and people coming for the Quarter alone miss most of the authentic folk life that still hangs on in and around the city.

Mardi Gras pulls in the huge, unruly crowds but the best times begin in late April, give or take a few monsoon rains and hurricane winds. They open up great old Fairgrounds racetrack in late April and hold about the biggest party in the world. It's called the JazzFest and it has featured such names as Wynton Marsalis, Miles Davis, B. B. King, Harry Connick, Jr., the Neville Brothers, John Lee Hooker and the Count Basie Band.

The JazzFest draws about four thousand musicians each year and in addition to jazz they play Cajun, Afro-Caribbean, folk, Latin, some rock, rhythm and blues and bluegrass and zydeco, a blend of Cajun with black chank-a-chank. Local people come in and set up booths and cook the real soul food—Cajun and Creole, sweet potato biscuits, fried catfish and peppery corn bread, alligator nuggets, crawfish bread, po'boys, jambalaya, muffalettas, soft-shell crab, a dozen types of gumbo, boudin, bourbon-flavored bread pudding and Sazerac cocktails.

The JazzFest drew close to half a million people in 1991 when we were there. The crowd was big but spread out enough to let you breathe and take in the show. The food was better than you'll get in the expensive Quarter restaurants, and the several stages set up at the racetrack offered lesser-known but spirited singers and players: the Dirty Dozen Brass Band playing the favorite New Orleans funeral procession music, the zydeco of Boozoo Chavis, the blues of Ironing Board Sam, Hot Lick Cookies and Mr. Google Eyes.

The festivals and celebrations go on through the summer and into the fall. In May there's the Zoo-to-Do, a social season sponsored by the Audubon Society. There's a Civil War reenactment over on the Bogue Falaya River and a Greek festival in downtown New Orleans along Decatur Street. In June a Cajun festival brings on more food and music. A little later in the summer they hold pirogue races, a motor sports grand prix, an antiques fair and the always popular Bayou Lacombe Crab Festival. Still to come are the La Fete food festival, Black Heritage days, and the French Market Centennial, which will celebrate 200 years of the historic bazaars along the banks of the river in the Quarter in 1992.

The best times in this land of dreamy dreams are hidden sometimes back in out-of-the-way places. Using the city as a home base, you can venture out a couple of days and find dozens of festivals and exotic goings-on. They have a praline fest down in Houma, a crawfish cook-off at Breaux Bridge, and a *rendezvous des Cajuns* with live TV Cajun-style at Eunice. St. Joseph's Church bazaar in Loreauville puts on a bourre cardsharp tournament, or you can take a swamp tour at Lockport. Up at Mamou they have a big Cajun music festival where you can see the old, old Cajun men with long white beards playing delightful accordion music. They stage the great American crab cook-off in Marshland. You can see displays of Louisiana French art at the Zigler Museum in Jennings.

Or you can just wander into any friendly little town of Cajun country from over in Lake Charles to Baton Rouge. Way down on the Gulf they hold the largest fishing events and tarpon rodeos at Grand Isle, and at Cameron you can see a big fishing festival, where just for fun they throw in a marshmallow-tossing contest and let kids and overgrown boys chase greased pigs. But surprisingly, the most soothing trek we took was a swamp tour recommended by several New Orleans insiders. We set out for some Cajun bayou country, got turned around several times and finally found a bayou landing at Petit Caillou after trying to follow some Cajun road signs. The people are most anxious to help you find your way if you're lost and they never get put out with you, but down here you just have to learn to get the feel of things; it's called Cajun trust. You think you're completely lost when all of a sudden you're exactly where you want to be. We were ready to throw up our hands and we pulled over to ask a young Cajun couple the way to Bayou Petit Caillou and they said, "You're here, this is it."

The tour of the deep swamp was conducted by a tough old Cajun lady who calls herself the queen of the bayou. She was upset the afternoon we got there because it was starting to rain hard again; we were the only ones wanting to take the tour that day and we waited around for the rain to slack off and finally the bayou queen said, "We caunt wait, cher, any longer. If it gets dark I might even get lost down in dare."

So we struck out in her boat down an oil company canal and into the famous Louisiana swamps, passing all manner of water birds, herons and egrets and a big hawk or two and of course the uncurious pelican that just sits on a dead tree stalk and stares at you as you glide past. We dodged around cypress stumps and beneath mazes of hanging moss and right through outgrowths of the thickest ferns we'd ever seen. We were glad our guide knew the swamp, but then she knew everything in the bayou country and was something of a celebrity and told us she'd guided famous people through these glades. She talked to alligators that waited in the brackish water. "They hear us coming," she said, and then added with a serious little laugh, "Cher, keep the hands inside the boat. I tell everybody that and we haven't lost any fingers yet."

The rain was coming down strong again and she told us we'd have to turn back. We spent only part of an hour in the swamp and she was so apologetic that she could only sigh deeply and look at the swamp as if it had something personal against her today. The gators refused to come out and see us no matter how she coaxed them and sang to them. As soon as we got back to the boat dock the rain stopped and we were completely soaked, miserable but feeling fully refreshed. "You have a bad trip to my swamp," she said, and she didn't want to take the full price she usually charged, but we insisted. "Ah, cher, you longed to see the alligator and I didn't give them to you. You come back sometime and I will take you to a special place where you can get right to those babies. Their eyes glow in the dark, you know that, cher? They are so lazy and they think when they see you that you are a coming feast." We had a good laugh with her. Not for a minute could you ever lose trust in her Cajun wise blood.

Coming back toward the city, we wandered around until we could get onto the Pontchartrain Causeway. It's twenty-six and a half miles long and newcomers don't want any part of it, we were told, because there are so many horror tales that it's become part of the local folklore. We had skirted the great salt lake to Covington, home of Walker Percy, who might have surely won another Nobel Prize in literature had he lived a little longer and produced another novel like his *Love in the Ruins.*

As we bounced along in the land-yacht over the long bridge we thought that Percy's visions were uncanny: everything down in this dreamy land was like love in the ruins. The twenty-six and a half miles go straight and straighter and we found ourselves looking out at the few boats and tankers without thinking of any sudden storm that might knock out a section of this bridge and plunge us down into the deep private sea that surrounds New Orleans. People have been washed off the causeway, lifted off it. In papers you read that people jump from this bridge. It's not a beautiful bridge; it's low and monotonous, with crossovers every few miles for emergencies and cowards. But once you're on it you have to keep going, and New Orleans rises on the other side steadily, looking like a lost Byzantine city.

We came back into the city through the Garden District. After all the mansions we'd seen down the river, the Garden District didn't seem any more impressive. It's full of huge old antebellum houses, with architecture that ranges from elegant to downright tacky. Everybody who comes to New Orleans on vacation makes the tour of the Garden District. The well-known streetcars of New Orleans bisect the district's wide boulevard and the landscaping itself is the most pleasing aspect. Just two or three streets over the poorer section of town commences, but tourists turn around before they get that far.

Back in the Quarter, we walked several blocks down into a seedy section to find a café people had told us about. We strolled through what amounted to slums, with begging street people and the homeless and the dope peddlers hanging on the corners or lying in the junky yards of shabby, run-down old frame houses. New Orleans has its problems with the drug culture. A writer friend of ours used to live in New Orleans and liked living in the Quarter but the last time we talked to him he told us he was moving out. "It's just too dangerous," he said, "and I was not getting any work done and didn't feel free to go out at night just to walk around for some atmosphere." He's the one who told us about the café we were headed to. "Best red beans and rice in New Orleans and you can't come to town without checking out Buster's."

So we checked out Buster's. Our writer friend had joked that maybe we'd need a gun for protection if we ventured off the beaten path. It wasn't that bad, but it was a shoddy show. We found Buster's, an old wreck of a house with some street people loitering in the front yard. Two of them, a loving young couple wearing shorts so tight their genitalia protruded, mooched some change off us, and when we were inside ordering the specialty of the house, the couple came in and put our change in the jukebox. We wanted red beans, rice and ribs, and one of us got them. The black girl waiting on us came with only one of our orders, leaned down to the one not getting food and said, "What are you having?"

"Why, I'm having the same thing he is."

"No, you ain't."

"Why not?"

" 'Cause we're out."

It was New Orleans, it was Buster's, and you can't come to New Orleans without checking it out. The young couple, our panhandling Romeo and Juliet, had played a jazzed-up version of "Summertime" on the jukebox and people were clapping their hands and singing along. The couple didn't mind leaning over people's tables and asking if they could have a roll or an extra rib, so we gave them our one order. Nobody in the place seemed to mind them. It was a way of life, New Orleans-style.

People walk in the Quarter. The sidewalks are narrow and the streets, built for the nineteenth century and before, are not passable by automobile, but that doesn't stop the vehicles. There are big hotels over near the Superdome and a lot of tourists stay there and take a taxi to the nightlife and the restaurants. Some kind of hustle is always going on down Bourbon Street, a gimpy hooker or panhandler or street preacher or an impromptu striptease by overeager college girls on a weekend lark. Beat cops walk the street now and again but mostly they give directions to Antoine's or Paul Prudhomme's.

There were other, less supercilious aspects of New Orleans. To talk about that and things Southern, we had contacted a man well known for his journalistic acumen. His name is Roy Reed and we followed his writing for years in *The New York Times*. He was a foreign correspondent for the *Times* and the newspaper's chief voice in the South during the civil rights movement.

Roy Reed started his career as a reporter for Harry Ashmore at the *Arkansas Gazette* when that paper stood up to Governor Faubus during the 1957–58 school crisis. Like Hodding Carter, Ashmore and his small band of reporters took on the demagogues and outlasted them. Roy went on to cover such scenes for *The New York Times* as the IRA guerrillas in Belfast and vigilante mobs in Selma. Over the past twenty-five years Roy became a legend in newsrooms around the country; he was the reporter whom James Reston often hand-picked to cover a story. Until he retreated a few years ago to his farm at Hogeye in the Ozark Mountains, Roy lived in New Orleans and used it as his base in covering important stories across the South. In his newspaper days Roy interviewed presidents and prime ministers, but one of the more colorful figures he ever dealt with was right here in Louisiana. That figure was a political boss named Leander Perez. It was a name to make you grit your teeth.

Perez was a throwback Dixiecrat and political boss in Plaquemines Parish, as bad a stronghold for white supremacy as ever existed in the South. There he sat on his white steed, his grouchy, sour face filling up the TV screens in the early days of racial defiance. You thought maybe Leander was worse than his bite, that he was merely posing like Orval Faubus or George Wallace and secretly loving all the publicity. But Perez wasn't. He was just what he looked like, an overbearing, obnoxious bully.

Roy Reed went to Plaquemines Parish to interview Leander Perez once. Before the interview was over Roy thought Perez and his cronies might take him out and lynch him.

"He was called the Judge," Roy recalled. "I don't think he was ever elected to anything, maybe self-appointed . . . in the Louisiana scheme of things."

The interview became a face-off. Perez couldn't stand it that he was eye to eye with the symbol of everything he hated, because Roy Reed was a "nigger-lover" and communist agitator and worse, a reporter for *The New York Times.*

"He invited me to lunch," Roy said, "and it was a ploy, a trap. All his local cronies came along too. They had a way of marching into lunch single file in the order of their political importance. They started in right away throwing jabs at me.

"At the luncheon Leander loosed a full frontal attack on me and the newspaper and the Kennedys and the freedom riders. He baited and accused me of this and that and the other cronies joined in until the venom was coming out of their eyes. I discovered that to be deprecating would be a wrong move, so I started slamming it right back at them. They weren't used to someone standing up to them, especially a newspaper reporter who could hide behind newsprint. I caught them off guard and pretty soon I saw that they were having a high old time.

"In the end one of the cronies clapped me on the shoulder and allowed that I was one of the best fellers around."

Roy told how Perez then took him aside as he was leaving and sounded a meaner note. Perez had boasted on national TV that

A streetcar named Desire.

he would tolerate no freedom riders or organizers trying to get the blacks out to register and vote. Now he was not posing for the camera; he was deadly serious. "Just let them nigger-lovers come on down here and we'll throw them out on my island where there's nothing but cottonmouths and alligators."

Roy added a postscript to the Leander Perez episode. The Plaquemines boss lived long enough to see his stronghold begin to crumble. Right under his eyes a wave of Yugoslav immigrants moved into the parish and with their numbers began to make political inroads. "Today a sizable colony of Yugoslavs live in the parish," Roy said. "They are in charge now and have political control, and the Perez cronies are a thing of the past."

In spite of himself, Perez must have admired Roy Reed's mettle and his grit. He doesn't fit the stereotype of the puffy, chain-smoking journalist; he's in his fifties now but looks years younger. He's never shunned a story and never backed off from one that involved going up against the power structure. For one story alone that Roy Reed broke, he should have been awarded the Pulitzer Prize. It involved the chemical corridor just up the river.

Roy Reed was *The New York Times* reporter who wrote the first account of the horrors of the cancer corridor. It was Roy's work that actually gave the corridor the name it will never escape. Roy's story pinpointed the imminent dangers and cited the many offenders, documenting the cases of victims already known.

The story hit every front page in the country. Soon journalists were coming in from everywhere to follow Roy Reed's lead. It all began back in 1969.

"The bottled-water industry boomed in Louisiana," Roy said, almost with a shrug. "I guess it's still booming."

More than twenty years have passed and the corridor is still there and the chemical companies and oil refineries are doing business as usual. The government has not only left them to their own self-regulation, it has patently encouraged their environmental overkill in the name of progress and growth. The only difference that's come about since Roy published his accounts is that the people know about it and their psychological numbness has had time to wear down to indifference.

"The worst atrocities on the corridor have taken place since 1969," Roy said. "It's trendy now to do a story on the corridor."

The story was such a glum one for Roy, especially since we had New Orleans and the river to talk about, that he got a little angry at having to shrug so many times. We turned back to the city.

Modernity may be taking away some of the town's old character, but Roy says there are sustaining qualities about New Orleans that can't be changed. He wrote in an essay once that the whole city lives on the verge of events. "There's a secret wildness in New Orleans beneath the summer humidity. The main source of it is nature, which is as close as the brackish tides that encroach on the very suburbs. The people understand that their petty divisions could be swept away in an hour if the river's levee should give way."

Events in the city begin *at* the river and *because of* the river. "The Mississippi River," Roy Reed says, "is the most interesting continuous drama in New Orleans."

* * *

It's probably that secret wildness after all, not the nasty lure of the Quarter, that brings people back to New Orleans. We didn't get a hurricane during our stay, not even very high winds. We did get incessant rains. Natives of the Quarter came and went with a composure that the tourists find engaging. There was a very different look to the eye of the native, an expectancy maybe, a readiness oddly bordering on goodwill.

We sat again in the courtyard of the Maison de Ville and watched the ferns and banana trees being beat to pieces in the drenching. In August 1969 the hurricane of the century, Camille, tore up the Gulf Coast. Winds up to two hundred miles an hour swept Louisiana and Mississippi and Alabama. The surge was felt up the river as far as Iowa. Hurricane parties were going on here in the Quarter and all along the coast. Over at Pass Christian an hour away a festive hurricane party was under way when Camille hit. More than seventy-five people died.

We didn't get a hurricane party either. Flash flooding was going on around New Orleans as we drove out via the Elysian Fields road, heading south as far as we might go. We passed one red streetcar out Elysian way, just sitting there by its lonesome.

CHAPTER 26

Sultry Coast

"On that day the realm of France received the vast basin of the Mississippi, from its frozen northern springs to the sultry borders of the Gulf, all by virtue of a feeble human voice."

—*From Francis Parkman*, La Salle
and the Discovery of the Great West

We lost our fellow traveler, Old Highway 61. It vanished in the middle of Tulane Avenue in the heart of New Orleans. We had followed the highway along the river all the way from St. Paul, and we thought we'd be a little lost without it, but we still had a hankering to satisfy, and some last business.

So far as we know, Mark Twain never sailed to the end of the river, even though his boyhood dream was to steam down the Gulf and up the Amazon. In *Life on the Mississippi* Twain scarcely mentions the estuary, and he never brought up the Acadian people of the lower river. If he were here today, we're sure he'd want to see what that's all about.

We followed the river out of town, through the suburbs of Gretna and Belle and Bertramville. We saw along the river other chemical plants, so the corridor continues almost to the sea. We knew the river ran almost another 150 miles below New Orleans but we were not expecting much industry; we were wrong. We saw more plants on the river, and we noticed their wastewater flowing back into the water and turning it again to the milky foam we had seen all down the river.

We entered the steamy world of Plaquemines Parish, once the stronghold of Leander Perez. The countryside looked more wholesome than we had imagined and the little hamlets were friendly, the people easy to talk to. We had noticed, too, a prevalence of

David Duke posters in the parish and those we talked to said, al-most to a person, "Duke's our man down here because he talks our language." The former Ku Klux Klanner was no joke in Loui-siana, and we sensed that he was becoming a political factor, so in some ways the old Leander Perez influence was still alive, though Duke got less than 40 percent of the vote in the election.

We were on another river road now, the last one, State Highway 23, which takes the river traveler almost to the rim of the Gulf. Over to the west lay the big Barataria Bay, where LaFitte's priva-teers operated and found haven. But we weren't looking for pirates or seersucker demagogues—we wanted to see if we could find the home ground of a genuine hero. Back in 1927 when the great flood was threatening to wash New Orleans into the sea, a young Cajun named Ted Herbert (pronounced "A-BARE") had single-handedly saved the city.

When the flood came in 1927 Herbert was an unlikely hero; he was just a young fun-loving boogerlee, a "no count Cajun" who worked as a salvage master along the river. The ramparts were holding the river out of the city but were threatening to break at any moment. The river was riding sixty feet above the old levee, which was now acting as an underwater dam and causing the river to back up around New Orleans. Herbert donned his deep-sea sal-vage suit and dived down sixty feet to plant a dynamite charge; his first attempt failed and the engineers ordered him not to make another. But young Herbert went down again. In all he made five dives and on the last one he succeeded. The explosion shot water and mud hundreds of feet into the air; the river rushed in torrents, taking the little town of Caernarvon and most of Plaquemines and St. Bernard parishes with it, though Herbert had saved thousands of lives in New Orleans.

We looked around for the town of Herbert's heroic deed in 1927 but it didn't exist anymore. We inquired after Herbert himself but no one we talked to could remember him. There's a statue of An-drew Jackson in New Orleans, but none of Ted Herbert. Some-where along the river, we thought, they ought to put up a historical note about the incident and how one man saved a famous city.

Down in these snake-infested back bayous and swamps, the Af-rican phenomenon of voodoo found a ready-made home. Thou-sands of snake worshipers were taken as slaves and transported to the West Indies in the seventeenth and eighteenth centuries. And they carried their god with them to the New World. Robert Tallant in *Voodoo in New Orleans* and N. N. Puckett in *Folk Beliefs of the Southern Negro* tell us that voodoo meant not only the god and its worshipers, but also the rites and practices and priests and priestesses. In Louisiana voodoo has been forbidden by law since it first appeared, but that hasn't stopped it. Black slaves practicing voodoo were much feared; the whites became terrified of the possibility of rebellion under the banner of this strange cult.

It is said that the first gathering place for voodoo in New Orleans was in an abandoned brickyard in Dumaine Street. The king and queen would first take their places, followed by the priests and the worshipers; bonfires blazed high as the ritual of the snake, the sacrifice and bowl of blood began. The authorities of New Orleans threw the snake worshipers out of the city, but the religion only thrived in these swamps.

The sugarcane commences again as soon as you get out of the urban sprawl of New Orleans and you see, tucked off the roads, some of those snow-white burial vaults. Out west of the city the houses and farms are not at all like those of the upper delta; they are impeccably kept, not affluent, but prideful.

We took a short side trip over to Morgan City and passed over the Atchafalaya River again. At Morgan City the river was full of tankers and cranes and offshore rigging. It is here that the Mississippi River wants to come. In the big flood of 1948 it did come this way, and some hydrologists say that it will come one day to stay.

Morgan City sits on a bay of the Gulf and is a busy shipbuilding port surrounded by oil rigs. Just outside of town, the sugarcane starts again. The land was soaked and brimming; it looked as if it couldn't take any more, the way it might look as a flood comes. We found an old man sitting alone at a marina and asked him what he thought of the big river flooding here someday. He laughed a good Cajun laugh and said, "It'll come and make a new sea for us."

The Atchafalaya River marks the mythical boundary of Acadia. From here up through New Iberia to Alexandria and west to Lake Charles is the spiritual domain of the Cajuns, with the unofficial capital at the little French town of St. Martinville, where Evangeline State Park is. The heritage of Louisiana's Cajuns dates to 1763 when England took over Canada and evicted French families from Nova Scotia, dropping them in the humid wilds of southern Louisiana. These Acadians were immortalized in Longfellow's poem *Evangeline,* and though Longfellow took poetic license by having the French families endure a hellish trip by raft down the Mississippi, the romance of the ordeal still lives here. In truth, about five thousand Canadian French made the sea voyage from Canada to the Gulf Coast; many more declared their willingness to remain in Canada under English law.

The Cajuns were strong people and made a passable life for themselves in and around New Orleans but were pushed off their land little by little until they had only this less fertile western plain. Still, the Cajuns love Longfellow and sing of "Ah Von Jay Leen" in their songs.

As we ranged back southward we touched on what was once known as the German Coast. Survivors of Law's grand ruse in the eighteenth century claimed the mudbank coast and the swampy edge of the river above New Orleans; in the 1720s and 1730s German, French and Dutch immigrants put down roots here; they represented noblemen, convicts, prostitutes and people escaping creditors or religious oppression. And they created the stout and spirited "German Coast" that exists today.

We passed drainage canals and bayous and as we circled around on back roads, we saw the land losing its richness, though the Cajuns out west somehow have made a treasure of what was left them.

At the top of the river we had seen a broad world of water; as we descended to the lowest reaches of the basin, we found another water world. Maybe that's an additional quality of the Mississippi, for it's doubtful that any other great river of the world works quite the same way.

We came in sight of the Gulf near Grand Isle and saw nice summer houses and fishing lodges and stretches of good white beach. Here and there we came across Chinese names on stores in the little towns. In the nineteenth century the Chinese immigrants were not called coolies at first; they were "imperials" because of their reputation for docility and neatness. The Burlingame Treaty of 1868 sealed the Chinese immigrants' doom; that treaty, pushed through by the railroad barons, allowed the Chinese to be herded into this country like so many sheep, or like lemmings to be drowned in the sea. One of the old bad sayings of the railroad days was that "under every railroad tie lay a dead coolie."

It was off Grand Isle here that hundreds of Chinese were shoved and dumped overboard, and who knows why. Maybe the sailors bringing the Chinese thought their task was over as soon as they saw land. The old accounts of the incident say that only a handful of the five or six hundred Chinese pushed overboard made it to the shore. In a way those who drowned may have been the lucky ones, for those who came to land later met almost certain death through maltreatment or disease. They were brought in to work on the plantations or to dig canals or to build the levees. In 1869 a Chinese labor convention was held in Memphis; the idea was to bring in labor more cheaply than could the peonage system that was then in operation.

Grand Isle today is a resort and a tranquil setting, a good place to bring the family for a seaside vacation. We spotted a couple of good-looking Chinese restaurants in the area. We stopped and asked and some local folks said the Hunan was especially good.

We reconnected with State Road 23 for the final push to the estuary. The area becomes swampier the farther south you go and the rain forest thickens. It's what you would imagine the Amazon basin must look like, only here the delta is becoming more a salt sea. The salt water seeps inland for miles and settles like a gigantic net, trapping the wastewaters that have come down with the river. There is no fishing through this marsh; they tell us fish can't live in the marshes because the salt water has mixed with the waste and that simply smothers fish to death.

We saw French names on mailboxes along the state road. That seems appropriate somehow, French descendants living down along this lowest reach of the Mississippi. We stopped at a store in a tiny place called Happy Jack and asked directions. We seemed to be going into more primitive territory and we asked a pretty girl in the store if we could get down to Pilottown by the state road.

"I'm not at all sure," she said. "I know you can go by boat. There's some shack people living down in the swamps, Cajuns, and they will give you directions. Just remember that Cajun directions are just guides."

We kept on going and passed other hamlets, the towns of Empire and Triumph. Those names clearly were ironic. The last towns on the river were names for the whole long dreamt-of mouth of the Mississippi.

The state road played out past the little place called Venice. It was not a town, just some structures built high on stilts, with people living off down the bayou. The area was swampy and we felt as far-flung as we'd ever been on the journey. A muddy side trail ran off into a dense marsh.

We could make out the Gulf and the wildlife refuge in the distance. A tanker was steaming up toward New Orleans and another one was coming about a quarter of a mile behind it. We couldn't see all three channels of the river, but we knew we were on the estuary, about the way we'd pictured it.

The Mississippi is certainly no wild river here. There's no roaring into the sea, no sound of any kind except the faint call of seabirds. The river lay spreading itself as thin as silt. Whatever name it needed to be called, Mechesebe or Mississippi or Father of Waters, it was rolling easy now, hardly making a stir.

We are told by scientists, environmentalists and official governmental agencies that just off this shore, out there where the oil rigs sit, the water is a hypoxic region covering up to four thousand square miles. All scientific evaluation agrees that this hypoxic region is probably forever. No fish live there, no plant life grows. The scientists and experts have given the area a name. They call it the dead zone.

Very close to where we were standing, La Salle and his party of explorers stood about three hundred years ago. They were joined by those "civil and free hearted" Indians of the river. La Salle's men had cut down timbers and erected a cross in the clearing by the river. In his book on La Salle, Parkman described the scene as solemn. La Salle stood on one of the three channels of the river and with the wide Gulf in sight he claimed the Mississippi and all the lands contiguous to it for France.

The explorers bowed their heads and chanted the *Te Deum* and the *Exaudiat* and the *Domine Salvum*. Emotionally, La Salle knelt and prayed. His French soldiers fired their muskets as he planted the French flag. Parkman says the shots echoed over the marshes and coastline, raising flocks of birds to blacken the sky over the Gulf.

As we stood near the same location, we heard no bird cry, though on the horizon we could make out a faint smoke trail from one of the oil tankers. We were quite alone and we didn't think there was a civil and free-hearted soul within miles. Having come this far, maybe we had expected more than what we had found. The beginning was a nice, clean little lake. We couldn't see to tell for ourselves if this lowland watery world was a river or a marshland. More than 150 years ago Mrs. Trollope, the intrepid Mississippi traveler, had entered the estuary here and her pen had captured the river's terrible, majestic power. She saw a mighty river pouring forth its "muddy mass of waters and mingling with the deep blue of the Mexican Gulf." She wrote that she had never beheld a scene so utterly desolate; "had Dante seen it he might have drawn images from its horrors."

We could see the Gulf high on the horizon and there surely was no blue water now. How odd that Mrs. Trollope would have Dante on her mind when she first saw the mouth of the Mississippi; we had an image from Dante in our minds too, but we were thinking of that dead zone out there. Drastic changes had come over the river since Mrs. Trollope's time. We had seen the river's mouth from the air before and had once upon a time ridden a fast powerboat out one of the channels. Still, as we stood on this lonely spot we were not so much in awe as we were curious. When did the river stop its violent pouring into the sea? Was it after all of man's attempts to conquer it, or had the river slowed itself in its capricious way, just to taunt those who wanted to tame it?

It was another sentimental idea to be discarded along with wastewater or images from Dante. The river, we knew, defied explanation, and that thought was no romance.

So we had come as far as we could go and we simply stood in a misty fog and waited for the right impulse. We had come to plant no flag and make no claim. We might have been tempted to speak some words, but we couldn't find a voice. We thought about the beginning, where there had been no hint of vitality, no trace of richness and no cloud of menace. There was a menace here; we couldn't see it—it was out there in another zone. Yet we oddly began to feel, in spite of all, a sense of beginning.

Afterword:
Getting out of the River

"You can't pluck a flower without troubling a star."

—Adage

After we had followed the long meandering length of the river for days and weeks, our minds became rivers themselves, with a thousand images swirling in the current. In *Life on the Mississippi,* Mark Twain spoke of finding good places to get out of the river, and though he never explained, we know he wasn't talking about exciting ports or good times waiting on shore. Maybe he was thinking that being a man of the river is so complex that you have to get off of it on occasion just to figure out what it means.

When we had been off the river for a time, we began to have some fitful stirrings. Distant images came visiting our dreams; faces and voices and places got mixed in our dream-current until we could see them as a sum of the whole river:

Old codgers on courthouse lawns South and North, not as wise as they would have you believe but sometimes the best voices of the river.

A Japanese graveyard put down on the delta where the apple tree people now rest by the river.

The civil and free-hearted folks in their church. Were these not the true inheritors of the native land?

A poor black girl trying to sell herself for a lottery ticket—and after all, she wasn't the real loser in that game.

Those hot-tar prison boys doing a hell of a job.

The Cajun singers and dancers.

A poet watching eagles from a bluff that looked down on a place of massacre.

Old grandfathers with their grandkids at a baseball game.

A lost and hungry girl at a jitney store.

The enduring voice of a 100-year-old woman defying the sorry bastards who were ruining her land.

The loneliness of an old, dying couple hanging on bitterly to the idea of home.

One last image hung in our brains, that of another kind of river captain. He was the master of his own kind of doomed vessel and so entrenched behind his bulwarked chemical corridor that he has become the darkest side of the dream.

Maybe the Mississippi River is too big, after all, to command the attention it would require to save it. Those who tried to conquer it have made it many rivers, an aqueduct for the nation's business. And it has always been a conduit for the wastes of the cities.

No one can believe that the Mississippi will ever be clean again or even safe to go near. Plant life that used to flourish along the river has vanished little by little and species of fish are disappearing one by one. People living along the levees still have to drink the "cured" water of the river, still have to bathe their children in it and cook with it. And will have to go on using it.

We have a comfortable disease in the world called progress, the poet e. e. cummings said. And maybe the most remarkable thing about the river is that it makes you think about yourself and what you're doing. Whenever we felt a bit sanctimonious coming down the river, we had to remind ourselves that we were traveling in a big old polluting hog of a car, an unforgivable waste of energy.

The first pollution of the river began at its birth when the glacial melt created it and charged it with an original energy. A marvelous purification system was installed at that time by nature in a state of things as close as life can get to paradise. But since the river couldn't long flow through paradise, it became a useful tool in man's economy and his moral scheme of things. Modern technology has discovered ten thousand ways to generate wealth from the river's energy. Civilization would not have got anywhere without its rivers. The managers of the living world now long exiled from paradise are the ones who get to decide how the river is to be used, or abused. But there's one little ethical spanner in the works, a haunting moral issue called the interconnectedness of things.

The state of the river today is encapsulated in the adage that you can't pluck a flower without troubling a star. When technology uses the river's power and returns only wastes, it is creating a fatal mind-set that catches us all. It is killing the flower because it sees no profit in the star.

When Mark Twain went down the river in 1882, the Mississippi's permanence was as unquestioned as God's grace. Our trip started out as something of a sentimental journey, and we told ourselves we simply wanted to relive a great old book and celebrate its author. But we kept finding new worries, and there was something more than a little disturbing in all the fret over the Father of Waters, the sting of an idea that we didn't recognize before we went to the river, a lingering notion of interconnectedness. We went to the river thinking it was a magnanimous old war-horse, something akin to a god. And it wasn't. It was a troubled star.

The journey led from brightness down through the heart of a new kind of darkness and into the evil pits of a dead zone. And if there was any safe passage left, it was in the idea that we're all connected and have been thrown into this together.

References

Adler, Jerry, with Todd Barrett, Ginny Carroll, John McCormick, Michael
   Reese and Mary Hager. "Troubled Waters." *Newsweek* 16 April 1990,
   p. 72.
Anderson, Nancy, and Dwight Anderson. *The Generals.* New York: Knopf,
   1988.
Arkansas Gazette [Little Rock]. 2–6 October 1919, p. 1.
———. 21–28 November 1919, p. 1.
———. 20 March 1990, p. 1.
Ayres, Alex, ed. *The Wit and Wisdom of Mark Twain.* New York: Merid-
   ian, 1987.
Brown, Michael. "The National Swill." *Science Digest* June, 1986.
Butler, Anne M. *Daughters of Joy, Sisters of Misery.* Urbana: University of
   Illinois Press, 1985.
Carter, Hodding. *The Lower Mississippi.* New York: Holt, Winston and
   Rinehart, 1944.
Cash, Wilbur Jack. *The Mind of the South.* New York: Random House,
   1941.
Catton, Bruce. *A Stillness at Appomattox.* New York: Doubleday, 1953.
———. *Grant Takes Command.* Boston: Little Brown, 1968.
Coulter, Merton E. *The South During Reconstruction.* Baton Rouge: Loui-
   siana State University Press, 1947.
Daniel, Pete. *deep'n as it come.* New York: Oxford University Press, 1977.
Devol, George. *Forty Years a Gambler on the Mississippi.* 1895 Reprint. New
   York: Johnson Reprint Corporation, 1968.

De Voto, Bernard, ed. *The Journals of Lewis and Clark.* Boston: Houghton-Mifflin, 1953.

Dickens, Charles. *My American Notes.* New York: Oxford University Press, 1951.

Drago, Harry Sinclair. *The Steamboaters.* New York: Dodd Mead, 1973.

Fatout, Paul. *Mark Twain on the Lecture Circuit.* Bloomington: University of Indiana, 1966.

Faulkner, William. *Old Man.* New York: Random House, 1961.

Grant, Ulysses S. *Personal Memoirs.* Edited by Mark Twain. 1893 Reprint. New York: The American Publishing Company.

Greenpeace. "The Mississippi River and the National Toxics Crisis." *We All Live Downstream.* Washington, D.C.: Greenpeace USA, 1989.

Hodge, F. W., ed. *Spanish Explorers in the Southern United States.* New York: Barnes and Noble, 1977.

Hogan, William Ransom, and Edwin Adams Davis. *William Johnson's Natchez.* Baton Rouge: Louisiana State University Press, 1951.

Jackson, Donald, ed. *Black Hawk, An Autobiography.* Urbana: University of Illinois Press, 1972.

Jaggers, Annie Laurie. *A Nude Singularity: Biography of Lily Peter.* (Forthcoming.)

Kaplan, Justin. *Mr. Clemens and Mark Twain.* New York: Simon & Schuster, 1966.

King, Edward. *The Great South.* Baton Rouge: Louisiana State University Press, 1972.

McCool, B. Boren. *Union, Reaction and Riot, A Biography of a Rural Race Riot.* Bureau of Social Research, Division of Urban and Regional Studies. Memphis: Memphis State University, 1970.

McPherson, James M. *Battle Cry for Freedom.* New York: Ballantine, 1989.

McLeod, Reggie. "An Environmental Snapshot of the Mississippi." *EPA Journal* November/December, 1990.

Morrison, Samuel Eliot. *The Oxford History of the American People.* New York: Oxford University Press, 1965.

Olmsted, Frederick Law. The Cotton Kingdom (Two Volumes). New York: Mason Brothers, 1862.

Paine, Albert Bigelow. *Mark Twain's Letters* (Two Volumes). New York: Harper and Brothers, 1917.

———. *Biography of Mark Twain.* New York: Harper and Row, 1980.

Parkman, Francis. *La Salle and the Discovery of the Great West.* Boston: Little Brown and Company, 1918.

———. *The Conspiracy of Pontiac.* New York: The Library of America, 1991.

Puckett, Newbell Niles. *Folk Beliefs of the Southern Negro.* New York: Negro University Press, 1968.

Quick, Herbert, and Edward Quick. *Mississippi Steamboatin'.* New York: American Editions, 1889.

Rabalais, Nancy N., and Eugene R. Turner. "Changes in Mississippi River Water Quality This Century." *BioScience* (Volume 41, No. 3), March, 1991.

Reed, Roy. *Looking for Hogeye.* Fayetteville: University of Arkansas Press, 1986.

Rolvaag, O. E. *Giants in the Earth.* New York: Harper & Row, 1955.

Saxon, Lyle. *Lafitte the Pirate.* Gretna, Louisiana: Pelican Publishing Company, 1989.

St. George, Judith. *The Amazing Voyage of the New Orleans.* New York: Putnam, 1981.

Stampp, Kenneth M. *America in 1857, A Nation on the Brink.* New York: Oxford University Press, 1990.

Tallant, Robert. *Voodoo in New Orleans.* Gretna, Louisiana: Pelican Publishing Company, 1990.

Thiers, Adolphe. *The Mississippi Bubble, A Memoir of John Law.* New York: Greenwood Press, 1969.

Times-Picayune [New Orleans]. 26 May 1991 (Editorial), p. 24.

Twain, Mark. *Adventures of Huckleberry Finn.* New York: W. W. Norton and Company, 1977.

———. *Life on the Mississippi.* New York: Penguin, 1984.

Utley, Robert M. *The Indian Frontier of the American West, 1846–1890.* Albuquerque: University of New Mexico Press, 1984.

Utley, Robert M., and W. E. Washburn. *Indian Wars.* New York: Houghton-Mifflin, 1977.

Wilson, Charles Reagan, and William Ferris. *Encyclopedia of Southern Culture* (Volume 3). New York: Anchor Books, 1991.

Wright, Louis B. *Gold, Glory and the Gospel.* New York: Atheneum, 1970.

Wright, Richard. *Eight Men.* New York: Classic Reproductions, 1987.

Index